Choreography of the Masses

jovis

Volkwin Marg (Ed.) for
Akademie der Künste, Berlin

CHOREOGRAPHY
OF THE MASSES
IN SPORT.
IN THE STADIUM.
IN A FRENZY.

CONTENT

INTRODUCTION

Klaus Staeck and Johannes Odenthal

It is one of the key tasks of the Akademie der Künste to design and defend public space as a fundamental prerequisite for a democratic development of society. As our places of social congregation are increasingly sold out to private investors and sponsors, we are less and less involved with designing and more and more with defending, which is an alarming state of affairs. Because as our society cast off the shackles of feudal and clerical overlords, it became an important task and challenge to keep the social sphere free and open to individual expression, and to uphold a symbolic gesture in support of the new social order in the urban setting as well as public images. The importance of buildings has shifted from cathedrals and palaces to parliament buildings, railway stations, shopping arcades and cafés, libraries and museums. And of course to stadiums. Unlike in any other place, tens of thousands of people congregate in stadiums for a joint demonstration of social order. And this is the point where the explosive political relevance of these large building projects of the 20th century becomes apparent, especially for the time we live in. Because the organisation of the masses in stadiums is celebrated by both, the dictators of this world and peaceful civil society. Whether it is used for sports competitions, concerts or parades: the stadium becomes the medium for collective self-expression and political propaganda in modern times. The importance of architecture and its influence on social processes becomes apparent when we compare the 1936 Olympic Stadium in Berlin with the stadium built for the 1972 Olympic Games in Munich. The self-portrayal of National Socialist power at the 1936 Games was broadcast to the world using film as the medium. The title of our exhibition Choreography of the Masses takes its cue from Leni Riefenstahl's propagandistic screening of sport; this is counterpoised with the tent-roof architecture of the Olympic Stadium in Munich and the staging of the *cheerful Games* as a response by a democratic society.

When, on the occasion of the European football championship, our member Volkwin Marg suggested an exhibition of stadium buildings to the Architecture Section, we became immediately aware of the topicality and importance of this contemporary building project. In cooperation with the architectural historian Gert Kähler and the project developer Michael Kuhn we have created an interdisciplinary cultural history of the stadium, in which construction projects are presented in the context of sports and social theory: a critical appraisal that focuses on the increasingly powerful role of the media in sports and the fan culture from a historic and social perspective.

Our special thanks go to the curators for their considerable commitment, as well as Minister of State, Bernd Neumann, who has helped making this exhibition project a reality by providing financial support.

THE CURATORS DISCUSS THE EXHIBITION

MICHAEL KUHN Hans Scharoun, an important architect and member of the Akademie der Künste, who the Berliners have to thank for the Philharmonie, wrote this maxim on the sketch for a design while still at school, in 1910: "An independent architect should not be guided by the sensational, but by his reflections." The Olympic Games, world and European championships of games such as football – which these days is very popular – and even the current Eurovision Song Contest, are affected by the choreography of the masses. This also has an effect on how architects design stadiums and arenas – it presents an opportunity to reflect on the issues involved.

VOLKWIN MARG In its deepest essence, mass choreography is politically motivated – it therefore follows that architecture is similarly motivated – because architecture is not the free art of an artist who can decide for himself, but is tied to the client-briefing for the creation of public spaces, for which the architect is responsible in all aspects both with regard to the client and to society at large. And, when an architect is asked to provide the stage for mass social activity he will have to ask what it is that drives people in this mass activity.

GERT KÄHLER Furthermore we are witnessing a breathtaking development in an age in which technology is providing new means of telecommunication in an almost explosive manner, which will influence social behaviour in a way that cannot be foreseen, from telephones to printed mass media, broadcasting and television through to laptops, mobile phones, electronic customer files and biometric data recording. What used to be physical masses of people turns, in a parallel development, into virtual masses in our modern-day computer-world.

VOLKWIN MARG Modern communications technology only multiplies the efficiency of information exchange but it also affects the ancient roots of the psychological make-up of our society. It is said that man, both as an individual and as a social being, has long been psychically pre-programmed and the evolutionary biologists, brain physiologists and social psychologists more and more frequently talk about man as a pack animal.

Herd, horde, pack and swarm behaviour is the subject of current research which for example investigates mirror neurones and their imitation reflexes. Analogies with insects and other animal swarms cause scientists to suspect a *swarm intelligence* also in man, leading to *social* or *moral* swarm behaviour, although the latter requires an advanced acculturation process developing from an inherent psycho-social code. To me that sounds like wishful thinking which would like to point to some natural psychological pre-condition or make-up whereas in fact such values have to be passed on from generation to generation as a cultural process.

MICHAEL KUHN However that may be, the choreography of masses has been practiced for thousands of years and mass behaviour has been accounted for either empirically or intuitively. Therefore this exhibition points to the socio-political background of stadium construction, of sporting competition and behaviour in games throughout the last 2,500 years in Europe, since the Olympic Games in ancient Greece.

GERT KÄHLER This retrospective is particularly interesting for a critical comparable appreciation of current mass events in which the original practices are continued as in former times, this may be the paramilitary fighting disciplines of ancient Greece during the Olympiads, or the appeasement of the masses with bread and games during the Roman Empire, which nowadays are adopted through television and mass sports events; it may also be the planned subordination of subjects to royal absolutism through national games (as before the French Revolution) or to an authoritarian state, national physical exercise or colonial leisure pursuit in nationalist and colonial competition of the 19th century; or it could be a completely new current strategy: that of changing citizens into even bigger consumers in a consumer society with its fixed focus on profitable growth in production.

VOLKWIN MARG These age-long practices illustrate the extent to which the architecture of stadiums for choreography of the masses is a mirror of the prevailing social conditions and an over-arching quasi-superstructure in the Marxist sense, while at the same time being subject to change as part of the change in production methods or political authority.

However, the psychological mode of behaviour of man as a pack animal seems to remain rather static compared to these changes in society. At least that is what some clever heads have perceived and pronounced before. These statements have lost nothing of their currency.

For this reason, we have included them in our citations for the exhibition, for example, Goethe's impression of mass behaviour in the Roman arena at Verona, cited from his Italian diary dated 1786, for example Étienne-Louis Boullée's tract, *Architecture. Essai sur l'art* on the project of his colosseum in Paris which was designed to subordinate the subjects to the absolutist monarchy of Louis XVI (Boullée is wrongly classified as an architect of the revolution because the text was not published until 1791, after the French Revolution), for example, Gustave Le Bon's summaries from his 1895 book *La Psychologie des Foules*, which make a concise incontrovertible argument as if they were the briefing of the propagandist Goebbels, or an up-to-date manual for the advertising industry.

GERT KÄHLER The private scholar Le Bon, who is the originator of the science of mass psychology, is not the only one; I am thinking here of brain researcher Hugo Karl Liepmann who, back in the 1920s, diagnosed unconscious processes which run in parallel with other processes in that part of our brain which supposedly is reserved for conscious thinking.

Or of Richard David Precht's book, *Die Kunst, kein Egoist zu sein* [The art of not being an egotist]. In his chapter "Warum Kopieren vor Kapieren kommt" [Why copying comes before understanding], he points out the three criteria of swarms, which were postulated by the IT expert Craig Reynolds in 1986: "Move towards the centre of those you see around you! Move away as soon as somebody comes too close! Move roughly in the same direction as your neighbours!"

VOLKWIN MARG That sounds as if he had read Elias Canetti's 1960 book, *Crowds and Power*. That opus magnum by the Nobel Prize winner was the result of his 20 years of study of the subject. It should be read again and again, in spite of its over 500 pages, because it really is still topical!

It is a pity that this exhibition only allows us to offer very few citations and we are only able to include a few pages (from the 32nd edition by

Fischer, the paperback publishers) as excerpts for inspirational reading. For a start, the first chapters of the book are brilliant essays, each in their own right: reversal of the fear of physical contact; open and closed crowds; the crowd as a ring (such as in an arena); the discharge; addiction to destruction; the eruption; panic; the characteristics of crowds … and so on. … As an architect especially, I started to reflect much more after reading this book, and was more aware of the ambivalence of my designs.

MICHAEL KUHN But that did not stop you from designing and building stadiums?

VOLKWIN MARG No, but it made me more thoughtful about it. I became aware that, as in music, there are architectural compositions which convey a sense of law and order and others that encourage a more liberal demeanour.

GERT KÄHLER For this reason we have selected the two demonstrative German Olympic schemes of mass choreography as an introduction to the exhibition, as stage backdrops so to speak for opposing social visions: the Olympic Stadium in the Berlin Reichssportfeld of 1936 and the Olympic Stadium at the Olympiapark in Munich of 1972.

MICHAEL KUHN These are symptomatic architectural reflections of opposing visions of society. While I am on this subject, may I ask you: when you converted the Berlin Stadium by the architects Walter and Werner March – the first stadium conversion by gmp for the 2006 World Cup – did you try to inform visitors about the National Socialist intentions behind the mass choreography by establishing a permanent exhibition, but at the same time try not to touch or even destroy the well-known historic monument from the Nazi era with its historic burden? Since then you have been building stadiums in a wide range of countries worldwide, the last one for the 2010 World Cup in South Africa, and now for UEFA EURO 2012 in Warsaw and Kiev. What scope do you and your partners have to influence the architectural backdrop for the mass choreography in very different social and political environments?

VOLKWIN MARG I have already said that of course, architecture is not apolitical. Let's take the last two examples. In Warsaw, we conceived the national stadium as a cradle for Polish pride in national survival in the face of foreign adversaries – both German and Russian. Poland's largest space for public assembly becomes a triumphant landmark opposite the inner city which was rebuilt from the rubble and which became a World Heritage Site. That is the message of the young Polish democracy. From the outside, the national stadium conveys an image of lightness and transparency rather than heaviness and closedness. Whatever will be displayed in a multi-purpose arena in front of massive crowds of spectators, the architectural ambiance will always convey a cheerful mood, on the inside as well.

In contrast, the project in Kiev was about providing a shell for a historic building monument from the Soviet era in the midst of the old city centre, which is surrounded by a chaotic assembly of old as well as new tower blocks – some illegally constructed without permission, something that went on even while we were converting the stadium, somewhat analogous to the State's constitution. The new glass envelope surrounding the old stadium does not close it off towards the city centre, but is completely transparent and presents the audience's life in the stadium in the midst of the city. We have covered the grandstands around the Olympic running tracks with a lightweight, translucent membrane that is reminiscent of a star-studded sky. The enormous size of the stadium – which can accommodate 78,000 spectators – does not necessarily call for the intimidating architectural heaviness of former times. An unwelcome element in these manifestations of public life is – in both Warsaw and Kiev – the currently obligatory double barrier both for the stadiums themselves as well as for the concourse in front, which is predestined for alternative urban uses, for fear of out-of-control crowds or possible terrorism.

GERT KÄHLER Both these projects are national stadiums which are supposed to represent their country on the occasion of large public mass events. A frequent criticism is that the architectural input into this kind of development helps to control the masses and thereby stabilises political regimes which exert their power without sufficient democratic legitimacy.

VOLKWIN MARG Such abuse can happen, but political conditions can also change: the pace of architecture and society follows different patterns over time – the former is built for 100 years, the latter is subject to constant change. For example, the original Polish national stadium was created under the influence of Russian Stalinism, but its most recent use was for the mass celebrated by the Polish pope with 100,000 faithful.

The conversion of Ukraine's national stadium, which dates back to the Soviet era, was designed by us as a direct result of the national emancipation from the Soviet Union, when Yulia Tymoshenko (who is now locked up) was head of the government, and it was opened by the current President, Viktor Yanukovych. So who is helped by this architectural input? What the future holds, I do not know. Future change through communication? Or change through isolation?

MICHAEL KUHN This issue arises in all those countries where illegitimate forms of government – illegitimate in the sense of our democratic constitution – are in opposition to the majority of the population; that could be in Asia, in Africa, in South America, or in the Gulf States; I am particularly thinking of the Eurovision Song Contest in Azerbaijan.

VOLKWIN MARG Again, the question arises: change through communication or change through isolation? What can help the population to overcome internal social problems and contradictions, what helps those in power suppress these contradictions? We Germans had a very vivid experience of this confrontation of opinions 20 years ago during the Cold War – and have finally come to terms with it in a pragmatic way.

Through communication or through isolation?

I see the more urgent problem elsewhere, i.e. in what Gert Kähler called the transformation of citizens into consumers. We are contributing to our own deformation of the citizen society, which we are busy exporting, and that is something that is conveniently overlooked. Even the term *consumer*, which has become commonplace, shows a revealing cynicism. Whether we are building filling stations, railway stations, airports or stadiums, we are exposed to the ruthless commercial dictate of reckless product advertising, which is not only an acoustic and optical imposition but also dictates our cultural life as well as the choreography of the masses.

GERT KÄHLER With reference to Canetti, [the German philosopher Peter] Sloterdijk has pointed out that the original crowd of congregations and gatherings has changed into a programme-related mass which undergoes an emancipation process by congregating in one place. The notion is that of becoming mass as an individual. This also refers to the millions of television viewers. But I would not express it quite so incontrovertibly as you say it. Because on the other side, the side of the citizens, we are also witnessing more and more commitment: through citizens' initiatives, as *Wutbürger* [enraged citizens], in voluntary positions, in clubs and social projects. The question is – a question I don't dare to answer – whether in fact these phenomena are a constant aspect of society, in other words not really a sign of change.

And then again, there is yet another aspect which was touched upon with the term *swarm intelligence*: it relates to the ambivalence of the masses and the question as to whether swarm intelligence is something that applies to human crowds: on the one hand there is the *dumb* mass which follows a leader and on the other there are social forms such as cities – which after all are also agglomerations of people – which through competition and the networks of their residents have led to man's most outstanding achievements.

VOLKWIN MARG In my view, the transformation of citizens into consumers is the most disastrous development of our take-what-you-can-get society which, without consideration for the desirable maturity of citizens – not to mention concern for our limited resources – exposes them to advertising and subconsciously programmes them for a superfluous and harmfully increasing material metabolism. Media dictated by viewing quotas, rapid changes in fashion and mass events are increasingly focused on just this one aim. By paying for the tickets and buying what has been advertised, citizens are even made to pay for their manipulation. In this perfidious manner it is a new phenomenon in history.

MICHAEL KUHN How is that evident in contemporary stadium design and the treatment of spectator crowds?

GERT KÄHLER Like the mass media, events – not just of a cultural nature, but also leisure and sports events – are no longer financed from the entrance fees alone, just like filling stations cannot be run from the sale of petrol and airports from the landing fees and passenger service; they need the profits from the sale of merchandise, product advertising and television viewing quotas to be commercially viable The higher the number of consumers or the quota of viewers, the higher will be the profit of the respective businesses.

VOLKWIN MARG In stadium design this leads to a calculated separation of spectators into consumer classes:
- "VIP-VIP" class with separate entrance, lift and special viewing box;
- VIP class with separate car park, entrance, lobby and personal viewing box;
- Business class with separate entrance, shared viewing boxes, business restaurants and separate grandstand sectors with arm chairs;
- Press class with separate entrance, its own grandstand sector and lift to the so-called mixed zone, which is shared with the players;
- Normal standard class with kiosks for refreshments in open grandstand corridors;
- Fan class with standing places behind the goals, with the home fans at one end and the away fans at the other end to diffuse potential conflict.

GERT KÄHLER Of course, this segregation of spectators is strongly reminiscent of the Roman Colosseum. The difference is that in ancient Rome the masses were divided by their social status (as well as gender), whereas nowadays it is money that separates the classes. In consequence, the newly-defined consumer classes differ in access arrangements, layout and fitting-out standard, down to the last detail. On the one hand, people seem to have an emotional need to merge with the mass as a whole, on the other hand they want their group to be segregated and separate from others.

In any case, the short-lived mass satisfaction does not last beyond the match as everybody goes their own way after the event, left with nothing but the hope of another shared excitement in the future. Canetti has described this very impressively in great detail.

VOLKWIN MARG The frequency of these events has increased. Olympic Games every four years (two years if you count the Summer and Winter Games), world and European football championships alternating every two years, the Eurovision song contest every year, European and Bundesliga games now sometimes several times a week.

MICHAEL KUHN Sport dominates the media, which need high viewing quotas for their advertising revenue, which in turn is financed from boosted mass consumption. In order to maximise advertising revenue, the advertising banners are made higher and moved ever closer to the pitch so that the organisers have to accept that the lower rows are no longer occupied because of the restricted view (players can only be seen down to their knees).

GERT KÄHLER What ultimately matters is not the number of spectators at the game but how many viewers can be captured at home in front of the television. This is very apparent in television shows that are organised in the studio by the broadcasters.

To give an example: the Eurovision song contest is expected to attract about 150 million European viewers. Brainpool, the company responsible for the installation of the stage set for this one-off singing competition in Baku, is expected to invest 50 million Euros – all financed by the advertising revenue; naturally, the broadcast will take place at prime Central European viewing time. For the man in the street in Azerbaijan, which is located far to the east of Europe, this intoxication of overwhelming television aesthetics cannot therefore start before midnight local time.

VOLKWIN MARG Of course, the total television experience needs acoustics as well as visuals. In a sports stadium the atmosphere is generated by the spectators themselves, with their synchronised chanting, screaming or booing, or the self-created rhythm of a Mexican wave. Cheering and groaning is amplified by the reflective properties of the grandstand roof and, even more so, by the roof in fully covered arenas.

This acoustic spectator backdrop is no longer important for the Eurovision Song Contest, because for the purpose of the television broadcast, the audience is only needed so that it is possible to show an adequate crowd clapping their hands. The crowd doesn't even have to be big.

And the singers and musicians don't even need the clapping. Most of them only pretend to be making music because most of the sound track and the lighting sequence have been recorded and are produced via playback. In other words, in terms of acoustics, the spectators become a virtual mass because the broadcast relies on the pre-produced surrogate for the 150 million viewers in their television armchairs.

MICHAEL KUHN I see what you mean, these are really somewhat alarming aspects of mass choreography. Nevertheless, in spite of all criticism, the experience of a proper stadium is still fascinating, whether it is full or empty. Also for the architects and engineers who design and build it.

VOLKWIN MARG Yes, these are the largest public spaces and, full or empty, they have become collective symbols of our cities and states, you could say the cathedrals of our secularised mass society, catalysts for the ambivalent transformation of individuals and mass.

GERT KÄHLER And they present a unique challenge in terms of organisation and choreography, involving ambitious designs and high expectations for the interpretation of the respective *genius loci*. That becomes very apparent from the examples compiled in the exhibition, examples that have been built by members of the Akademie der Künste.

VOLKWIN MARG As part of their service to society, architects and engineers are constantly searching for new ways of combining aesthetics, function, construction and relevant meaning. When they succeed the result is architecture in self-assured diversity.

PROF. DIPL.-ING. DR. H. C. ARCHITEKT VOLKWIN MARG

Born in 1936 in Königsberg/East Prussia
Studied Architecture at Technical University Braunschweig
Since 1965 Freelance architect, together with Meinhard von Gerkan,
gmp · von Gerkan, Marg and Partners
1972 Appointment to Freie Akademie der Künste (Free Academy of Arts), Hamburg
1974 Appointment to German Academy for Urban and Environmental Planning
1975–1979 Vice President; 1979–1983 President of the Association of German
Architects (BDA)
1986 Appointment to the RWTH Aachen University, Department of Architecture,
Chair for Urban Planning and Material Studies
2007 Establishment of the gmp foundation to enhance architectural education
2010 Appointment to Freie Akademie der Künste (Free Academy of Arts), Berlin
Numerous publications, exhibitions and lectures in Germany and abroad on
architecture, urban planning and cultural politics

APL. PROF. DR.-ING. GERT KÄHLER

Born in 1942 in Hamburg
Studied Architecture at Technical University Berlin
1981 Conferral of Doctorate, 1985 Habilitation
Since 1988 working as freelance journalist and scientist
Visiting professorships at Braunschweig, Berlin, Aachen
Member of the German Academy for Town and Regional Planning (DASL)
Member of Freie Akademie der Künste, Hamburg

MICHAEL KUHN

Born in 1974 in Parchim
Vocational training in business and a design-related trade was followed by architec-
tural studies at Hafen City University (HCU) Hamburg
In 2002 he joined the practice of von Gerkan, Marg and Partners
Since 2010 he is Head of Department for PR and Communication
Involved in managing the formation of the Academy for Architectural Culture (AAC)
Curator for national and international exhibition projects, such as the Architectural
Museum of Pinakothek der Moderne in Munich, MAC Quinta Normal Santiago
de Chile, Exhibition Hall in Ho Chi Minh City and Hanoi, Vietnam, MAC Niteroi,
Rio de Janeiro, Brazil

SPORT
IN ANTIQUITY

SPORT IN ANTIQUITY

The modern term *sport* has its origin in Great Britain as late as the 18ᵗʰ century; physical exercise and competition were deemed to be part of man's innate nature: they were necessary for hunting for food and for defending one's tribe against another. Only once these two aspects had become secure was it possible to practice movement for its own sake and peaceful competition, i.e. sport in today's sense – which is at the same time training for combat. From the existential necessity it is clear that pure physical strength is not the only issue and that instead, other factors come into play such as applied intelligence, strategy, trickery and the cunning application of equipment.

Since time immemorial our continued existence or destruction has depended on intelligently applied physical prowess. This is also reflected in ancient religions – those who enjoy the protection of the gods are superior to others. For this reason, battle, victory and defeat have always featured in the ancient myths and were experienced in front of spectators in religious unity. All this needed a place, a venue suitable for such rituals.Competition, cult experience and a sense of place merged into an indivisible whole.

The ancient occidental world provides us with an illustration of this relationship. In that sense *sport* is both a religious event and shared emotion in a stadium or arena, but also competition which gives rise to cheating and a perverse tendency towards sensationalism – with brutal fights to the death.

TIMELINE ANTIQUITY

GREECE

About 1700-1400 BC During the prime time of the Minoan culture of Crete numerous artefacts with images of racing carts, fist fighters and wrestlers are created.

About 900-700 BC The aristocratic culture of the Greeks produces vase paintings showing physical exercise and contests.

776 BC First evidence of lists of Olympic Games winners.

648 BC Horse-racing and pankration (a mixture of boxing and wrestling) are added, thus completing the core of the Games' contests.

586-573 BC Additional games with sports competitions are established at Delphi, Corinth, Nemea and Athens.

490 BC Battle of Marathon: following the Greek's victory over the Persians, a runner is said to have run the 41.9 kilometres to Athens to convey the message.

About 160-180 In a travel guide, Pausanias describes the competition sites at Olympia and thereby creates the basis for later excavations.

ROME

753-509 BC Kingdom

6th century BC Etruscan graves depict wrestlers, boxers, gladiators, javelin and discus throwers, jumpers, dancers, horsemen and cart drivers.

509-27 BC Republic

366 BC New rules are issued for the Ludi Romani at the Circus Maximus, which include cart races, horse-riding, wrestling and dancing.

264 BC The first gladiator fights take place in Rome.

73-71 BC A revolt at a gladiator school triggers the Spartacus uprising, which lasts until 71 BC.

27 BC-AD 284/285 Roman Empire (through to the Crisis of the Third Century; from 235: period of the Soldier Emperors.

80 Inauguration of the Flavian Amphitheatre (now: Colosseum).

122-146 In 4,257 quadriga races, Diocles achieves 1,462 wins, 861 second and 576 third places. Total winnings: 35,863,120 sesterces.

284/285-6th/7th century Late Antiquity

549 Under the Ostrogoth king Totila, races take place for the last time in the Circus Maximus.

GREECE

This is the gate through which the athletes entered the stadium – just as they do today: a dark tunnel opening to the bright light and to thousands of spectators.

The sacred Olympic grove.

GREECE

In ancient times (since about the 8th century BC), Greece was not one coherent central state, but consisted of a number of city states albeit with a shared understanding of a common culture.

Even in a slave-owning democracy such as Athens, there was an urban upper class of free, male citizens, and frequently power was held by tyrants. Athens and Sparta fought for predominance, both in warring battles and in physical competition. Unity of mind and body was pursued as an ideal of beauty, which was deeply ingrained in the common understanding. Education of the mind was based on the elements of rhetoric, reading, writing, philosophy, the natural sciences and the arts – while physical education was achieved through practicing physical prowess and training in combat.

The sphere of the gods mirrored that of the human world and was deemed to control the fate of those living on earth. Originally, competitions between the city states were cult games in warrior disciplines. The athletes fought for themselves and their city which, should they win, rewarded them substantially – both materially and with fame and honour.

The religious origin of the Olympic Games becomes apparent through the fact that they were carried out in a sanctum – the games in Olympia were held in honour of Zeus. At the end, both combatants and spectators celebrated a feast as a service in honour of the gods.

The formerly exalted image of the ancient Olympic Games is today seen in a somewhat more sober light:

"The real Olympia was much more lively, much more controversial and much more complex. There was bribery and corruption, there was fierce fighting for victory and very vocal encouragement, sweat poured in streams, the referees were struggling to impose the rules of the competition, politicians and speakers gave inciting speeches, the victory was sold for political ends, each city tried to carve out its own share of the propaganda cake dished out in Olympia via victories, and in the heat of the brutal heavy athletics fights there were even occasional fatalities!"

KARL-WILHELM WEEBER, THE UNHOLY GAMES: LEGEND AND REALITY OF ANCIENT OLYMPIA, 1991.

OLYMPIC GAMES

With their competitions in the small place of Olympia on the Peloponnese, the Greeks have given the name to what is today the most important sports event worldwide. It is probable that the ancient Olympic Games developed out of death-cult ceremonies – in his heroic epic *Iliad*, Homer describes in detail the competitions held in honour of the dead Patroklos during the Greek's battle for Troy. According to local mythology, Pelops, after whom the Peloponnese was named, managed to win over the King of Elis only by vile trickery in a cart race – this deceit was supposed to have been the trigger for the ensuing competitions which were held in order to atone for his misdemeanour.

There were a number of different games in ancient Greece but the most important ones remain those at the city of Elis, which took place every four years in Olympia in honour of Zeus. Their beginning has been lost to us in the mists of time, but since 776 BC there is written evidence of the feast which originally only lasted for one day and later – as the number of sports disciplines increased – spread over five days:

Timeline at the ancient Olympic Games

Day 1
_ Grand opening with Olympic oath
_ competition of heralds and trumpeters
_ pentathlon
_ competitions in the boys' class

Day 2
_ Horseraces
_ men's pentathlon (discus, long jump, javelin, stadium race, wrestling)
_ memorial service for Pelops

Day 3
_ Procession and large sacrifice to Zeus
_ running competitions
_ joint sacrificial meal

Day 4
_ Combat athletics competitions including wrestling, boxing and Pankration
_ weapon run

Day 5
_ Procession to the Zeus Temple and award ceremony and sacrificial thanksgiving
_ festive meal

A 19th-century wood engraving of an Olympic cart race: highly dramatised (after a drawing by Heinrich Leutemann around 1865).

The athletes started training at their home towns and villages ten months prior to the actual games. At least one month prior to the games they had to make their way to Elis where their capabilities were tested in a *training camp* – as a type of *end qualification* determined by the judges.

In view of the time involved, it was obvious that only members of the affluent nobility could afford to leave their homesteads for such long periods – unless they were *professionals* that had been selected by a *polis* to compete for it. There was no *amateur* status applying to the games, which would have excluded professional competitors taking part for payment.

How hard the life of an athlete was is well described in the advice given by Epictetus of Hierapolis (about 55–120 AD):

Advice for an applicant to the Olympic Games

"So you want to become an Olympic champion … but before deciding you should know what is awaiting you there. You will be asked to commit to a strict order. Food will only be available at precisely regulated hours and be restricted to very specific types; neither cake nor sweets nor ice-cold water or especially wine, are permitted. The scheduled exercise hours must be adhered to, whether you feel like it or not, and whether it is scorching hot or cold and wet. You are completely at the mercy of your sports instructor. When finally the competition starts, you have to roll about in the dirt and risk dislocating your arm or spraining an ankle. You will certainly swallow dust and receive blows, and at the end, if things go wrong, you will be the loser. So by all means, if you are still interested, go there and fight."

THIS ADVICE IS THOUGHT TO HAVE BEEN GIVEN BY EPICTETUS OF HIERAPOLIS (ABOUT 55 TO 120 AD).

Painting of a boxing fight on an amphora.

OLYMPIC BUILDINGS

The buildings that have been unearthed by archaeologists in Olympia today present a confusing range of layers from different periods which are hard to decipher for the visitor. However, throughout the centuries there was a link between the temple and the stadium, a link between religion and sport, which also involved the spectators. In the classical era (about 400 BC) the stadium was able to accommodate up to 50,000 people, i.e. the games were a mass event which attracted even more spectators than today's games in terms of percentage, because the Greek city states were hardly any bigger than today's small to medium-sized towns.

A characteristic feature of the stadium is its rectangular layout. On their way into the stadium the sportsmen passed a row of Zeus statues which had been paid for by convicted cheats of the games; to this day one can read the nature of their demeanour engraved into the plinths of these statues. Then the athletes stepped through a small tunnel (*krypta*) which opened out into the stadium – an architectural device leading to a grand opening – thus orchestrating the entrance of the teams, as it is often practiced today. The stadium had a running track that was 192 metres long and easily 30 metres wide, which, in the simplest case, was run once – the home strait providing a view of the Zeus Temple and gods. Along one of the long sides, in the middle, there was a stone-built podium for the judges, opposite which was an altar, with spectators standing on the tiers.

1   Gymnasium
2   Hera Temple
3   Treasuries
4   Stadium
5   Zeus statues
6   Zeus Temple
7   Therms
8   Domicile of the priests

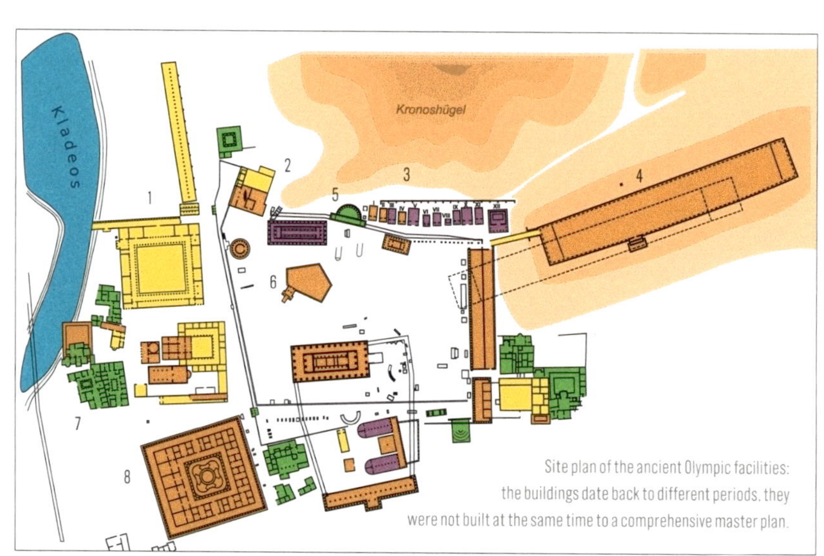

Site plan of the ancient Olympic facilities:
the buildings date back to different periods, they
were not built at the same time to a comprehensive master plan.

Stylized drawing of an Olympic sprint race (amphora, around 530 BC).

SPECTATORS IN OLYMPIA

The games took place in July or August – the hottest time in Greece. And they were an enormous show – it is estimated that 20,000 to 50,000 spectators had to be catered for. People lived in tent cities, but even the supply of water was difficult. In view of the fact that the Greek cities were often involved in disputes, travellers to and from the games were protected by the so-called *Olympic Peace*, which nowadays is popularly cited, but which in fact was only a truce limited to one month before and one month after the games.

The only spectators allowed were men and unmarried girls (i.e. presumably children). Eligible participants in the competitions were only Greek males, i.e. free citizens. However, women had their own games (*Heraia*) which took place between the Olympic Games.

The huge number of spectators in Olympia indicates the importance of the games for Greece – just the journey to and from the games could take several weeks. It is therefore easy to imagine that the games had a social and political significance beyond the sporting event and the religious content for the visitors – who endured such hardship and the inconvenient stay in Olympia: that of an exchange of news, and a political stage.

"There are enough tiresome things in life – why would you want to go to Olympia? Will you not be cramped together, bothered by noise, screaming and a scorching heat, and scarcity of water for a refreshing bath, only to then be exposed to rain that soaks you through to the skin? But you happily endure these hardships in return for watching the gripping competitions."

EPICTETUS, 2ND CENTURY AD.

Marble sculpture of wrestlers, around 200 BC
(after a Greek original).

FAME, HONOUR AND DISGRACE

The competitor's goal is described in the *Iliad* as "always being the first, and outshining the others". That was the personal goal which was supposed to be achieved, while complying with the rules. The fact that there was an oath that bound the competitors to these rules, and that there was a whole catalogue of punishments, is a clear indication that the rules were not always complied with – otherwise the punishment would have been superfluous. In Olympia, a particularly frightening statue of Zeus with bolts of lightning in his hand was where competitors swore the *Olympic oath* which bound them to fair competition, to defined rules. In spite of that, there was racketeering and bribery because only victory counted: there was no silver or bronze – the winner took all. On the last day of the games the winner was ceremoniously garlanded with olive branches, which had been cut by a boy with a golden sickle.

When the winners returned home they were triumphantly welcomed and, much like today, some of the glory also rubbed off on the home town. The rewards were high: a statue of the winner might be placed in the Olympic grove, there might be coins with an image of the athlete, as well as commemorative ballads by poets, not to mention material rewards. Overall, an Olympic winner was able to lead a life without material concerns – he was treated to free meals and he enjoyed the benefit of theatre seats and other socially attractive gifts.

However, those that were caught cheating had to pay a stiff fine, the money from which was used to finance the Zeus statue which was erected as a stern reminder to the athletes entering the stadium.

Those guilty of a false start or similar *small* transgressions, were – only – punished with a whipping …

The Olympic Games at the holy Zeus site, Olympia.
A copper engraving by Matthaeus Merian (1593–1650), with later colouring.

Weapon run: this contest cannot deny its military provenance (amphora, mid-6th century BC).

SPORT AND WAR

Although the citizens of the different city states perceived themselves culturally as Greeks, they were nevertheless constantly involved in political rivalry; for example disputes between Sparta and Athens took the form of prolonged wars (e.g. the Peloponnesian War from 431 to 404 BC). These were also a reflection of different social codes of behaviour. The Olympic Games reflect interesting changes over time. Initially the Spartans usually had the upper hand because the hard, pre-military education of their young men – which was obligatory for all! – gave them special prowess in terms of strength and endurance. The likelihood of winning was much reduced for other cities, where training did not start until ten months before the games.

However, as individual disciplines became more specialised – especially those which were ignored by Sparta as being insignificant from a military point of view – the citizens of other towns qualified and even became more successful than the Spartans during the 6th century; general fighting fitness for the purpose of war became separated from general physical education, which was aimed at training specialised performance sportsmen for various disciplines. Public funding specifically for sport was indicative of the desire to increase the importance of the town through Olympic wins – not unlike the so-called *competition of systems* at the time of the Cold War, thousands of years later during the 20th century. On the other hand, the fact that the military background of sport remained an obvious aspect for the Greeks can be seen in the discipline of the *weapon run*: a race undertaken with military equipment (similar to today's biathlon).

Nevertheless, how unimportant the common task of defending the country was compared to the fascination exerted by the games is illustrated by the anecdote that when the Persians under Xerxes invaded the country (around 480 BC), only a small military contingent could be mustered – because the Greeks were celebrating the games: "Woe are we! That a people should prefer games to fighting its foes in battle!" the Persian Great King was said to have exclaimed.

Sacred relief depicting a cart race (beginning of the 4th century BC).

The numerous depictions of sports contests on vases and amphorae – which were items of daily use – indicate the ubiquitous presence of sports in Greece.

SPORT AND SOCIETY

Physical competition for its own sake was also an issue of controversy in ancient Greece. In an elegy, the poet Xenophanes (b. 570 BC) compares the merits of a sportsman with citizenship and commitment to one's own *polis*:

"Nay, should a man win victory by the swiftness of his feet / Or in the five-contest, there where the precinct of Zeus stands / By the streams of the river Pisa in Olympia, or else in wrestling / Or by possessing skill in the painful boxing / Or again in that dreadful contest which they call pankration: / He would be more glorious to look upon in the eyes of his fellow citizens / He would win the privilege of a seat of honour at the contests / He also would have bread from the public stores granted to him by the city / And even a gift to serve him as an heirloom / Even if he won with his horses he would obtain all these / Though he is not worthy of such rewards as much as I am. / For our art and wisdom is better than the strength of men and horses / Nay, this is an utterly abysmal custom, and it is not right / To prefer strength to a capable mind / For suppose there is a man among the people good at boxing, / Or at wrestling or at the five-contest, / Or even in swiftness of his feet (which is most honoured / Of all men's deeds of strength in the contest): / Not for that reason would the city's affairs be better managed. / Short-lived, indeed, would be the joy of victory / By an athlete in the contest at the banks of the river Pisa: / For this is not what fills the city's storehouses."

XENOPHANES (B. 570 BC).

ROME

The victorious gladiator: his opponent lies in the dust and the Vestal Virgins demand his death
(lithograph after a painting by Jean Léon Gérôme, about 1870).

ROME

There probably weren't another people more enthusiastic about sport than the Romans – which no doubt was due to some extent to their original war-like attitude and military discipline. Rome itself, which drew special benefit from the imperial conquests, was inhabited by a mass society which was not sufficiently occupied with tasks or *jobs*; it was therefore necessary, under the motto *panem et circenses*, to spend public funds in order to keep the scores of people streaming into the capital city quiet. Bread and games. During the time of the emperors, around 200,000 people relied on public bread rations for their livelihood and were entertained by public shows. There is a pertinent comparison with the present and its social care and entertainment programmes.

As in Greece, the origin of these events was of a religious nature and was connected to the cult of the dead which had been passed on by the Etruscans. Part of the games also often involved processions through the streets. This tradition was the justification for holding these events on public holidays. The Emperor Claudius (41–54 AD) already had decreed 159 days as public holidays and in the late period of the empire there were almost twice that number. The games were free of charge for the spectators; they were organised for the plebs and sponsored directly by the emperor and rich citizens.

But these public games were only some of the sporting activities in Rome. The whole scenario was extraordinarily complex, there were public shows and private *fitness programmes* with athletic disciplines and ball games involving all free citizens, sometimes even women – although the latter not much in public. So there were both: sport as a leisure pursuit practiced by many citizens, and the large events which tried to outperform each other.

These Roman mosaics show a number of different gladiator fighting scenes:
man against beast, man against man – certainly bloody …

"Never were citizens anywhere – not even in Athens at the peak
of its power – able to spend so much time in pursuit of useless
occupation. Even the highly technological United States, with its
five-day week, cannot compare to Rome; because Roman workers
who no doubt had got up at daybreak, were not called upon to
work beyond midday. The transition from an active, useful life in
early, republican Rome to the passive, parasite-like life which
finally prevailed, took place over several centuries. Finally though,
visiting public shows on water and on land, with men and animals,
became the main purpose of life and all other activities were
carried out in its support, either directly or indirectly."

LEWIS MUMFORD, THE CITY IN HISTORY:
ITS ORIGINS, ITS TRANSFORMATIONS AND ITS PROSPECTS, 1979.

Sacred relief showing a gladiator fight.

SHOWS TO THE DEATH

A special feature of public Roman shows were the *munera*. These were not about peaceful competition between trained athletes, but the objective was to destroy the opponent, in particular in fights with animals and between gladiators. In today's parlance these were *shows*, albeit with a highly bloodthirsty aspect. Wild animals were set upon each other and gladiators, usually slaves or freedmen – who could thereby achieve star status – fought each other.

There were even sea battles (*naumachiae*) representing real battles which took place inside the Colosseum in Rome which was flooded with water for the purpose. Then there were the *agones*, which were similar to games in the Greek tradition. These were competitions which we might call track and field competitions, and horseraces. These were not for slaves – who were not admitted – but for free men from reputable families; like in Greece, there were substantial prizes to be won which secured competitors a respectable income.

"MORITURI TE SALUTANT"

Convicted criminals, gladiators recruited from the army of slaves, or wild animals – these were the victims of the battles in the *circus*. However, as the number of events increased and the public expected more and more, the protagonists were later professionals who were trained in gladiator schools – fighters with military weapons who were *groomed* to kill each other. Following the orderly procession into the arena, the emperor in his box was greeted with "ave imperator, morituri te salutant" (greetings to you emperor, from those destined to die).

Frequently, and in order to increase the excitement of the fight, the protagonists used different types of weapons in their battle. If somebody was wounded, the spectators shouted *habet* (he has had enough) and his life depended on the emperor's mercy and that of the spectators. Most commonly the thumb pointed downwards, because one wanted to see the victim's fight to the death. At the end, the dead body was dragged out of the arena on a hook and burnt.

The more gladiators were trained in the schools, the more trained fighters there were to threaten the existence of the current social order, armed men who had to be kept in good humour; the Spartacus gladiator uprising (73–71 BC) was a result of these conditions.

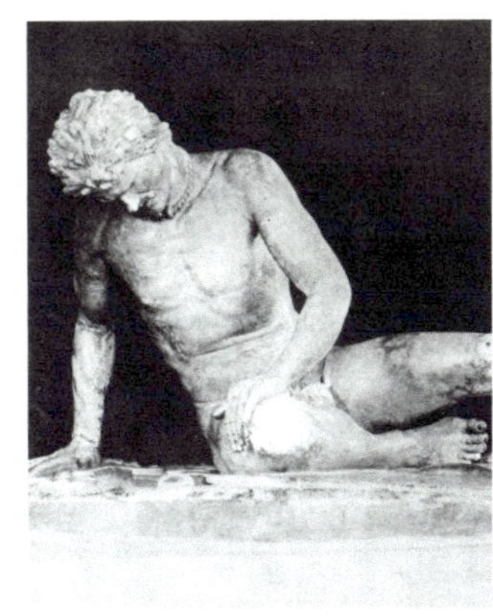

The dying gladiator
(statue, Capitoline museums).

Roman mosaics.

Kirk Douglas, with grim resolve, fighting as Spartacus in Stanley Kubrick's film (1960).

This painting by Antoine Caron (1566) is called "The massacres of the triumvirate" and shows rather unrealistic scenes of street fighting. The picture shows the Colosseum in construction which is not quite in accordance with the actual time sequence.

SPORTS SHOWS AND WAR

The extent to which the carnage in the arena became similar to that of military combat and the extent to which the people enjoyed the excitement of both is illustrated by a report on the situation in December of 69 BC. The troops of the later Emperor Vespasian tried to occupy the city of Rome in a battle against the troops of the then ruling Emperor Vitellius. There were fierce street battles, especially in the poorer quarters of the city, which took place at the time of the *Saturnalia*, a kind of carnival celebration. The Roman historian Tacitus wrote: "The people stood directly next to the fighting troops as spectators and, just like in a gladiator battle, they screamed and clapped, encouraging sometimes one side, sometimes the other. Every time one of the sides was pushed back into the loser street, the people noisily demanded that those hidden in the shops, or those who perhaps had fled into a house, should be brought out and made *a head shorter*.

(…) The whole city was a cruel and repulsive sight: battles and wounded people right next to bath houses and snack kiosks, as well as blood and heaps of dead bodies directly next to whores and rent boys. (...) This was not the first time that armies with weapons had battled in the city (…) and although there had not been less cruelty at that time, people's indifference now was inhuman, and the festivities were not interrupted for one second: as if this were an additional entertainment during the festivities, people were gregarious and relished the spectacle without really caring for either party, happy at the State's misfortune."

So while a decisive battle for the power in the State was taking place, the general public merely focused on the spectacle. The people wanted – and got – *panem et circenses* instead of a political mandate.

CART RACES IN THE CIRCUS MAXIMUS

The Circus Maximus was the largest arena for racing events in Rome. It measured 600 metres in length and 140 metres in width. During Caesar's reign (100–44 BC) there was space for 145,000 spectators, and it is claimed that it was later extended to accommodate 385,000. It was extended step by step by various emperors; initially by Caesar, then by Augustus (from 31 BC sole reigning successor of Caesar) who had an obelisk erected on the *spina* (the centre which separated the two racetracks); a second obelisk was added in the 4th century. Trajan (emperor from 98 to 117 AD) had the *circus* fully reconstructed in stone, including a box for the emperor.

The *circus* was built for cart races with teams of horses: the start was at the straight, narrow end and the race involved seven laps around the track. Initially an event involved 12 races, later on 24, and before the start a procession took place in which images of the gods were carried into the arena. The *circus* was also used for animal and gladiator fights.

Today, the Circus Maximus is still used for large events, such as rock concerts or the reception of a winning football team such as the Italian 2006 world champions; to this day the *genius loci* is determined by the historical aura with its reminder of antique spectacles.

Above: large wooden model of ancient Rome gives an impression of how huge the sports facilities were in the context of the city.
Right: mosaic with quadriga as used in the races (3rd century AD).

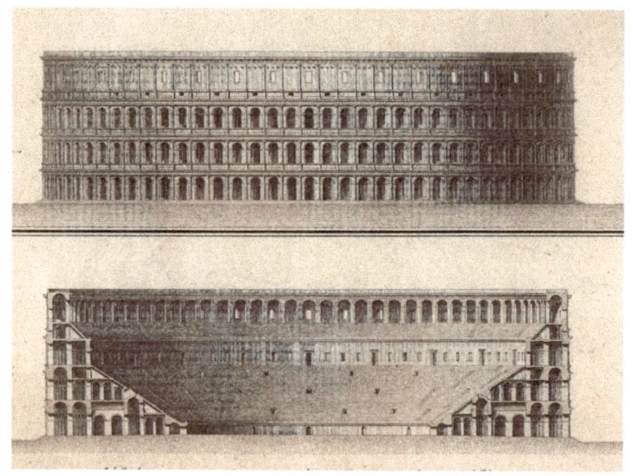

Reconstruction of the Colosseum in plan, section and elevation (copper engraving, early 19th century).

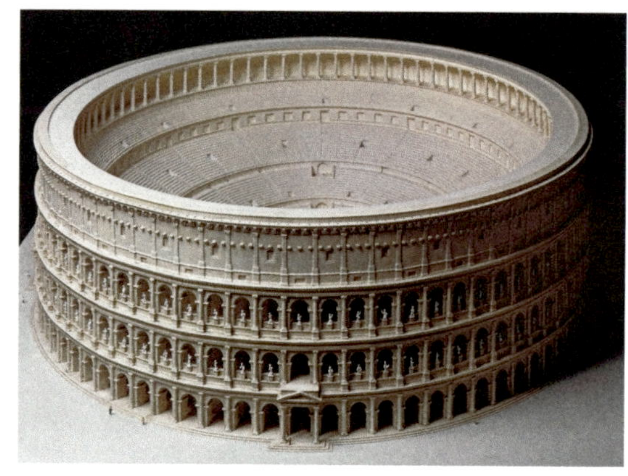

A model representing the Colosseum.

COLOSSEUM: BATTLES FOR ENTERTAINMENT

The Emperor Nero (from 54 to 68 AD) had originally planned to expand the palace between the Roman Esquiline and Palatine hills following the city's great fire. However, after his downfall, his successor Vespasian commissioned a huge amphitheatre in that location, presumably using the gold Rome had acquired in the Jewish-Roman War (66–70 AD). It consisted of three storeys of arcades that, with their 80 arches, formed the structure surrounding the elliptical base. Vespasian's son Titus commissioned a fourth, enclosed storey to be built on top. The spectators were protected from the sun by a sun sail which, with the help of marine soldiers, was rigged up on a rope structure which was suspended from 240 brackets with masts and ropes.

The building was completed in 80 AD and the opening was celebrated with 100 days of games – including gladiator battles, re-enacted sea battles and animal hunts in which 5,000 animals were killed.

The building had space for 50,000 spectators. The system for controlling the flows of spectators was extremely sophisticated, both in terms of safety – it was possible to vacate the building within a few minutes – as well as in terms of allocating visitor spaces in accordance with a strict class society: four entrances were reserved for the emperor and dignitaries. Normal citizens used the 76 other entrances (equipped with a sort of *ticket* for the respective tier) with tiers being separated by social status. Fourteen of the lower rows were reserved for knights, the bottom row for senators. The *plebs* – the ordinary people – sat on the top rows, furthest away from the action, and higher up still the women of paupers were allowed to stand. But a strict order also applied within the rows: there were certain areas for married men and others for unmarried men, for envoys from foreign powers, for boys and their educators – the Colosseum was a precise reflection of Roman society.

The section illustrates the ingenious guide system for people through and within the Colosseum.

Pictures do not really convey the enormous size of the building,
which still impresses today.

The Pope on his traditional via crucis on Good Friday with a stop in front of the Colosseum
(2010): the close connection between sporting ecstasy and religious fervour can be seen.

Another wooden model of Rome at the time of Emperor Constantine (around 300 AD): the Field of Mars has already been densely developed with a number of different facilities, mostly for sport.

The famous "bikini girls" mosaic showing girls playing games is proof of the fact that women occupied themselves with sport too, and that ball games were already in existence, as were bikinis (4th century).

CAMPUS MARTIUS: GAMES AND SPORT

The Circus Maximus and the Colosseum were monumental buildings used for huge – and violent – mass events. However, they only reflect some of the events and significance of competition in historic Roman society. Large parts of the population practiced sport – in our current understanding – i.e. for relaxation and as a leisure pursuit; physical fitness was a socially recognised objective for the individual. At the time of Augustus (emperor from 31 BC to 14 AD), a contemporary wrote: "Now there is no area in Rome which is more beautiful than the Campus Martius which, it seems, has been beautified by nature and art in competition. The size of this ground alone deserves our admiration, as it allows such a large quantity of carts and horses to race without impeding each other, not to mention the enormous quantity of people who every day congregate to play ball games or practice wrestling and throwing the discus."

The area measured more than 250 hectares and was used by many people for sport as a leisure activity without spectators. It was situated inside a loop of the Tiber River, outside the city walls, and originally had been used for grazing cattle and also as a military exercise ground. Since 55 BC when the first solidly built theatre was erected there for no less than 10,000 spectators, it was successively occupied by a number of buildings, one of them the Ara Pacis Augustus (a monumental peace altar), the Pantheon (a place for worshipping all gods, built from 118 to 125 AD) as well as sports buildings such as the Stadium of Domitian (built 85 AD for 30,000 spectators), which can still be recognised from the layout of today's Piazza Navona and the remains of which one can still see at six-metres depth.

The large bath houses (*thermae*) which existed in all Roman cities and towns were another type of sports building although they were not places of competition, and in that sense were similar to the *gymnasion* and *palästra* which had been adopted from Greece and adapted to Roman needs. Large villas had their own fitness room (*sphairisterium*) in which the affluent practiced with their personal trainer.

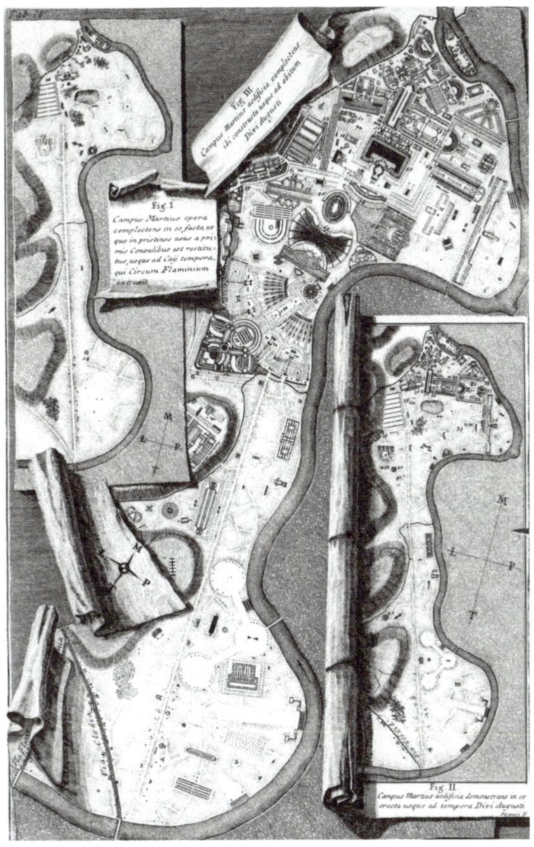

The Field of Mars as seen by Giovanni Piranesi (1720–1778),
who was an archaeologist and architect.

Giovanni Piranesi was delighted in drawing the disintegration of the Roman buildings,
such as the Forum Romanum shown here with the Colosseum in the background.

The field-and-track stadium on the Field
of Mars was converted to form the Piazza
Navona in the Baroque era (copper
engraving by B. F. Leizelt, beginning of
the 18th century).

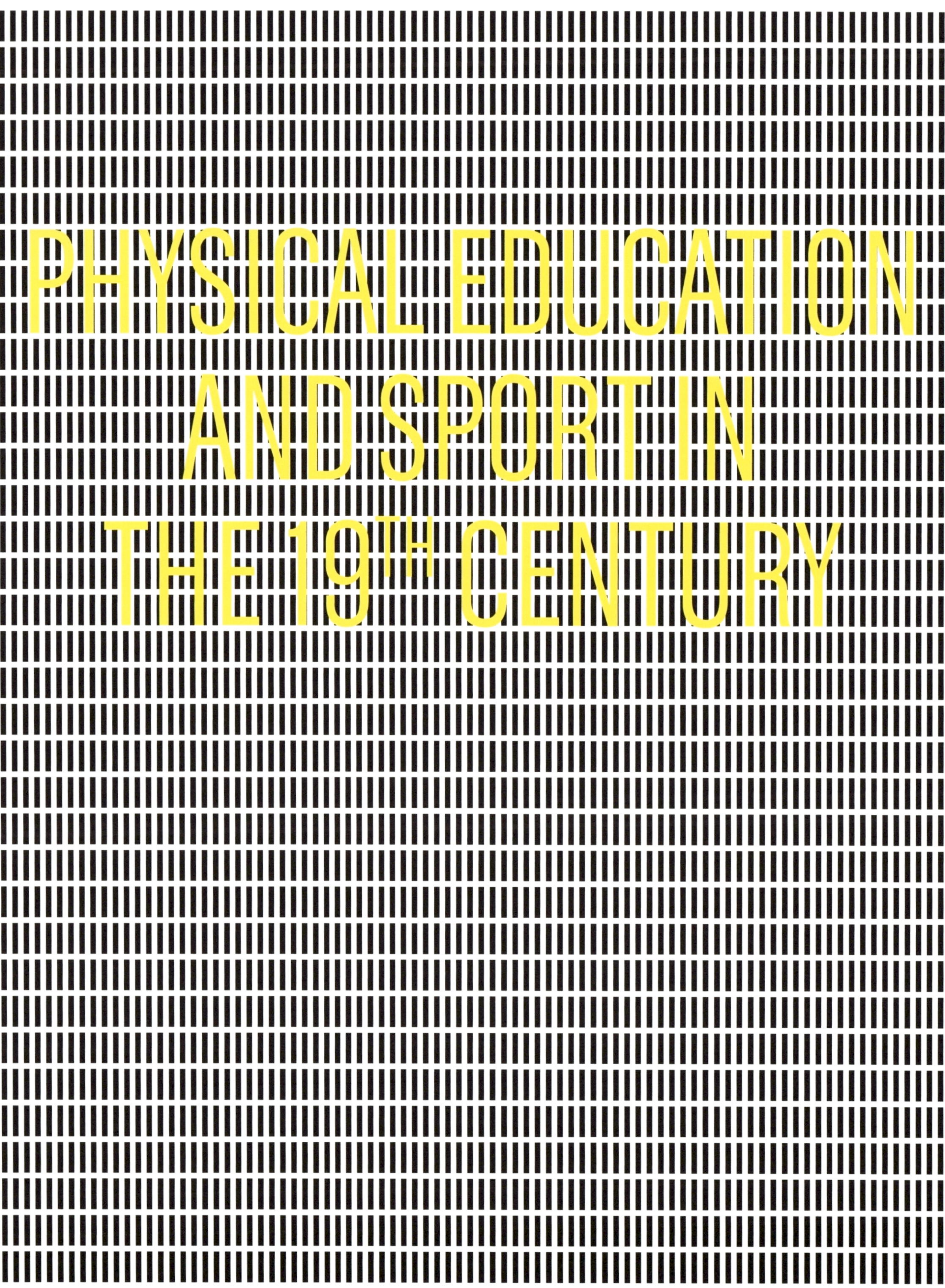
PHYSICAL EDUCATION AND SPORT IN THE 19TH CENTURY

PHYSICAL EDUCATION AND SPORT IN THE 19ᵀᴴ CENTURY

Physical education – what an irritating word for something that, in our opinion, should be fun! Nevertheless, in the 19th century it was a fitting term, particularly on the European continent. The British took a somewhat different view early on; in their upper classes they pursued a certain goal and changed physical exercise into sport in today's sense.

All the same, play and sport in order to exercise and strengthen the body were common on both sides of the channel: children running after a ball or competing in sack races, future warriors practicing fencing or horse-riding – all this we can imagine taking place in the Middle Ages. But in the 19th century a new aspect emerged in the context of physical exercise. The Enlightenment and French Revolution created the basis of a new social awareness – physical activities without any further, secondary purpose as confirmation of a citizen's individuality. Gymnastics and sport, though seemingly similar, have their origin in different theoretical and social concepts. What they have in common, however, is that they relate to a new society – a society in which each person is considered as an individual being, who does not see himself as being defined purely by his social class.

Man unfolds in the totality of his mental and physical capabilities – thus connecting with the ideal of Greek antiquity. There are numerous treatises, starting with Jean-Jacques Rousseau (*Emile, or On Education*, 1762), that deal with the different forms of physical activity in order to free man from social influences and create a *natural* unity of body and mind. But the concepts were also formalised – for example, in the form of physical exercise as a means of national self-liberation in a Germany that was still dominated by the authoritarian tradition, or as a means of distinguishing the classes in a class society such as that in Great Britain, or ultimately, at the end of the century, as an Olympic ideal of peaceful competition between national states in the style of ancient Greece. All the same, this ideal set new standards. On the other hand, it was never fully achieved – one might say that otherwise it would not be an ideal.

Very soon after, the workers' and women's emancipation movement lead to a new assertion of the right to exercise new forms of body culture in society. As physical exercise became a common activity throughout all social strata, physical training emerged as sport and also as a mass phenomenon.

TIMELINE
19TH CENTURY

1789 French Revolution

1793 Johann Christoph Friedrich GutsMuths publishes Gymnastik für die Jugend (Gymnastics for young people); his Spiele zur Übung und Erholung des Körpers und Geistes (Exercise and recreating games for body and mind) appears in 1796 and in 1798, his Kleines Lehrbuch der Schwimmkunst zum Selbstunterricht (Small teach-yourself manual on the art of swimming) is published.

1806 Napoleon defeats the Prussian army at Jena and Auerstedt; the Holy Roman Empire of the German Nation comes to an end.

1807 Reforms by Stein-Hardenberg are adopted in Prussia.

1807 Johann Heinrich Pestalozzi publishes Über Körperbildung als Einleitung auf den Versuch einer Elementar-Gymnastik (Body building as an introduction to elementary gymnastics).

1810 Friedrich Ludwig Jahn publishes Das Deutsche Volkstum (The German cultural identity); in 1811, the first gymnastics ground is created at the Hasenheide in Berlin.

1813 Napoleon is defeated in the Battle of the Nations near Leipzig.

1819 The Carlsbad Decrees for combating liberal movements in Germany come into force: gymnastics grounds are closed and Jahn is imprisoned; in 1820, gymnastics are prohibited in Prussia (gymnastics ban).

1836 Formation of the Hamburg Rowing Club.

1839 In England, the first Henley Boat Race takes place.

1841 The first inter-regional gymnastics festival takes place in Frankfurt am Main.

1842 The gymnastics ban in Prussia is lifted.

1843 Bavaria, Hessia, Württemberg, Lübeck, Bremen and Oldenburg include gymnastics in the school curriculum; Prussia follows suit in 1844.

1844 The gymnastics festival in Magdeburg attracts 1,000 participants.

1848 Revolution in Germany: barricade fighting (with gymnasts taking part) breaks out in Berlin, Dresden and Frankfurt am Main. The German National Assembly convenes in St. Paul's Church in Frankfurt; Friedrich Ludwig Jahn is elected as delegate.

1850 Acts in Prussia, Saxony and Bavaria suppress and control clubs and associations.

1855 The first German indoor swimming pool is opened in Berlin.

1858 With the rise to power of King Wilhelm I there are hopes of more liberal policies.

After 1860 School gymnastics is becoming popular in towns and cities.

1860-1863 The Prussian "parallel-bars dispute": gymnastics with equipment is abandoned in Prussian schools.

1862 The British found the first polo club in India; the first European club is founded in 1868.

1863 The Football Association (FA) is founded in England, the world's first football association.

1867 The Queensberry rules, which define the rules of boxing, are established in Great Britain and are still largely in use today.

1868 The Deutsche Turnerschaft (DT) German Gymnastics Association is set up in Weimar.

1869 Formation of the German Social Democratic Workers' Party.

1870/1871 The Franco-Prussian War leads to the foundation of the German Empire.

1871 The Rugby Union in Great Britain establishes common rules for rugby.

1872 England and Scotland stage the first ational football match.

1874 Gymnastics is made compulsory in girl's grammar schools in Prussia.

1877 The first cricket Test match takes place between England and Australia.

1878 The German Reichstag passes the Socialist Acts.

1888 The Lawn Tennis Association is founded in Great Britain.

1888 Emperor Wilhelm II ascends to power.

1888 The first professional league, the Football League, is created in England.

1890 The Imperial school conference in Berlin demands one daily hour of gymnastics, and achieves three hours a week of gymnastics at Prussian grammar schools.

1893 The Arbeiter-Turnerbund (ATB) (Workers' Gymnastics Association) is formed in opposition to the Deutsche Turnerschaft.

1893 Karl Fischer forms a rambler group at the Berlin-Steglitz grammar school which, later on, leads to the Wandervogel movement which is constituted as an association in 1901.

Around 1900 In Berlin, sport develops into a professional and spectator activity that attracts large numbers of people. Newspapers and magazines publish reports on sports events.

GYMNASTICS IN GERMANY

GYMNASTICS IN GERMANY

Today, the term *gymnastics* is generally considered to refer to one particular form of sport, to one of a number of different disciplines. However, in their origin, sport and gymnastics developed from very different political and social situations.

The early years of the 19th century were characterised by Napoleon's war campaigns and the French occupation of Germany – but what, at the time, was the meaning of *Germany*? The *Holy Roman Empire of the German Nation* had ceased to exist in 1806 following the abdication of the Emperor. Following the Napoleonic defeat, numerous small and medium-sized states were established in addition to Prussia and Austria – the country had disintegrated into small units. Furthermore, with its motto *Freedom, equality, fraternity*, the French Revolution in 1789 had developed democratic ideas. And the start of industrialisation with its emerging *Fourth Estate* – the proletariat, and the rise of the middle classes, promoted new social concepts.

The gymnastics movement initially came about as a protest against Napoleonic occupation, i.e. it had aspects of liberation. At the same time, from the very beginning, it had a nationalistic core. Gymnastics was not seen as personal, purely physical exercise but had an ideological/political dimension – both with national as well as liberal elements, which were violently opposed to each other. The national elements were particularly supported by the Wilhelmian Reich (since 1871) because the emperor recognised the connection between gymnastics and physical military prowess. For this reason, the typical sports buildings in the 19th century were not arenas for mass events – these were not yet in existence – but gymnasia in schools and military exercise grounds: discipline and order was the maxim; there was little regard for the enjoyment to be had from physical activity.

GUTSMUTHS —
GRANDFATHER OF GYMNASTICS

At the beginning of the 19th century, German gymnastics which, from its very beginning, was associated with national and even nationalistic tendencies, was decisively influenced by two persons: by Johann Christoph Friedrich GutsMuths (1759–1839) and by Friedrich Ludwig Jahn (1778–1852). Both these names can still be found in the names of gymnastics clubs, for example in *Guts-Muths 1861 Gymnastics and Sports Club* in Berlin or in *Jahn Regensburg*. Since Jahn had been spending some time at the newly founded Schnepfenthal Educational Institute where GutsMuths was a teacher, it would be fair to call them the grandfather and father of gymnastics.

In 1793, the first of numerous schoolbooks by GutsMuths appeared, *Gymnastics for Young People*, the first dedicated book worldwide on gymnastics in schools; this was supposed to *reaffirm a patriotic outlook* – physical education was associated with nationalism and combative prowess. During the time of the Napoleonic wars, this acquired a special meaning.

Almost at the same time, in 1789, the French architect Étienne-Louis Boullée had designed an arena for 300,000 people in Paris for the *ancien regime*, on the later Place de la Concorde.

As part of the reforms introduced by Freiherr vom Stein (1757–1831) in Prussia, which were meant to help modernise the state, GutsMuths' theories were adopted into school curricula.

Statue of Christoph Friedrich GuthsMuths in his native town of Quedlinburg.

"FRESH, DEVOUT, HAPPY, FREE" — TURNVATER JAHN

While Germany was still under Napoleonic oc-cupation, in 1811, the son of a Brandenburg pastor, Friedrich Ludwig Jahn (1778–1852), published his book entitled *Deutsches Volksthum* (cultural iden-tity of the German people) – a somewhat strange title considering the fact that a distinct German state did not exist at the time. In view of the book's main thrust, which primarily dealt with the struggle for freedom in an occupied and dissected country without national unity, rather than gym-nastics as physical exercise for its own sake, the latter could not be put into practice in the schools, for political reasons. In order to be able to practice gymnastics under French occupation, Jahn went out to exercise in the open; his first exercise place was located in the Hasenheide (a heath) in Berlin (1811). At a time when obligatory attendance at school, although in existence, was by no means commonly complied with, his appeal went out not only to school students but also to all young men. There was only the simplest of sports equipment; parallel bars, the high bar and others were only developed over time; on the other hand, people did not confine themselves to gymnastics as we understand it today – instead they also ran, threw, climbed and jumped: young men were meant to be trained into patriotic soldiers for a national *people's war* – a type of subversive training of partisans.

So the issue was not just gymnastics for its own sake and neither was it to achieve records, or to be the first in a race. It was about paramilitary training, which quickly spread throughout the country. It was about the struggle for liberation from Napoleon.

Picture of Friedrich Ludwig Jahn dated 1852 (contemporary lithograph).

The Hanau vigilante group consisted of gymnasts who were a driving force in the struggle for freedom and democracy during the 1848/49 revolution.

After Liberation and Restauration following the Vienna Congress of 1815, the liberation aspect was no longer politically acceptable; Jahn suffered persecution and went to jail, gymnastics were banned in Prussia and the lawyer and writer E. T. A. Hoffmann (1776–1822) wrote:

> *"Jahn has been accused of spreading dangerous principles with his gymnastics ideas; it is thought that what he conveyed to the gymnasts in word and teaching has resulted in dangerous attitudes threatening the peace of the state."*

It was not until 1840, when the gymnastics ban was lifted, that gymnastics could again be practised in Prussia, and numerous clubs were formed. Nevertheless, the controversy over the ideological orientation of gymnastics continued: on the one hand there were the *nationals* and on the other hand, the *liberal republicans* – and later the workers with their own concepts. In the 19th century sport was a matter of political attitude, expressed in the motto *Fresh, devout, happy, free* (in German: *Frisch, fromm, froh, frei*) expressed in the emblematic gymnastics cross with the four Fs.

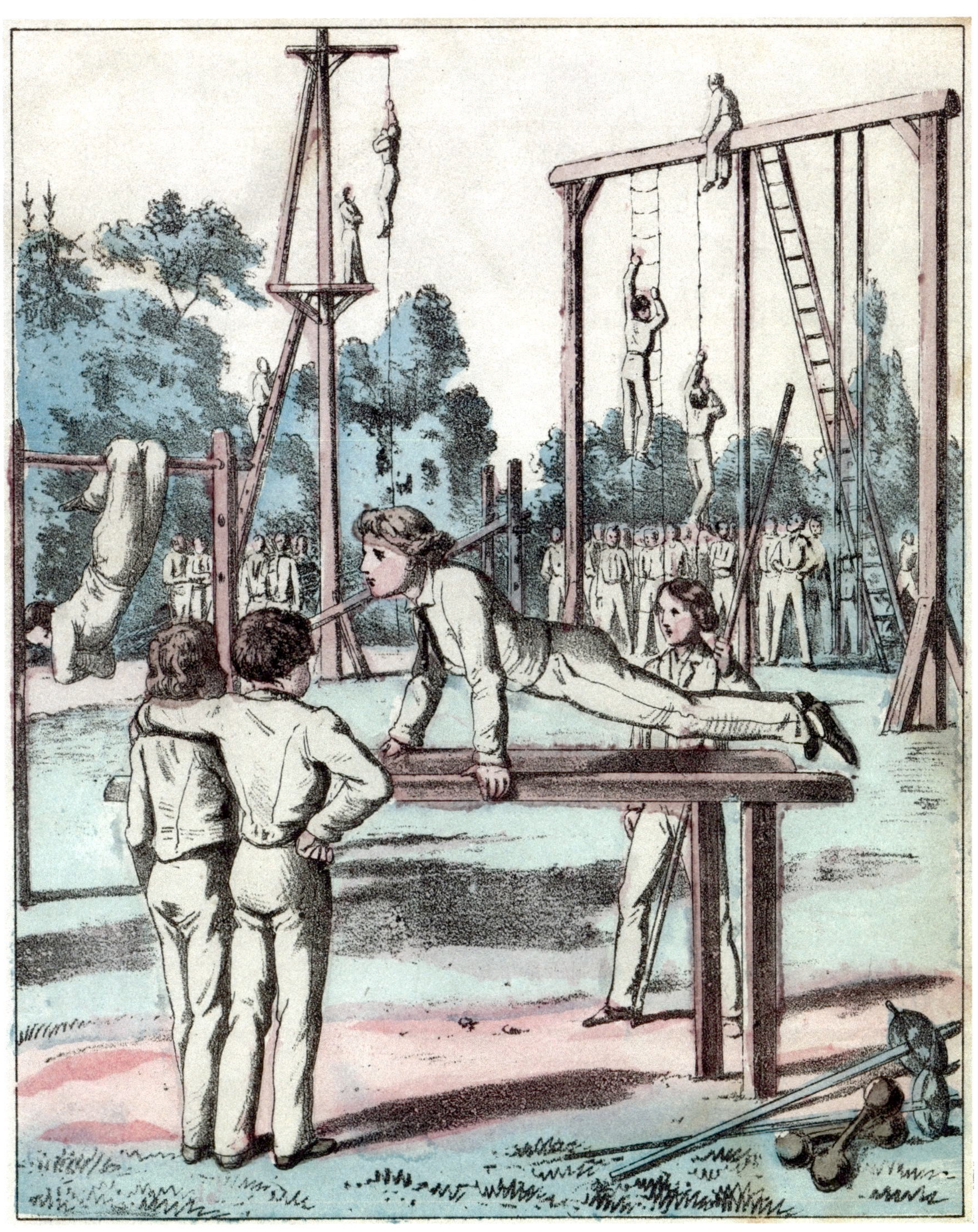

Gymnastics using the parallel bars, high bar and rope (contemporary lithograph, 1849).

THE PRUSSIAN "PARALLEL-BARS DISPUTE"

It is ironic that gymnastics equipment such as the parallel bars and the high bar, which had been introduced by Turnvater Jahn and which, after the ban on gymnastics had been lifted, was also available in schools, led to another political dispute. The Prussian captain Hugo Rothstein, (1810–1865), was critical of this equipment and, instead, wanted to introduce the Swedish *Lingsche Gymnastik* with paramilitary group exercises, due to its supposed high educational value. It was not an academic question – after all, one could have just left everybody to exercise their own choice. But gymnastics with equipment had been introduced to the Prussian military – and that's why it became a political issue. The dispute took place at the highest level in the Prussian Landtag (parliament). The outcome: the military went without gymnastics equipment while schools retained it.

Nevertheless, group-oriented discipline and submission of the individual were the main requirements for cadet-training establishments as well as schools. In a guide book for gymnastics in primary schools it says that "With the help of physical exercise, pupils are to be trained in focused attention, quick and exact execution of commands, controlling the will and submission for the benefit of the greater whole."

Above: Soldiers doing gymnastics (barracks of Artillery Regiment 11, Kassel, about 1900).
Below: New developments after 1900: football is accepted even by the military (Prussian main cadet school, group photograph of the team).

GYMNASTICS AND
THE MILITARY

Following the formation of the German Reich
in 1871, many gymnastics clubs were organised
under the umbrella organisation called Deutsche
Turnerschaft, which was strictly national and
anti-French in its orientation; gymnasts with a
liberal-democratic attitude were outsiders, the
revolutionary tradition of 1848 had been forgotten. On that basis the gymnastics movement qualified for acceptance by state institutions, i.e. the
schools and the military: strict rules, drills, commands and obedience became the basic principles
of gymnastics.

Books like this one carefully explored the new "desire for movement":
not sport or gymnastics, but "military gymnastics" as an independent discipline.

WILHELM BUSCH: THE CONSEQUENCES OF STRENGTH

With keen élan jumps from his bed
The eager gymnast Hoppenstedt.

He grabs the dumbbells free and fresh
Thus practising his lazy flesh.

At first the biceps gain in height
To give the arm its real might.

One-sided though is every man,
Who not with both hands practise can.

Strength is required in the neck,
To lift the full weight off the deck.

He never fails, especially,
To train leg muscles' energy.

Meanwhile below is Mr Meck
Who's pointing upwards at the deck.
The strength increases. – But below
Old Meck knows nothing of the show.
Then crack! – too great becomes the weight;

The ceiling yields – and gives a break.
And Hoppenstedt with a big clutter,
Drops down into the dish of butter.

Catastrophe is on all sides,
While Hoppenstedt slips down and slides.

He rushes out in hurried haste,
With pot and butter all apaste.

Disaster struck the smallest though
Poor little dog, Fidelio.

"It was not until 1863–1864 that the City built the central gymnasium at Prinzenstrasse 70, with a hall measuring 1,034 sq m and two smaller fencing rooms as well as various rooms for theory lessons and administration. The building also provides accommodation for the city's Chief Gymnastics Instructor, another gymnastics instructor, the gymnastics helpers and the porter. (…) The largest gymnasia by square area can be found in the secondary education establishments, i.e. grammar schools and secondary schools (…)."

CITATION FROM A BOOK ON NEW ARCHITECTURE IN BERLIN, PUBLISHED IN 1896.

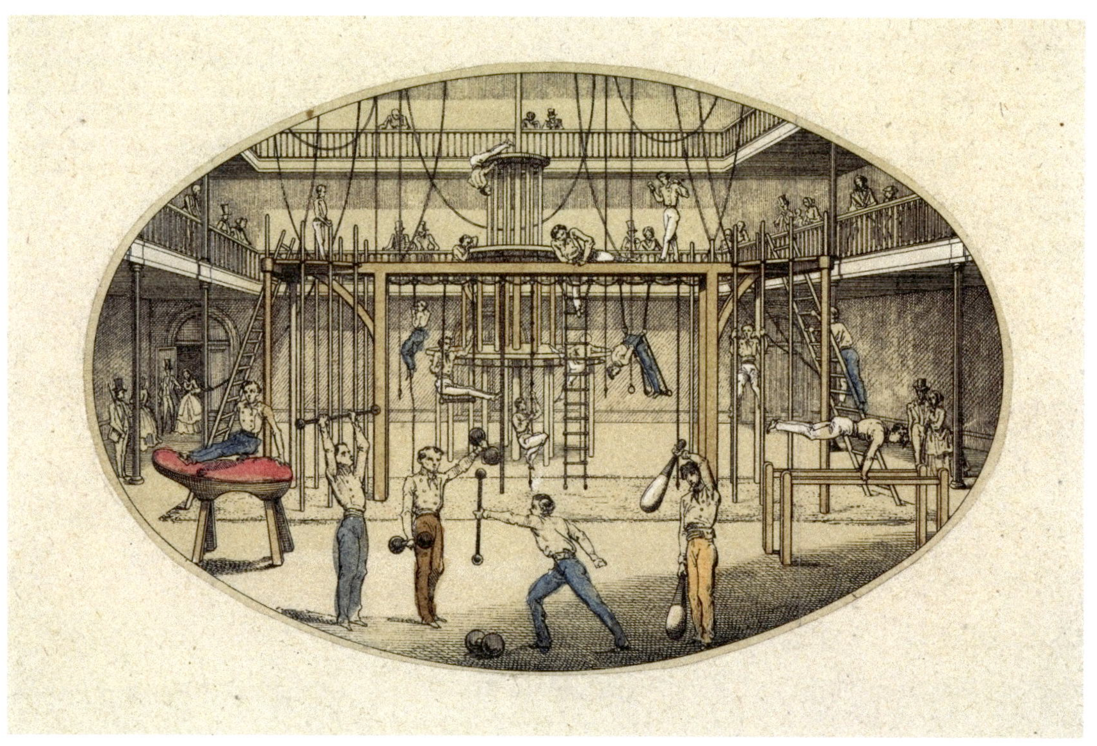

Apparatus gymnastics in a gymnasium (about 1845).

GYMNASTICS AT SCHOOL

Conclusion: gymnastics in the schools was strictly hierarchical, with pupils in the grammar schools – with their better education – benefiting from preferential treatment.

Part of the standard equipment included climbing frames and ropes – which were much in favour until far into the 20th century – on which fit and agile boys (of course no girls!) were climbing up swiftly and easily while those less physically able hung down like wet bags …

These were drab places, dominated by an authoritarian sense of order, devoid of any playful enjoyment.

Gymnasium of "Köllnisches Gymnasium" grammar school in Berlin, built 1891/92.

The first gymnasiums were dark and rather sombre places
(first gymnasium of the 1817 Mainz Gymnastics Club, photograph taken around 1900).

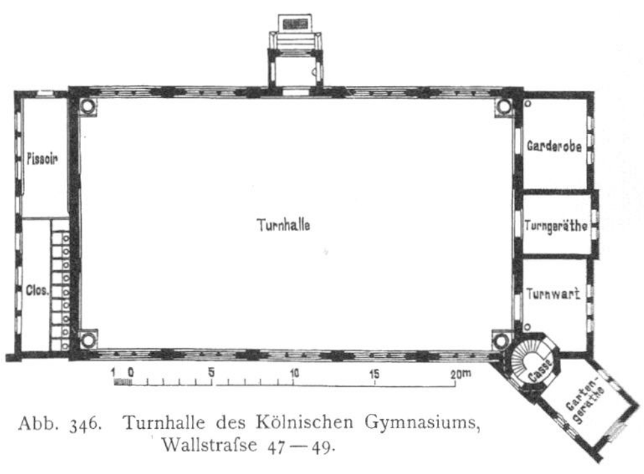

Abb. 346. Turnhalle des Kölnischen Gymnasiums,
Wallstrafse 47 — 49.

... and it was no different in Berlin: even the layout of the gymnasium seems to follow a military order.

These modern swimming baths, where the gender separation is clearly visible, were designed by Fritz Schumacher, the great Hamburg Oberbaudirektor (Senior Director of Construction). The baths opened in 1914.

"A BATH A WEEK FOR EVERY GERMAN!"

This postulation by the Berlin dermatologist Oskar Lassar (1849–1907) made in 1874 was not really a friendly request for more bath time fun or *wellness*, but rather a bid for more personal cleanliness of the proletarian class. The medical establishment slowly recognised that many diseases and epidemics could be prevented by better personal hygiene (in 1892, almost 10,000 residents of Hamburg died of cholera as a result of infected river water and a disregard of the rules for the prevention of epidemics). In the workers' quarters, slums or medieval city districts of the time it was difficult to establish preventive hygiene measures as many homes did not yet have piped water installations or toilets. This meant that the ordinary people had to be educated.

The first German *people's bath* had been established in Hamburg in 1855 – with bathtubs and showers, without a pool. It goes without saying that the swimming pools built towards the end of the century had separate pools and changing rooms for women and men – it was inconceivable that the genders be allowed to catch sight of each other. And the German term *Badeanstalt* did not come about by accident – these places were created with nothing but cleanliness in mind.

Bade-Anstalt 1. Ranges

Städt. Hallen-Schwimmbad Heidelberg

Bergheimer Strasse 45, 3 Minuten vom Bahnhof
Haltestelle der Elektrischen Strassenbahn: Hallenbad—Thibautstrasse.

Zwei Schwimmbäder für Männer und für Frauen
220 qm, bezw. 120 qm Wasserfläche.

Wannenbäder und Brausebäder.

Dampfbad (Röm.-Irisch). Elektr. Bad
Montag, Mittwoch und Samstag Vormittag für Damen vorbehalten.
Fichtennadelbäder, Solbäder, Kohlensaure Bäder, Sauerstoffbäder, Fangopackungen.

Die Anstalt ist das ganze Jahr geöffnet, und zwar:
a) vom 1. Mai bis 31. August: morgens von 7—1/2 9 Uhr abends; b) in den Monaten April und September: morgens von 1/2 8—8 Uhr abends; c) vom 1. Oktober bis 31. März morgens von 8—8 Uhr abends.

Kassenschluss für Schwimm-, Brause- u. Wannenbäder 1/2 Std.	vor den an-
„ „ Schwitzbäder 1 1/2 „	gegebenen Schlussbade-
„ „ Hundebäder 1 „	zeiten.

Preise der Bäder	Einzeln	Dauerkarten 12Bäder	3Monate
	Mk.	Mk.	Mk.
Schwimmbad (Preis ohne Wäsche):			
Erwachsene, gewöhnlicher Preis	—.40	4.—	6.50
„ ermässigter Preis	—.20		
(Mittwoch und Samstag von 1/2 6 Uhr ab.)			
Kinder unter 14 Jahren gewöhnlicher Preis	—.25	2.50	4.—
„ „ 14 „ ermässigter Preis	—.15		
(Mittwoch und Samstag von 1/2 3—1/2 6 Uhr.)			
Wannenbad (Preis ohne Wäsche):		11Bäder	
I. Abteilung	—.80	8.—	
II. „	—.60	6.—	
III. „	—.30	3.—	
Ein Kind unter 10 Jahren in Begleitung eines badenden Erwachsenen **halbe Preise.**			
Brausebad ohne Wäsche	—.10		
Dampf-, Warm- und Heissluftbad:			
Einschl. Massage und Schwimmbad (mit Wäsche)	1.50	15.—	
Elektr. Lichtbad mit Wäsche	2.50	25.—	
Medizinische Bäder			
Sauerstoffbad mit Wäsche	2.50		
Kohlensaures Bad mit Wäsche	2.—	30.—	
Schwimmunterricht (Karte gültig für 3 Monate):			
Erwachsene	7.—		
Kinder unter 14 Jahren	5.—		
Hundebad.			
Reinigen kleiner Hunde bis 45 cm	—.50	5.—	
„ mittlerer Hunde (über 45 cm)	1.—	10.—	
„ grosser Hunde (über 70 cm)	1.50	15.—	
Besichtigungsgebühr der Baderäume	—.20		

Wäscheleihgebühr: Badeanzug 15 Pf., grosses Badetuch 10 Pf., kleines Handtuch, Badehose, Seife, das Stück je 5 Pfg.
Wäsche-Aufbewahrung (gültig 3 Monate) kleines Fach Mk. 1.—,

Anmerkung. Die Anstalt bleibt am Neujahrstag, Karfreitag, Ostersonntag, Pfingstsonntag, Fronleichnamstag und Christtag während des ganzen Tages geschlossen. Jeden **Sonntag** sowie Ostermontag, Himmelfahrstag, Pfingstmontag, Stephanstag und Fastnachtdienstag Schluss ab 1 Uhr nachmittags.

Das Rauchen im Badegebäude ist nur in den hierfür bestimmten Räumen gestattet.

By today's standards, the entrance fees at this "first-class swimming baths" establishment were reasonable. Before visiting something as exotic as public swimming baths, a prior inspection of the premises was recommended.

The Arbeiter-Turn-Zeitung (Workers' Gymnastics Times) published in Leipzig was the official organ of the Workers' Gymnastics Association (1913).

The first German Workers' Gymnastics Festival took place in Leipzig in 1922.

WORKERS' SPORT:
"FRESH, FREE, STRONG AND TRUE"

The 19th-century gymnastics movement had its origin in the war of liberation against Napoleon and was therefore initially liberal-democratic in orientation. One aim of *political gymnastics* had been achieved by the time the German Empire was formed in 1871: a unified national state. It is therefore logical that organised gymnastics moved into a national conservative direction in order to preserve this achievement. However, the emerging *Fourth Estate* of the proletariat, the industrial workers, did not feel represented in these conservative clubs, in spite of the fact that many of the aims originally associated with the gymnastics movement were similar to those of the organised workers – the social and solidarity-forming function, and the rejection of competition and records. The social class segregation in the Wilhelmian State demanded its own associations and organisations: in consequence, the *Workers' Gymnastics Association* was founded in 1893 as a socialist organisation in opposition to the Wilhelmian State authorities.

Workers' sport in the sense of distinct, class-specific forms of organisation was an important part of sport until the time of the Weimar Republic – with its own associations, stadiums and even its own Olympic Games: at the end of the 1920s, about 1.2 million workers were organised in workers' associations. Mass events with orchestrated speech and movement choruses, and initiation plays were characteristic of sports festivals – the choreography of the masses took place on the lawns of new stadiums. These were also built in the 1920s, partly because the English team sports became popular in Germany too, and partly because large crowds of spectators wanted to see their competitions: a completely new building type was created, consisting of the pitch, a running track and spectator stands.

For example, in Cologne's *Grünzug Süd* parkland area to the south of the city, which had been designed by City Architect Fritz Schumacher, the city's mayor, Konrad Adenauer, initiated the construction of a large sports facility, including velodrome, swimming pool and three adjacent track and field grounds and grandstands which were separated by user classes, including one specifically for workers.

"Solidarity" was the key word in working-class sport. Although this sounds a little old-fashioned today, it was of crucial significance to workers at the turn of the century.

There was also a political aspect to workers' sport and gymnastics. They were an important element in the class struggle, provided an opportunity for finding solidarity in the club and for enjoying some longed-for leisure time.

SPORT AND IDEOLOGY

The pamphlet, with an appeal to organised cyclists and a strong warning against the consequences of *socialist cycling*, is an example of the political alignment and ideological overburdening of gymnastics and sport by the respective associations:

Appeal!

Cyclists! Sports enthusiasts!

"Social democracy, this notorious proponent of all endeavours against Christ and fatherland, is revealing its true face in ever more audacious and brash form; the orgies enacted by this overthrow party against Throne and Altar are becoming wilder and more and more outrageous. Social democracy does not shy away from anything that serves its purpose. All types of sports associations are used, under the cloak of pretended neutrality, to bait the naive and over-trustful public into buttressing the wicked aims of the Red International. (…)"

WORKERS' OLYMPICS OR:
DOES SPORT HAVE TO BE COMPETITIVE?

The first Workers' Olympics of the international Workers' Sports Associations took place from 24 to 28 July 1925 in Frankfurt am Main, in the new Waldstadion arena which has now been converted into the Commerzbank Arena. Twelve nations took place, but the games were not about individual victories and national ranking as in Coubertin's Games, which were rejected by the workers, but about a shared sports festival and the expression of *body culture* as part of humans as a whole. Therefore there were no flags, no national anthems, no winners; the 3,000 participants made their entrance into the stadium to the tune of the Internationale: "This is the final struggle …"

Two further Workers' Olympics took place, one in Vienna in 1931 with no less than 25,000 participants, and one in Antwerp in 1937, this time with significantly less participants – indicating the effectiveness of the destruction of the workers' movement in Germany.

Sport without flags and national anthems, but with mass displays (these are now being rediscovered and used for the opening of Olympic Games).

Fighting amazons as imagined by male sculptors (Greek relief, 4th century BC).

The first ladies bicycle race took place as early as 1868 – in Bordeaux, France.

SPORT FOR WOMEN
"FREE FROM ANY SECRETLY RAGING PASSION"

Combat and sport with and by women can be found as early as in Greek mythology – the amazons were warlike women who also fought men and had to be trained for that. Nevertheless, sport for women has always been a contentious issue – for men; in ancient times, women were not admitted to compete in the Olympics; they were not even allowed to watch. But in the 19th century there were, on the one hand, the developing desire by women to practice sports and, on the other hand, the restrictions imposed by men who feared the worst regarding *propriety*. To be more precise: regarding their own ideas of *propriety*. To this day, the emancipation of women in sport presents a challenge, with attitudes ranging from recognition and sexist behaviour. Women's boxing was the last to be recognised because it was considered *un-aesthetical*. Furthermore, today (in contrast to the 19th century) the scantiness of women's sports attire is controlled by regulations in order to rule out what is seen as *sexy* – by men.

The extensive restrictions applied in women's sport were less restrictive only in school gymnastics because these took place in girls' schools with their own girls' gymnasia: the first gymnastics institutions for girls in Berlin were founded in 1843. However, it took about another 50 years until gymnastics for girls became part of the mandatory curriculum in Prussian schools.

The small (sexist) difference: men's clothes do not have to fit tightly but women must not wear more than 7 cm of fabric between hip and leg: it is not the degree of cover that is regulated but the degree of exposure. Admittedly, the regulations shown here were for the 2004 Olympic Games; those for 2012 are less restrictive.

Elegant tennis dress. 1912.

The clothing of working women was
not quite as elegant.

Oxford versus Cambridge: the first rowing contest between two universities took place in 1829.

THE CREATION OF SPORT IN GREAT BRITAIN

THE CREATION OF SPORT IN GREAT BRITAIN

Serve and volley by an English gentleman.

England is often called the *home country of sport*. Here, sport has different roots and has developed differently compared to the rest of Europe. The development was influenced by a strong aristocratic class and a long period without war, which meant that no military training was required for the young. From the early 18th century, sports events were a common occurrence: especially rowing competitions, cricket and horse-racing. The term *sport*, which has its origin in the English language, derives from the Latin *disportare*, meaning to amuse oneself – which indicates that it referred to the leisure activity of a class that had spare time because it was privileged enough to be able to live off the work of others or off inherited wealth. It is therefore not surprising that even cockfighting was classed as *sport* – as it served as entertainment. But the English gentleman was not just a spectator, he took part in sports activities, even in boxing competitions, which were a lot harder in those days than they are today. There were paid boxers – i.e. professional sportsmen – but a gentleman would not take money as that would have looked like paid labour.

Betting was very popular as it was a means to make – or lose – a fortune faster than at the stock exchange. For the betting system to be widely accepted it had to comply with consistent rules; these were determined in *clubs*, access to which was restricted to the nobility. It was part of a gentleman's code of honour to be a good loser whilst, paradoxically, winning was the objective of the competition (and was an intrinsic part of the betting system).

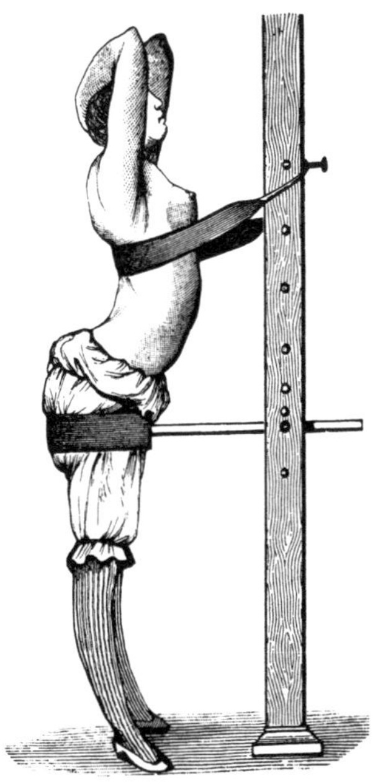

How the "posh" British ladies kept fit prior to 1900; those less well situated had to work.

DEVELOPMENT OF RULES DURING THE 19ᵀᴴ CENTURY

A seemingly surprising parallel exists, both in terms of time and content, between the development of sport in the 19th century and industrialisation, which started in England and proceeded to conquer the world. Like sports, industrialisation relies on competition and is based on gaining an advantage through skilful solutions (technical inventions in industry could be seen as a parallel to the *tactics* employed in sports). Furthermore, the industrialisation process was not regulated by class barriers or guilds, but was in the hands of a growing and increasingly confident middle class. The idea of maximum performance in industrial production has a parallel in the sportsmen's striving for records: to achieve a maximum of performance with the most efficient deployment of power and intelligence.

Increasingly, the rules were no longer defined in aristocratic clubs, but in democratically structured organisations, i.e. in sports associations (interestingly, here too, women were only admitted in exceptional cases). Nevertheless, the middle class wanted to distinguish itself from the lower class, which led to the idea of the *amateur* who would practise sports as a leisure pursuit rather than for payment. That was something only the aristocracy and the middle class could afford. It follows that the idea of the amateur, which for a long time was prevalent in the Olympic Games in the 20th century, originally came about as a way of excluding certain classes of participants.

The English ladies were not professionals: cricket match 1891.

A football game in 1827: presumably the referee would have shown one or several red cards if these had been in existence (lithograph by George Hunt, about 1830).

SPORTSMANSHIP AND FAIRNESS

"The English sportsman is proud of being a good loser. In that way, he manages to make his opponents feel guilty when they have won." What Peter Ustinov (1921–2004) – himself definitely not a sportsman – expressed here slightly sarcastically, has an odd background, which is somewhat difficult to understand. It is not only about complying with the rules – that is taken for granted. In a social setting where winning, success and records are the objective and, in the free market economy, are pursued with few scruples, the focus in sports is, on the one hand, to win and, on the other hand, for the winner to show his losing opponent due respect for making this victory possible. It sounds complicated, and indeed is complicated: for example, it means that an amateur sportsman should not train too hard – after all the original meaning of the word amateur is *lover*. By contrast, those who have to earn their living with sports, have to train – they are not amateurs, but professionals.

Nowadays, practically all types of sport require an intensity of training and time input that can only be afforded by professionals. Not so with one of the most typical of English sports, cricket, which is largely played by amateurs and has rules which for outsiders are difficult to understand. At international level, cricket is played in so-called *Test* series. This gentlemanly aspect takes the sting out of the competition between countries (the notion is "We are just playing for the fun of it!" rather than "Our nation is better than yours!"), reflecting the original idea in English sport.

It must be said, however, that these days top cricket in England is also played by professionals.

SPORT
AND
IDEOLOGY

Sport and ideology: in 1914, the Germans
derided the British as "softies" who were
only able to battle on the football or
rugby pitch. The British used the idea for
their own propaganda: a fighter in sport
is also a fighter at the front.

YOUNG MEN OF BRITAIN !!
THE GERMANS SAID YOU WERE NOT
IN EARNEST
Extract from Frankfurter Zeitung :–
"The young Britons prefer to exercise their long limbs
on the football ground, rather than to expose them to any
sort of risk in the service of their country."
"We knew you'd come–
and GIVE THEM THE LIE !"
PLAY the GREATER GAME
and JOIN the FOOTBALL BATTALION

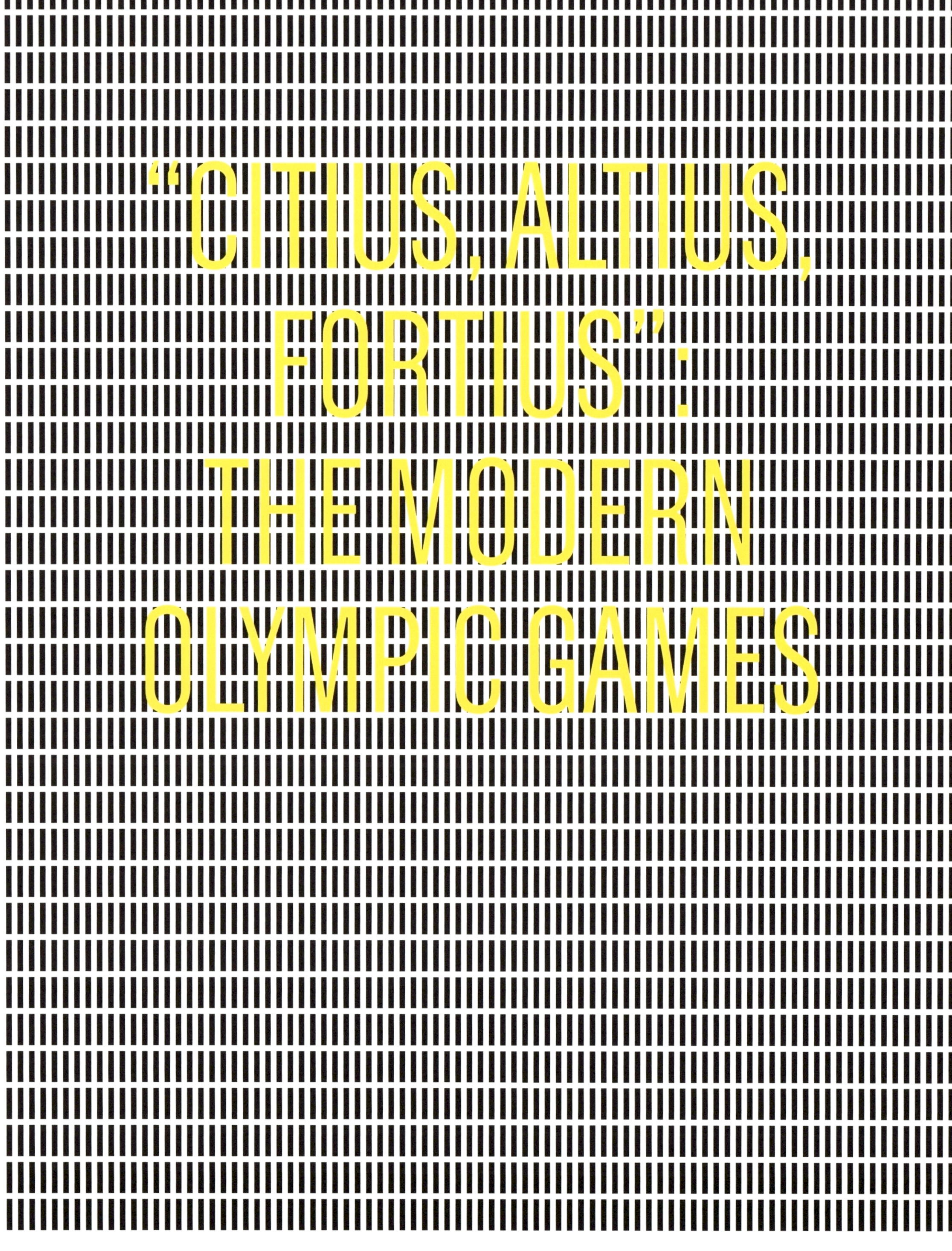
"CITIUS, ALTIUS, FORTIUS":
THE MODERN
OLYMPIC GAMES

"CITIUS, ALTIUS, FORTIUS": THE MODERN OLYMPIC GAMES

Following the ancient Olympic Games there were other games throughout history, in the sense of big festivals with contests in a number of different sporting disciplines, from medieval tournaments through to the Cotswold Olimpick Games in England, which are thought to have taken place since 1612. These were always a mixture of entertainment, games and competition at national level.

But what a wonderful idea to transfer the example of peaceful competition between free citizens of the Greek city states to the 19th-century nation-states in Europe, which were often hostile to each other! The Olympic Games were never quite forgotten – the temple complex at Olympia was discovered as early as 1766 – but a systematic exploration did not start until 1875 when Ernst Curtius took charge of excavations. That was four years after the Franco-German War and the formation of the German Empire.

The French Baron Pierre de Coubertin blamed France's defeat not least on the poor physical condition of his country's soldiers, but his idea for new Games was not really motivated by military concerns. Rather he wanted to shift the battle to the field of sports, as a peaceful competition: "The Olympic movement breaks down barriers.

It demands air and light for all, it promotes general physical education that is accessible to all and, supported by male courage and the spirit of chivalry, blended with events for the pursuit of aesthetics and literature, is intended to be the motor driving the life of the nation and the focal point in the life of citizens", wrote Coubertin in his *Nouveaux Programmes*.

In contrast to the practice in ancient Greece, the Games were now to take place in different countries, who would take turns to hold them. Initially, women were not admitted (which did not change until 1900) and the sportsmen had to be amateurs, that is they were not allowed to earn money from their sport.

It was from these beginnings at the first modern Games in Athens that the world's biggest sporting event evolved during the 20th century: starting with 250 contestants from 14 countries in Athens in 1896 it grew to 11,000 athletes from 204 countries in Beijing in 2008. With billions of television spectators, the Games are a huge commercial business. In addition, there are the buildings which, from the beginning, represented architectural statements about dealing with sportsmen and spectators – the choreography of the masses.

TIMELINE

1894 Baron Pierre de Coubertin convenes a sports congress in Paris: the International Olympic Committee (IOC) is founded.

1896 The first Olympic Games of the modern era take place in Athens in the restored ancient stadium of Herodes Atticus (the Panathinaikon).

1909 Berlin is selected for the 1916 Summer Olympic Games, but the Games are cancelled due to the World War I.

1931 Berlin is awarded the 1936 Summer Olympic Games.

1936 The IV Olympic Winter Games take place in Garmisch-Partenkirchen and the 1936 Summer Olympics (officially Games of the XI Olympiad) in Berlin.

1952 The Federal Republic of Germany and the Saar Territory take part (separately) in the 1952 Summer Olympics in Helsinki, but the German Democratic Republic of Germany (GDR) does not.

1956 All-German teams participate in the Olympic Games in Melbourne, 1960 in Rome and 1964 in Tokyo.

1966 The IOC selects Munich for the Games of the XX Olympiad to be held in 1972.

1968 Two separate German teams participate in the Winter Olympics in Grenoble and the Summer Olympics in Mexico City.

1972 The Games of the XX Olympiad take place in Munich.

ATHENS 1896

In the modern Games there are medals for the top three places; the back of the silver medal is shown here.

The first conference for the organisation of the 1896 Olympic Games; second from left, Baron de Coubertin.

ATHENS 1896

Surprisingly, the first modern Games in Athens were a big success, attracting 250 athletes and a great many spectators. Thereafter the numbers diminished somewhat until the idea finally caught on at the 1906 Intercalated Games, which again took place in Athens.

Following several attempts to re-establish the idea of the Olympic Games in Greece and elsewhere in Europe, the renewed initiative by the French aristocrat, Pierre de Frédy, Baron de Coubertin (1863–1937) proved successful. At a conference with representatives from different sport disciplines, which had originally been convened to determine a unified definition of amateur status, the last point on the agenda was a discussion on the *re-introduction of the Olympic Games*. Once this was agreed upon, the International Olympic Committee was formed. In 1913, the symbol of the Olympic rings was developed and introduced, also by Coubertin.

Coubertin's fundamental idea was that of mutual respect: *le respect mutuel*. The Games were actually meant to further world peace – at a time of political tensions in Europe, which ultimately led to World War I. The grand idea was Olympic peace and it truly was a grand idea. This should not be forgotten, in spite of all the criticism relating to undesirable side effects of the Games, ranging from political manipulation through to corruption.

The focus was on the sportsmen's performances, their mutual respect for each other, the relationship between winners and losers, and also on the spectators, who were expected to admire fair competition and understand it as an example of human interaction.

Title page of the official report on the Games.

He was one of the heroes of the Games: water-carrier Spyridon Louis, son of a peasant and winner of the first marathon.

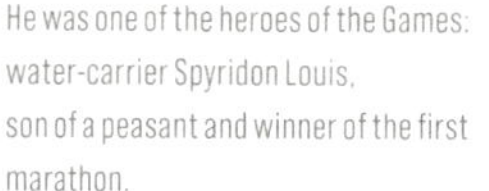

Pierre de Frédy, Baron de Coubertin, founder of the modern Olympic Games.

"LE RESPECT MUTUEL" – PIERRE DE COUBERTIN

The founding father of the modern Olympic Games was descended from a noble French family with a long history who had enjoyed a chivalrous aristocratic education. Although initially groomed to become a military officer, he turned his thoughts to educational projects with the aim of promoting holistic education that would bring body and mind in harmony, with sport playing an important role in that pursuit. These were ideas which had been practised in Ancient Greece and which resonated with the general enthusiasm for antiquity that was prominent throughout the 19th century. His philosophical outlook was focused on the ideal of a peaceful contest, something that only those with sufficient means could afford. Battling for money would have been dishonourable to him. To that extent his was clearly an aristocratic concept (and one that involved only men). *Knights* are men after all.

Under the pseudonyms of Georges Hohrod and Martin Eschbach, that is seemingly two authors, Coubertin himself became an Olympic winner in 1912, in the *literature* discipline, which at that time was still in the programme. He had submitted an *ode to sport* in which sport was celebrated as a gift of the gods and the elixir of life that would bring about beauty, justice, courage, honour, joy, fertility, peace and progress.

Unlike today, there was originally no distinction between the culture of the body and the culture of the mind. For example in 1936, the architects of the Berlin Reichssportfeld, the brothers Werner and Walter March, were awarded an Olympic gold medal, and art competitions were held until 1948. After that they were omitted because the artists usually made a living from their art and were therefore not amateurs, a strange notion.

The marathon finishing line: Louis is accompanied by Crown Prince Constantine and Prince George of England, while the spectators wave their hats in admiration.

Start of one of the 100 metre heats: please note the interesting start positions.

BACK TO THE ROOTS

After a long period of subordination to the Ottoman Empire, Greece regained its independence in 1830 and was assigned the German King Otto I from the Bavarian House Wittelsbach. The country was searching for a new identity, which it hoped to find in the classical age of its glorious past. The idea of a revival of the Games had been under discussion in Greece since the rediscovery of the Olympic sites and the excavations carried out by Ernst Curtius in 1875. It seemed only natural that the first Games should take place in Athens. Indeed the Greeks wanted them to take place there in perpetuity but could not secure support for this idea from the IOC.

Funding the event was – after initial difficulties – fairly easy: the Greek businessman and patron, George Averoff, donated the money for the reconstruction of the ancient Herodes Atticus Stadium and the operating costs were funded with the help of a series of commemorative postage stamps. The contests involved 241 sportsmen from 13 nations and lasted ten days. The most successful contestant was Carl Schuhmann, a German who won four gold medals in gymnastics and wrestling, two rather different disciplines! He also won a medal in weightlifting. The disagreement between *gymnastics* and *sport*, which had gone on throughout the 19th century, continued. The German gymnasts (together with those of other nations) declined to take part in events with the *sportsmen*, for social reasons; they were nevertheless reprimanded by the national German gymnastics organisation for taking part.

There were no national teams at the time, and no national anthems. Overall there was not much socialising: women and professional sportsmen were not admitted. Although there were victories, they were not celebrated with too much fanfare, as a gesture of noble understatement.

Above and right: The stadium was built on the foundations of the ancient stadium – hence its unusual shape.

REVIVING ANTIQUITY – THE HERODES ATTICUS STADIUM IN ATHENS

The stadium for the 1896 Olympic Games was a completely new edifice that was based on the exact layout of the previous building (the hippodrome of Herodes Atticus); large stadiums were a rarity elsewhere in Europe in the 19th century. A single sponsor, George Averoff, donated the money for the building, which was to be in marble throughout but, as with many later stadiums, it could not be completed in time and some parts were therefore clad in wood that was made to look like marble. The architect was Anastasios Metaxas, who based his design on the stadium of the Panathenaic Games (330 BC) in Athens, which had been excavated by the German archaeologist Ernst Ziller. It is a moot point whether the design should be attributed to Metaxas or to the original designer.

The stadium is located about one kilometre east of the Acropolis and is laid out in the shape of a horseshoe. The inside length is 236 metres and the track length is 333 metres with curves in a tight radius. It can accommodate about 69,000 spectators, with 50,000 seats. Tickets sold well and some events were completely sold out. The total number of spectators was 300,000.

Interestingly, the architect Anastasios Metaxas was also a target shooter and took part in the Games, placing fourth in several disciplines. It is quite likely that he is the only Olympic architect who was also a successful sportsman.

The Olympic Stadium – combining tradition with a new start.

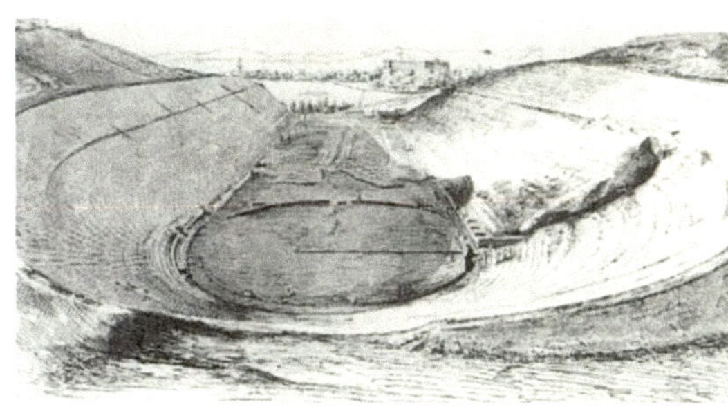

The former structure: the stadium as it was found and drawn by archaeologist Ernst Hiller.

BERLIN 1936

BERLIN 1936 –
GAMES IN THE NATIONAL SOCIALIST
"THIRD REICH"

There is no doubt that, following the Games that had revived the idea of the ancient Games, the 1936 Summer Olympics in Berlin were a first dramatic climax, from the point of view not only of politicising a sporting event using spectacular mass choreography, but also in terms of comprehensive urban and landscape design. This was the first time that the Games had been used entirely for the purpose of presenting the political ideology of a state, including extensive media features, such as the evocative films by Leni Riefenstahl, *Festival of Peoples* and *Festival of Beauty*, and – for the first time – television coverage. The dramatic staging of the event in the architectural setting was overwhelmingly impressive.

The power of the authoritarian state was expressed in the neoclassical style of the architecture. For the first time the Olympic fire was carried by runners from Olympia to the Games venue and the flame lit on a tripod that resembled the original Delphic design. At the Marathon Gate, with the Olympic flame above, the stadium was open and provided a vista onto the *Maifeld* ground, which was used for the parades staged by the Nazis, who had decreed the 1st of May as a holiday as a propaganda ploy against the socialists.

Along the line of sight, on the *Westwall* grandstand of the Maifeld, one could see, above the Temple of the Dead for the heroes of the slaughter at Langemarck (1914), the Olympic tower with the Olympic bell with the inscription: "I call the youth of the world".

This call to the nation's young people, in preparation for the planned Second World War, was part of a blatant but nevertheless brilliant choreography. It served a criminal cynicism which would, just three years later, lead to the cruellest genocide in history.

The architectural device of juxtaposing the spectator masses with the parade marching grounds was the expression of a dictatorship. The opposite was displayed 36 years later. The 1972 Olympic Games in Munich provided an opportunity to present Germany in a different light. Freeflowing forms of buildings, pathways and landscapes, transparency, cheerfulness and light pastel colours were the design features for a completely different choreography – the choreography of citizens moving about freely and cheerfully in an open democracy, without coercion.

Above: One of the posters for the 1936 Games in Berlin: it was clearly intended to seek a connection between sport and antiquity.
Below: The idea of combining the heroic Olympic glory of ancient times with Berlin and its quadriga on the Brandenburg Gate was brought to the world: a poster from 1936.

THE "GERMAN STADIUM" FOR THE 1916 GAMES – A FIRST ATTEMPT

By the beginning of the 20th century, the Olympic Games had become an established worldwide sports event; in general, sport had become a mass event. At that stage, in 1909, Germany was selected for the Games that were planned for 1916. For this purpose, the *German Stadium* was built by Otto March at the hippodrome in the Berlin Grunewald area and inaugurated on the occasion of the emperor's 25-year jubilee. A special feature of this stadium was that it was dug into the ground in order to preserve the view of the racetrack. The stadium – which was designed for 30,000 spectators – included a football pitch, a running and cycling track and also, within the stadium, a swimming stadium with a 100-metre pool.

The 1916 Games did not take place because of World War I (1914–1918). Instead, there were raging battles at Verdun, Langemarck and the Somme. The stadium was used as a military hospital during the war instead. Germany was blamed for the war and was therefore excluded from the Games in 1920 and 1924. In 1923, the German Stadium was chosen as the venue for the German Football Championship in front of over 60,000 spectators, which Hamburger SV won 3 : 0 against SC Union Oberschöneweide.

During the 1920s, the mass enthusiasm for sporting events led to plans to erect buildings for a *German Sports Forum* for the German Academy for Physical Education. The architectural competition was won by Werner and Walter March, the sons of the architect of the German Stadium; some of the planned buildings were completed during the 1920s.

In 1931, Germany was again selected for the Olympic Games, for which it had applied in 1929, this time for the 1936 Games.

The selection had taken place before the National Socialist party seized power. Once Hitler had taken over, there was a short period during which the new government considered returning the Games since their international character and the participation of different races and religions did not seem appropriate for the new Reich. It was not until Hitler recognised the opportunity that this event offered, with its high-profile publicity for presenting the new, National Socialist Germany to the world, that attitudes changed. All available resources were dedicated to the Games, which were intended to be larger and more impressive than any previous ones and to showcase Germany as an extremely successful sporting nation.

Propaganda races by German athletics clubs in the German Stadium, the predecessor of the Olympic Stadium (1923).

The major axis along which the buildings are placed stands out very well in the aerial photograph (left). It has been implemented without compromise through to the ground plates.

THE REICHSSPORTFELD –
OLYMPIC SHOWCASE FOR THE THIRD REICH

Between 1934 and 1936, the sons of the architect of the German Stadium, Werner and Walter March, built the new stadium for 100,000 spectators in the place of the old one, as well as a complete new sports facility, parts of which had already been included in the planned extensions to the German Stadium and were implemented in the new *Reichssportfeld*, the world's first Olympic Park. This new city park, the German Sports Forum, included a swimming stadium, the Dietrich Eckart stage, the Maifeld grounds with the Westwall grandstand for parades of up to 250,000 people and a bell-tower above Langemarck Hall, the inside of which was dedicated to glorifying the sacrificial death of 50,000 teenage war heroes. The Hall as well as the theatrical/monumental layout, with the buildings arranged along one long axis at the end of which one could see the bell-tower through the Marathon Gate, was intended to convey the National Socialist idea of power and glorification of death.

Carved in stone at the front of Langemarck Hall one can read the following lines by the German poet Hölderlin (which were written with reference to the wars of liberation from Napoleon):

*"The battle
is ours! So that you may live, oh Fatherland,
and do not count the dead! Dearest!
Not one too many has fallen for you."*

The opposite side displays a verse from a poem by Walter Flex, whose novel *The Wanderer between Two Worlds* (1916) had gained the status of a cult book:

*„Ihr heil'gen grauen Reihen
Geht unter Wolken des Ruhms
Und tragt die blut'gen Weihen
des heimlichen Königstums."*

*(You grey and holy phalanxes
march under clouds of glory
and bear the bloody sacrifice
for king and fatherland.)*

The bell-tower with Langemarck Hall – but what is the link between a memorial to dead heroes and Olympic sport?

Choreography of the masses was not restricted to the Olympic Games. The Nuremberg Rallies – or here, a KdF (Strength through Joy) event, "the working people engage in physical exercise" in the Deutschlandhalle, Berlin – were organised along the same principles.

After World War I the legend spread that many of the fallen heroes of the Battle of Langemarck were high school leavers who had rushed to the front with works of German literature in their rucksacks, including Friedrich Nietzsche's *Thus Spoke Zarathustra* and Rainer Maria Rilke's *The Cornet*.

The stadium's monumental architecture with its massive rows of pillars and a great deal of solid stone conveyed the feeling of gravitas, weighty mass, lockstep and the imperial power of Roman antiquity. The design was an expression of Hitler's idea that, in another thousand years, the ruins of his buildings would be witnesses to his empire's grandeur.

At the time, Olympic medals were also handed out for cultural achievements; for example, Werner March was awarded a gold medal in Town Planning for the masterplan and a silver medal in the Olympic art competition for the design of the stadium itself. He thus had the glory of being an Olympic medallist as an architect, not a sportsman.

Choreography of the masses was also practiced in other fascist countries – here, on skis in Mussolini's Italy (around 1935).

The German team enters for the opening of the Games.

Torch bearer about to enter Berlin, surrounded by enthusiastic spectators.

The "via triumphalis": Unter den Linden decorated with flags for the 1936 Games.

The route of the Olympic-torch run from Olympia to the respective venue; the run took place for the first time on this occasion, and has since been a regular feature of the programme.

THE GAMES – "THE FATHERLAND'S HIGHEST THRUST: OFFERING DEATH IF NEEDS MUST"

As already mentioned, the National Socialists were initially not at all enthusiastic about the Olympic Games; after all, they had only *inherited* them. But Hitler recognised the propaganda potential of such an event with its worldwide media coverage, giving Germany the chance to present itself as an open, peace-loving nation. The State therefore financed the entire project – a prerequisite for the extensive construction works; the fact that this also created many jobs for the unemployed was a welcome side effect. Hitler requested the creation of something *great and beautiful*.

The Olympic torch relay, which took place for the first time in 1936, was perceived as a gesture that would add a monumental, celebratory note to the event: 3,400 torch bearers carried the Olympic flame from Greece to Germany – an idea that to this day has proved to be a very popular choreography device. Finally, the opening ceremony culminated in an *initiation play* by Carl Diem who, after 1945, was Head of Sport at the Federal Ministry of the Interior for many years.

In the lines "In the games holy theme – the fatherland ranks supreme. The fatherland's high-est thrust – is offering death, as needs must" the notions of sport and contest are linked with the idea of sacrifice, death and fatherland in a sinister paradigm, which is also expressed in the Langemarck Hall under the bell-tower, both of which remained unchanged and without any comment until they were converted between 2004 and 2006.

Be this as it may, visitors coming to the Olympic Stadium as spectators often watched great sporting events in a stadium filled to capacity. Since the stadium's conversion for the 2006 FIFA World Cup by the architects von Gerkan, Marg and Partners, a permanent exhibition beneath the Langemarck Hall serves as a reminder of the burdensome inheritance left by the Third Reich.

Spectators using the Hitler salute.

1936 opening ceremony:
the German team marches in.

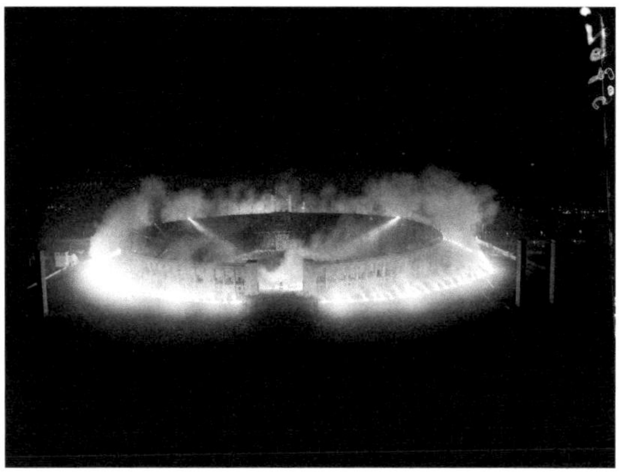

The closing celebration of the Games was also a dramatic event – the association with
flak searchlights became apparent three years later.

BOYCOTT OF THE GAMES

At the international level, the Games in National Socialist Germany were not without controversy; after all, the Nuremberg Race Laws had been passed in 1935, enshrining the persecution of the Jews in law, visible to all. Opposition stirred not only in the USA but also in other countries such as Great Britain, Belgium and The Netherlands.

On the other hand, Avery Brundage, someone who was not exactly known for his commitment to democracy and who later became the President of the International Olympic Committee for many years, was at that time the President of the Amateur Athletic Union of the United States. He travelled to Germany and was told that Jews were not allowed to practise sport in German clubs, to which he is reported to have said: "Jews are not admitted either in my sports club in Chicago." Which, incidentally, was also true for *coloured* people.

What then happened in Berlin during the Games was a brazen cover-up. One Jewish woman was admitted to the Games in Germany (another potential medal candidate was however not admitted) and anti-Jewish propaganda in the newspapers was prohibited for a short while: "The race issue shall not be addressed in any way when reporting on the sporting results; in particular, the sensitivity of negroes should be respected." [Peter Martin, *Charleston und Stechschritt. Schwarze im Nationalsozialismus* (Between Charleston and Goose-step: Black-on-Black in Nazi National Socialism), 2004]

This was intended to be a beautiful untroubled festival for sportsmen and spectators. The fact that about 50,000 people were being held as political prisoners received little attention during the Games. In his final address Goebbels predicted a new "epoch of real peace in all areas".

He had issued instructions to build the Dietrich Eckart stage using the design of the Greek theatre of Epidaurus, in honour of the poet who had been favoured by the National Socialists for his involvement in folklore and nationalistic issues. In an attempt to banish the past following the collapse of the Nazi Reich, the Reichssportfeld was renamed Olympia Park and the Dietrich Eckart stage was renamed the Waldbühne.

The festive performance, "Olympic Youth", in the Olympic Stadium on 1 August 1936.

Hitler salute and flak searchlights – it is no surprise the spectators, even those from abroad, were enraptured.

"Dome of light" over the Olympic Stadium during the closing celebrations.

PEACE PROPAGANDA FOR WAR

The official 1936 Olympics book includes a summary of what the Olympic Games meant for Germany's Third Reich and the politics of the National Socialists. The so theatrically and dishonestly hailed *spirit of Olympic peace* was intended to disguise the nation's rearmament, and it was only three years before Hitler's Germany attacked its neighbours. The following text appears cynical in hindsight and with the knowledge of the inferno that was being prepared:

"The Berlin Games are over, but they will not be forgotten. Too grand and noble were their design and execution dedicated to the Olympic idea by the Reich and the German people. It is Germany's pride and joy that it was able to present this festival to the world. It is its most honest desire to see this harmony, sportsmanship and comradeship which characterised these World Games, and the spirit of Olympic peace, kept alive and continue to spread its influence throughout the world.

(…) Almost every day, the Führer was with us. This lively and caring participation has filled our guests with surprise and admiration and they genuinely envied us for this man who, through his actions, has become the patron and promoter of these Games.

(…) The strong waves of love and admiration displayed by millions of Germans for the Führer during the Olympic Games have opened the eyes of many who might have been influenced by defamatory media, suggesting that Adolf Hitler would not dare to appear amongst the people. In Berlin they could see every day that he sits in the midst of his people who admire him and cheer him with intense passion. Huge numbers of foreigners have learnt to appreciate and respect the new Germany during these happy weeks and have become messengers of the truth."

Franz Miller et al., So kämpfte und siegte die Jugend der Welt Welt (thus fought and won the youth of the world).

A SENSITIVE RECONSTRUCTION OF THE OLYMPIC BUILDINGS

During World War II, the Blaupunkt company operated a factory for grenade and bomb fuses in the underground floors of the stadium; in 1952, the German Sports Forum became the headquarters of the British military administration of West Berlin and the Maifeld was chosen as the venue to stage birthday parades for the British Queen. The bell-tower with the Olympic bell, which had been badly damaged during the war, was blown up in 1947 and was reconstructed by Werner March from 1960 to 1962. As part of that work, the Langemarck Hall was reconstructed without any comment. The stadium itself was partly roofed over on the occasion of the 1974 FIFA World Cup.

A thorough renewal of the stadium did not take place until it needed to be reinforced for the 2006 FIFA World Cup. The project was the subject of an architects' competition in 1998, which was won by the architects von Gerkan, Marg and Partners; they respected the listed historic monument in their design by preserving the significant vista along the axis of the stadium, through the Marathon Gate, the open gap of the stadium with the Olympic flame, over the Mai-field grounds and to the bell-tower above the Langemarck Hall.

To achieve this, there is a gap in the grandstand roof above the Marathon Gate. The filigree roof seems to float above the heavy stadium without interfering with its contours. In an effort to deal with the heavy historic burden of this monument, the architects focused on informing the public about the historic context of the buildings rather than interfering superficially with the built structure as part of the conversion.

The architects went beyond what was required by their brief, and produced plans and found funding from the Federal Government and the City of Berlin for the conversion of the Langemarck Hall. With the help of the German History Museum it was possible to establish a permanent exhibition to explain the problematic history of the historic monument. In addition, the architects initiated, with the help of collected donations, the construction of an ecumenical chapel beneath the Coubertin box in front of which Hitler received the adulation of the public in 1936; the chapel is very popular today.

MUNICH 1972

MUNICH 1972 – THE "CHEERFUL GAMES"

The 1972 Olympic Games in Munich offered the unique opportunity to present the new Federal Republic of Germany in stark contrast to the Games held under National Socialist rule in Berlin in 1936. The jury, which was chaired by the architect Egon Eiermann, awarded **first** prize to the entry by Günter Behnisch & Partners, with its architectural, urban and landscape design that tried to reflect a free society in a democratic political system.

The jury appreciated not only the landscaping aspect of the design and the short distances between venues, but also the setting of the Olympic buildings in the Olympic Park, which allowed the free and unrestricted movement of citizens and guests from all over the world.

Instead of parading in marching columns and being forced into strict geometric patterns, people moved about in a free flow, around the hilly park, under translucent tent roofs, with the use of bright colours for orientation.

Tragically, this worldwide architectural message was marred by the attack on Israeli sportsmen by Palestinian terrorists in an attempt to take them hostage. This breach of the Olympic peace cast a deep shadow on the Games for young people from all over the world.

The closing celebrations of the 1972 Games in Munich: clearly more relaxed than those of 1936.

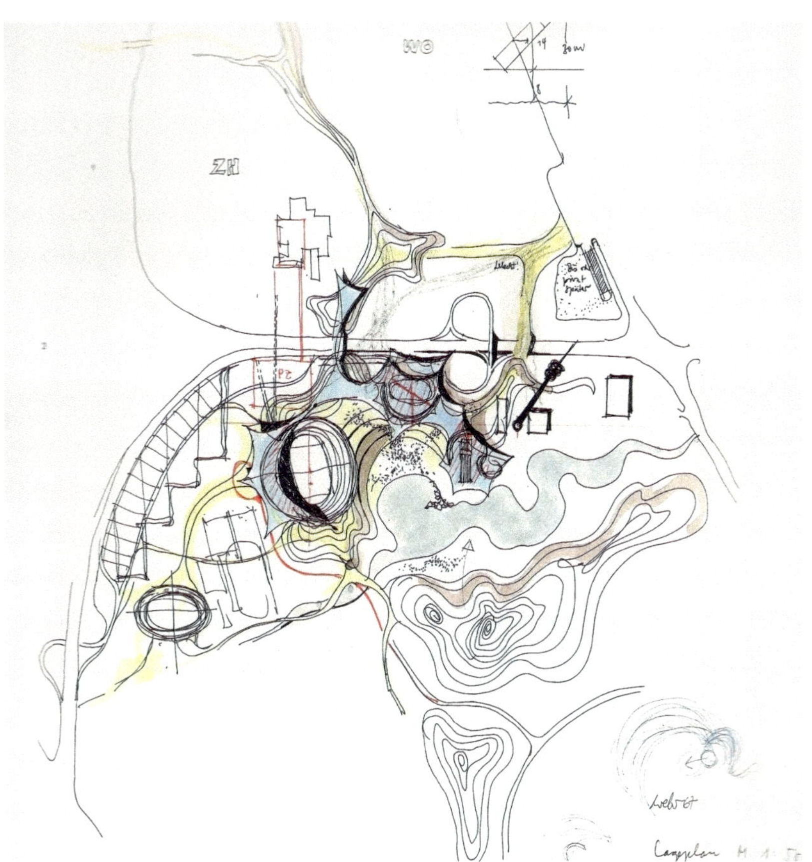

Sketch plan of the location of the Olympic buildings by Günter Behnisch.

BACKGROUND

Although Munich's population had exceeded one million residents since 1958, its transport infrastructure was poor and the sports venues were inadequate. The city suffered from the unattractive image of a *village of millions*. Munich's Social Democratic mayor, Hans-Jochen Vogel, wanted to modernise the city and also obtain funds from the Federal Government for his plans, because the state government was controlled by the opposition conservative CSU. In 1965, the President of the National Olympic Committee, Willi Daume, suggested that the city should apply to host the Games.

This proposal meant that certain problems had to be addressed: on the one hand there was the political question whether and how one could present oneself internationally after the period of National Socialist rule and the war and the image of the 1936 Games (as the *heartland of National Socialism* Munich had a problematic past), while on the other hand the administration hoped to obtain substantial funding from the Federal Government to pay for the necessary modernisation of the city.

In 1966, Munich was selected to host the Games, prevailing over its competitors Detroit, Montreal and Madrid. The core of the idea was to locate the Olympic buildings with the Olympic village close to the inner city on the Oberwiesenfeld, a former military and airport site, and to implement the notion of the Olympic Games in *parkland and with short distances*, as it says somewhat clumsily in the briefing for the 1966/1967 architectural competition.

First prize went to the Stuttgart architects Behnisch & Partners with Günter Behnisch, Fritz Auer, Winfried Büxel, Erhard Tränkner, Karl-Heinz Weber, Heinz Isler (construction) and Ulrich Hunsdörfer (traffic). The jury explained its reasons as follows: "The sculptural treatment of the terrain that characterises the design is not only an economic solution but also a favourable urban design approach for solving the task of accommodating the Olympic buildings on a site that does not naturally lend itself for that purpose." This shows that the roof was not a deciding factor at that stage.

One of the posters for the Games, again showing the distinct difference to those of 1936: "cheerful Games" versus heavy sentimentality.

Advertising poster in the "cheerful colours" of the intended "cheerful Games".

The tent roof covering the stadium: it has an impact on the behaviour of spectators – architecture influences people.

ARCHITECTURE AND TOPOGRAPHY

The brief for the architectural competition was preceded by the heading *Olympia im Grünen* (Olympia in Green Surroundings). The idea of a sculptured Olympic park on the Oberwiesenfeld with its mounds of rubble sparked the idea of turning away from the stern, axial layout of the Reichssportfeld in Berlin: the National Socialist paradigm was associated with a strict axial architectural layout whereas that of the Federal Republic was an inspired curvy landscape and architectural asymmetry. Later on, the winners of the competition commented as follows:

The aerial photograph shows the open, lightweight structure of the entire facility.

"The architectural response to the briefing request for an Olympia in Green Surroundings was 'an Olympic landscape'. This approach dominated all parts of the design, including the sports venues. Hollows in the terrain, similar to those in the Olympic Park, combined with a mountain, lake, pathways and trees. In other words: sport in hollows in the terrain, not in buildings. Traditional roof structures for sports venues were not suitable for this brief. (…) Nevertheless, these sports hollows had to be protected against wind and weather as well. A lightweight umbrella with a minimum of material seemed appropriate to us. This idea was best matched by a lightweight, pre-tensile space frame-structure consisting of steel networks with a translucent weatherproof skin.

(…) New design methods, new calculation methods, new production technologies, new details and much more had to be invented for the roof in Munich; extraordinary engineering was required and delivered.(…) It is therefore easy to overlook the fact that the key elements of our design are beneath and next to the roof; it is the sport and games landscape of the Munich Olympic Park."

GÜNTER BEHNISCH, "DAS DACH ÜBER DER LANDSCHAFT" (THE ROOF OVER THE LANDSCAPE).

In reality, a "little more" than the stocking fabric was required but the impression of lightness remains.

TENT ROOFS AND STOCKING FABRIC

According to the minutes of the jury's deliberations "The big problem with this design is the roof construction". So at the time it was not the roof that convinced the jury but the overall layout of the man-made park landscape; the roof was something like a symbol, a temporary roof cover, a kind of *big top* that would emphasise the playful aspect. Thought was given to alternative designs and to materials other than the polyester skin that had been proposed initially, for example wood boarding or lightweight concrete. Frei Otto, who had developed a similar structure for Montreal 1957, suggested that the architects use a pre-tensioned cable network covered with acrylic glass which would be translucent and cast only very little shadow – something like that had never been built for an area measuring 78,000 square metres. The estimated cost of the originally planned polyester roof was 17 million Deutsche Marks while the actual costs were about 190 million.

Eventually these tentative attempts at building a model led to the innovative tent-roof construction designed by the engineers Leonhardt, Andrä and Partners and their team members Jörg Schlaich and Rudolph Bergermann. This was a perfect match for the topographically modulated Olympic Park and became an unmistakable landmark.

The entire Munich Olympic Park was declared a historic monument, as was the 1936 Olympic site in Berlin. The latter was preserved in this way as a memorial to a despotic epoch in history, which had been overcome, and the former as an architectural manifestation of the built choreography of a free and freely moving society of citizens in a democracy.

One of the architects later gave an account of how the roof was designed:

"We got hold of ladies' stockings from my wife (…) which were knitted not in linear form but in a chain-like fashion. This material has about the same stretch characteristics in both directions; first of all it was roughly tensioned over an area and fixed with drawing pins, then it was supported with small wooden sticks, the outer edge contours were marked with a Pentel marker, the edge was folded and fixed with a needle and thread along this marking, then tensioned and knotted at the holding points; finally a bonded edging was applied to the folded edge and, once this had cured and become hard, cut into shape."

FRITZ AUER, "ZUR ENTSTEHUNG DES OLYMPIAPROJEKTES" (ON THE CREATION OF THE OLYMPIA PROJECT). UNPUBLISHED MANUSCRIPT 1999.

On the left, the "Women's Village" as used today, and on the right, the "Men's Village". The apartments are very much in demand.

OLYMPIC VILLAGES

Unlike the arrangements in Berlin in 1936, where the Olympic Village for the sportsmen was built far outside the city, later to be used as barracks, the Munich Olympic Village for women and men was developed directly next to the competition venues on the Oberwiesenfeld grounds. The women were housed in a compact low-rise development which later became an imaginatively painted student village (architect: Werner Wirsing), and the men in taller terraced houses which, after the Games, were sold as owner-occupied apartments and became a residential quarter (architects: Heinle + Wischer).

GERMANY (WEST) – GERMANY (EAST)

The contrast in political and architectural self-determination between 1936 and 1972 was not the only challenge; the other was that arising from the hostility between the ideologies of East and West, in Germany's case between the German Democratic Republic (GDR) and the Federal Republic of Germany (FRG). From 1956 to 1964, the German team at the Summer Olympic Games came from both German states, under a neutral flag and neutral anthem (*Ode to joy*), but the GDR had always aimed to demonstrate the superiority of the socialist system with its own team, given that sport with its global image as a benchmark for performance was an excellent instrument to achieve this. At the 1972 Olympics in Munich, the GDR sent its own team with its own national anthem and flag. For this reason and because the Games were taking place specifically in the FRG, the GDR made an enormous effort to raise its competitiveness in sports. And in fact the GDR sportsmen won 20 gold medals while those from the FRG only managed 13, which seemed to prove the superiority of the GDR system – at least in terms of selecting and training the team for high-performance sports, including doping. On this occasion, sport was not so much seen as an international contest but as a tool for political competition between different systems in the Cold War.

The final race in the 4×100 metres women's relay, in which Heide Rosendahl from West Germany prevailed over the East German world record holder and Olympic winner of the individual race, Renate Stecher, was perceived in the FRG as a *small victory in the competition between the systems.*

The GDR team joins the opening ceremony in marching formation; this is the first time that the GDR fields its own team and flag.

Mittwoch, den 6. Sept. 1972 · 30 Pf
Nach dem Blutbad im Olympia-Dorf
SONDERDRUCK
BILD
MÜNCHEN
16 Tote!
Alle Geiseln als Leichen gefunden!
Erschossen: Elf Israelis, vier Terroristen und ein Polizist
Ausgabe
Abendzeitung
Willkommen im Wienerwald
Wienerwald Gastlichkeit
B 20002 B
IOC-Chef Brundage
Die Spiele gehen weiter
100 000 kamen zur Trauerfeier
Wiederbeginn um 16.45 Uhr mit Handball
6. AUSGABE
tz
30 Pf
11 Israeli tot:
So kam es zum
Jetzt Teppichboden zu Sensations-Preisen!
Nicht lange warten TEPPICHBODEN 10.-
TEPPICH-DISCOUNT
Massaker im Flutlicht
Die blutige Bilanz: 17 Tote und mehrere Verletzte
Schießerei
Das Ende
Riegel
Leutnant Egon Kallensee (30) war Augenzeuge der Tragödie

... we now know that the good intentions and the architecture were overshadowed by a different reality – the attack on the Israeli team showed that there were graver matters than sport. The idea of the Munich Games, the "cheerful Games", is not affected.

SPORT AND
POLITICS

SPORT AND POLITICS

Mao Zedong, the Chinese Party Chairman, swimming in the Yangtze River; Walter Ulbricht, party leader of the SED (Socialist Unity Party) in the GDR, playing volleyball; black American athletes with raised fists during an award ceremony; the German Chancellor goal cheering in South Africa – images that are simultaneously political statements. In 1969 there was even a *football war* between Honduras and El Salvador.

When sporting achievement combines with the emotion of the spectators, sport inevitably becomes an object of politics, independent of its line of attack: that which formed the showcase for a National Socialist and racist state at the Olympic Games in Berlin in 1936, became symbolic of a free, democratic society in the same country in Munich in 1972 with the *cheerful games.*

Major events such as the Olympic Games or World Cup are especially susceptible to abuse as expressions of national pride, not least because they are generally financed by state funds. However, the connection between politics and sport exists at all levels: and thus an event such as the victory of the German team at the World Cup in Switzerland in 1954 becomes the rebirth of a nation!

This functions because many people identify with the athletes, thus leading to an emotionalisation – clearly a primary instinct which posits a *we* against the *others*. This has nothing to do with a contrived nationalism – it functions with one's own village club, the favourite team in the national league and through to the national team.

Politics attempts to utilise these emotions for its own ends.

SPORT
AND WAR

British and German troops meet up in no-man's-land between the trenches during the unofficial cease-fire.

SPORTING
CHRISTMAS PEACE

"Just imagine: while you were at home eating your Turkey, I was chatting out there with the men who I had been trying to kill just a few hours before", wrote an English soldier to his wife back home. He was referring to a truly remarkable event during the middle of World War I, as British and German troops lay tightly facing each other in the trenches of Flanders. Christmas 1914 – and only 1914 – a spontaneous ceasefire took place at various points along the front, something akin to a *Christmas truce*: the opposing troops sung Christmas songs together, exchanged gifts and played sports with one another – legend has it that in a football match between Germans and English near Frelinghien-Houplines the Germans won 3 : 2. On November 11 2008, a commemorative monument was unveiled at this site, a football match between the military units was held in remembrance of the event.

The *Christmas action* took place without prior arrangement and was far from welcomed by the commanders. However, an estimated 100,000 soldiers from both sides participated. The sporting contest was clearly (unconsciously) interpreted as an expression of a possible peaceful coexistence – a utopia.

During a memorial celebration, Peter Knight and Stefan Langheinrich, descendents of World War veterans, re-enact the scene of the 1914 Christmas cease-fire.

SPORTING COMPETITION WITH "REAL" WEAPONS

The counterpart to the ceasefire during Christmas 1914 is represented by the posters pictured here which called on sportsmen to volunteer for military service. An aggressive sport such as rugby appeared especially suitable. The depiction of *sport/sportsmen* and *war/soldiers* also provided a visual expression of the intended link.

That this was not just an English speciality is shown by the poster from Nazi Germany. When it comes to recruiting physically fit soldiers, sport in every country presents an important argument: sporting competition with *real* weapons – if that isn't an incentive!

"Therapeutic forms of sport": drawing by a Theresienstadt inmate.

Liga	Elektriker	Gärtner	Ghettowache	Hagibor Prag	Hagibor Therstd.	Jugendfürsrg.	Kleiderkammer	Köche	S.K. Linden	F.C. Wien
Elektriker			1:9		3:1		1:5		6:4	
Gärtner				3:1				2:0	3:0	3:1
Ghettowache	9:1			3:6		3:2				6:3
Hagibor Prag		1:3	6:3				2:2	1:9		
Hagibor Theresienstadt	1:3						1:6		7:5	1o:4
Jugendfürsorge			2:3				1:3	1:9	5:2	
Kleiderkammer	5:1			2:2	6:1	3:1				9:2

The Theresienstadt concentration camp even had its own football league – Liga Terezin.

"GHETTO GUARDS AGAINST COOKS 2:3" – SPORT IN THE CONCENTRATION CAMP

"Every Sunday there are football matches. Sunday between Norway – Czechoslovakia and Germany – and Poland. Norway won, Poland lost. These matches are sometimes played with passion. The blood boils and sometimes the players attack each other with their fists. In the match between Poland and Germany two players had to leave the pitch because they used their fists, after two others had already been carried off – unfit for competition. (...) A fine match! Directly adjacent people are lying dying. Sachsenhausen!" This was written by Fridtjof Nansen's son, imprisoned in Sachsenhausen concentration camp between 1942 and 1945. In actual fact organised football took place in the concentration camps on pitches specially laid out for this purpose – even in front of spectators, namely the guards and their prisoners. Theresienstadt had its own football league; matches were held such as *ghetto guards* against *cooks*. From 1943 onwards there was even a *Football Section* which devised special rules. And between the members of different countries *international matches* were held - all in order to strengthen the labour power of the prisoners. Once again, in the words of Nansen: "For many the fact that they were footballers was their salvation. They were treated with kid gloves, were assigned good jobs and received lots of food. In Poland the camps were the only places where it was permitted to play football; it was forbidden in the occupied country – although it was played in the underground."

However, there was another type of *sport*, namely the systematic physical mistreatment of concentration camp prisoners by means of *gymnastic exercises*, as commonly used during *honing* as part of military training. With the prisoners – who were already weak, generally ill and undernourished – this was an especially sadistic torture.

Football match in the Dachau concentration camp.

"Football war" between El Salvador and Honduras: the real issue was land seizure, not sport, but an international football match was the trigger for about 2,000 deaths over four days.

KIEV DEATH MATCH

Football as the continuation of war by other means: in the Summer of 1942, the Germans, who had occupied the majority of the Soviet Union, attempted to establish a semblance of normality. A team from the German air force was set to play against a soviet team in front of spectators in the Kiev Stadium – the same stadium that is currently being reconstructed for the UEFA EURO 2012 – the team from Bread Factory No. 3. However, what no one knew on the German side: it was largely composed of players from Kiev's best football club. They won 5 : 1, the return match yielded a similar result: final score 5 : 3.

According to legend the Kiev football players were never seen again, in other words they were taken directly to a concentration camp. However this has not been proven. The direct connection between play and terrible reality, namely that none of the players survived the period of occupation, remains speculation.

After the first leg and the defeat of the Germans, there was even a public poster for the return match – including a list of the Soviet players.

The entrance to the stadium

FOOTBALL WAR

A real *football war* took place in 1969 between El Salvador and Honduras, triggered by qualification matches for the coming World Cup (admittedly the actual reasons are to be found elsewhere): there had already been fighting between spectators during the first-leg match in Honduras, so during the return match the Honduran team were driven into the stadium in armoured vehicles for their protection. A further match in Mexico would decide the qualification. El Salvador won. This resulted in attacks on Salvadorian citizens in Honduras, which in turn occasioned the Salvadorian army to attack – supposedly in order to protect its own citizens in a foreign country. The war only lasted a few days, 2,000 people lost their lives, 6,000 were wounded, relations between the two neighbouring countries were poisoned for years.

The whole episode didn't really have anything to do with football, instead it was a channelling of the countries' internal economic problems into foreign political aggression; it was about illegal land seizure and immigration – concrete economic interests were at stake.

SPORTS BUILDINGS AND POLITICS

Jeu de Paume is a precursor of tennis, for which designated "tennis court houses" were built early on. Here the building is used for the Tennis Court Oath by members of the Third Estate, who pledged to continue meeting until a constitution had been written (Jacques-Louis David, "Le Serment du Jeu de Paume", 1789).

SPORTS BUILDINGS AND POLITICS

Sports buildings, stadiums and arenas, are in the first place: buildings. Large buildings as they are designed for large numbers of spectators. Consequently, they are also practical for non-sporting uses which require space for many spectators. When a political manifesto is read out to a large audience in a stadium then this no longer has anything to do with the sporting aspect of its construction, but solely with the practical character of its exterior. In turn, the Sportdome in New Orleans served as emergency accommodation following hurricane *Katrina*, as is often the case with gymnasiums following other natural catastrophes.

On the other side, sporting events have at least one thing in common with political rallies, but also with non-political events such as pop concerts or papal masses: the respective event – a football match, a World Championship, a papal mass, a party conference – is designed to generate a feeling of community, something akin to a *mass ecstasy*, an emotionalisation of the spectators. The sports building with itscircular or elliptical form is specially suited to this end as the terraces provide an architectural amplification of this community feeling – a choreography of the masses. When one looks around one as a spectator one feels part of a whole, the Mexican wave confirms it: it only functions when everyone participates.

If politics is able to awaken this feeling, then it is successful.

The same scene by a different artist: Jean-Louis Prieur (draft) / Pierre-Gabriel Berthault: "Serment du Jeu de paume" (the Tennis Court Oath), 1789.

"Total war – shortest war": Goebbels was right in his speech at the Sportpalast, only not in the sense he intended.

Another way the Sportpalast could be used: start of the 1927 six-day race.

Joseph Goebbels, Hitler's Reich Propaganda Minister (1897–1945).

"DO YOU WANT TOTAL WAR?"

February 18, 1943, during the middle of World War II: Josef Goebbels, Propaganda Minister to the National Socialist government in Berlin, gave a speech at the Berlin Sportpalast, where six-day races and boxing matches were held, to a carefully selected audience – a speech designed to mobilise the German people following the defeat in Stalingrad.

"The English say that the German people are war-weary. I ask you: are you prepared to follow the Führer as the phalanx of the homeland, standing behind the fighting army, and to wage war with wild determination and without hesitation, through all the turns of fate until victory is in our hands?

(…)

Fourthly: the English maintain that the German people are resisting the government's total war measures. It does not want total war, but capitulation. I ask you: do you want total war? If necessary, do you want a war more total and radical than anything that we can possibly imagine today?

(…)

Eighthly, I ask you: do you, especially you women, want the government to encourage German women to place their full strength at the disposal of the war effort, and wherever possible, to step into the breach in order to release men for the front, thus helping their men at the front?

(…)

The Führer has commanded, we will follow him. If we have ever believed staunchly and unshakably in victory, then it is now, in this hour of national reflection and inner resolve. We see it before us, within our reach, all we need is to grasp it. We only need to find the resolve to place everything else at its service. That is the order of the hour. And so the slogan is: now, people rise up and let the storm break loose!"

JOSEPH GOEBBELS, 18 FEBRUARY 1943.

Detainees are guarded in the Estadio National of Santiago de Chile following the 1973 Pinochet coup. The concentration camp was cleared shortly before Chile's participation in a World Cup qualification match.

A football match at the stadium in 2006.

PRISON ARENAS

Since Roman antiquity, the killing of people was nothing foreign to arenas and sports buildings. However, that this would return in the *civilised* period of the second half of the 20th century was not necessarily to be expected – the buildings are too much in the focus of media attention and a watchful public. And what was socially acceptable in ancient Rome is no longer the case today. Nevertheless: a stadium is highly suited to imprisoning a people.

In 1973 the Chilean General Augusto Pinochet organised a putsch against the Socialist government of Salvador Allende, legally elected in 1970 and now in severe difficulties. The new dictatorship pursued its political opponents with the utmost cruelty – around 40,000 prisoners were herded together in the National Stadium of the capital Santiago alone, which was effectively converted into a concentration camp. Prisoners were also tortured in schools and other suitable locations. The stadium itself was later released and returned to its former use. A secret prison served in its place. This was due to the qualification match for participation in the 1974 World Cup held at the end of the year against the Soviet Union – the stadium was needed.

The counterpart to the misuse of a stadium as a prison took place in 1974 in Greece, which at that time had just freed itself from the dictatorship of the so called *colonels*: in the Athens Stadium a celebration was held on the occasion of this liberation, with a concert from Mikis Theodorakis, the steadfast composer and opponent of the dictatorship.

SPORT AND NATIONAL IDENTIFICATION

SPORT AND NATIONAL IDENTIFICATION

Exactly why is it so exciting when Germany plays football against Holland or Austria? Both opponents are relatively small countries, and according to logic a small country cannot produce so many good footballers as a large one. Consequently, the outcome of the match must be clear from the outset.

From the perspective of the smaller country the situation is also clear – as in the case of David and Goliath: tripping up the larger opponent is a pleasure and alleviates the inferiority complex of the smaller country. However, when the supposedly small one plays the better and more attractive football then this in turn eats away at the large one – relations are reversed. Thus a highly complex web of emotions is at play here (and this is without even mentioning the political past!).

However, this only functions when the results are equivalent to the emotional effort, when they are achieved against all odds: a victory like that of Austria against Germany at the 1978 World Cup in Argentina had such potential – no one would remember the opposite outcome.

Furthermore, depending on the perspective, the same event is not assessed the same – what for the Austrians was the *wonder of Córdoba* was the *humiliation of Córdoba* for the Germans.

ERRATA

APPENDIX

This catalogue is published to accompany the exhibition
Choreography of the masses.
In sport. In the stadium. In a frenzy.
6 June 2012 to 12 August 2012
Akademie der Künste
Pariser Platz 4, 10117 Berlin

An exhibition at the Akademie der Künste,
Berlin, in cooperation
with gmp · von Gerkan, Marg and Partners
Architects

www.adk.de
www.gmp-architekten.de
www.choreographie-der-massen.de

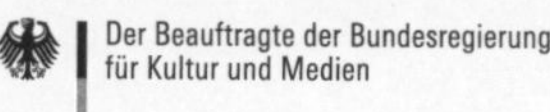
Der Beauftragte der Bundesregierung
für Kultur und Medien

EXHIBITION

Curators Volkwin Marg, Gert Kähler,
Michael Kuhn
Project management – Akademie der Künste
Johannes Odenthal, Carolin Schönemann
Assistant – Akademie der Künste Jacqueline Saliba
Project management – gmp Hanne Banduch,
Heidi Knaut, Michael Kuhn
Exhibition design Hanne Banduch, Heidi Knaut
Graphic design ON Grafik, Hamburg
Digital image processing Beatrix Hansen (gmp)
Editorial/copy editing Bettina Ahrens (gmp),
Martin Hager (edition8)
Translation Hartwin Busch, Colin Shepherd
Proofreading Mandi Gomez

EXHIBITION FILMS

Film excerpts for
"Sport in antiquity", "Sport and politics"
Concept and coordination Guido Brixner (gmp)
Production visionate interactive OHG, Hannover

In a frenzy – a film montage
Director and montage Hannah Leonie Prinzler
Sound composition Titus Maderlechner
Production Multivision Hamburg,
Knut Sodemann
Media technology vision_b, Berlin

PUBLICATION

Exhibition furniture and fittings
Act!worX, Berlin
Jörg Scheil (Akademie der Künste)
Andreas Northe, Cabinetmakers, Hamburg
Matzat Museum Technology, Berlin
Gärtner Internationale Möbel GmbH, Hamburg
P.O.P. Werbeteam GmbH, Hamburg
Wilking Metallbau GmbH, Berlin
Exhibition graphics and prints
René Birkner
DZA Druckerei zu Altenburg GmbH,
Altenburg
Reproplan graphics GmbH,
Hamburg/Berlin
Architectural model building Monath + Menzel
Architekturmodellbau, Berlin
Werner Modellbau, Braunschweig
Logistics Dieke Eiben (gmp)
Loans management Catherine Amé
(Akademie der Künste)
Public Relations – Akademie der Künste
Anette Schmitt, Marianne König,
Stephanie Eck
Public Relations – gmp
Christian Füldner

A microsite accompanies the exhibition
www.choreographie-der-massen.de
Responsible for the content Michael Kuhn (gmp)
Content management Nicole Schindler (gmp)
Realisation SHAKEN not STIRRED, Hamburg
Design ON Grafik, Hamburg

© 2012, Akademie der Künste, Berlin,
gmp · von Gerkan, Marg and Partners
Architects
jovis Verlag GmbH, Berlin, the authors
and photographers
All rights reserved.

Publisher Volkwin Marg for Akademie
der Künste, Berlin
Author Gert Kähler
Coordination Bettina Ahrens (gmp),
Michael Kuhn (gmp)
Editorial/copy editing Bettina Ahrens (gmp),
Martin Hager (edition8)
Translation Hartwin Busch, Colin Shepherd
Proofreading Mandi Gomez
Graphic design and typesetting
ON Grafik, Hamburg
Cover design
ON Grafik, Hamburg
Repro organisation DZA Druckerei zu
Altenburg GmbH, Altenburg
Printing and binding DZA Druckerei zu
Altenburg GmbH, Altenburg

Bibliographic data from the Deutsche Nationalbibliothek:
The Deutsche Nationalbibliothek lists this
publication in the Deutsche Nationalbibliografie;
detailed bibliographic data are available on the
Internet: http://dnb.d-nb.de.

jovis Verlag GmbH
Kurfürstenstraße 15/16
10785 Berlin
www.jovis.de

ISBN 978-3-86859-170-5

p. 79 **centre** ullstein bild – Imagno

p. 79 **bottom** ullstein bild – Hanns Hubmann

p. 80 **top left** Bundesarchiv

p. 80 **centre top** ullstein bild – Herbert Hoffmann

p. 80 **top right** Bundesarchiv, Graphic: Blez

p. 80 **bottom** ullstein bild – Wolff & Tritschler

p. 81 **top left** ullstein bild

p. 81 **top right** Bundesarchiv

p. 82 **top left** ullstein bild – TopFoto

p. 82 **centre top** ullstein bild – Wolff & Tritschler

p. 82 **top right** ullstein bild

p. 83 ullstein bild – Wolff & Tritschler

p. 85 **top** bpk/Hanns Hubmann

p. 85 **bottom** Johann-Karl Schmidt and Ursula Zeller (eds), *Behnisch & Partner: Bauten 1952–1992*, Stuttgart 1992

p. 86 **top** Bundesarchiv

p. 86 **bottom** ullstein bild – Schäche

p. 87 **top left** Gert Kähler

p. 87 **top right** ullstein bild – Schlage

p. 87 **bottom** ullstein bild – Robert Hetz

p. 88 **top left** Gert Kähler

p. 89 **top right** ullstein bild – Minkoff

p. 89 **top** Gert Kähler

p. 89 **bottom** ullstein bild – Werner Schulze

p. 90 ullstein bild – dpa

p. 91 ullstein bild – Lehnartz

p. 95 **top** Wikipedia/ Harold B. Robson

p. 95 **bottom** Wikipedia/ Alan Cleaver/Lizenz: CC-BY-2.0

p. 96 **top** ullstein bild – histopics

p. 96 **bottom** Bundesarchiv, Graphic: Prien Kroll

p. 97 **top** http://www.juedische-allgemeine.de/article/view/id/4108 (beide)

p. 97 **bottom** Foto: Friedrich Franz Bauer/ Bundesarchiv

p. 98 **top** © Bettmann/CORBIS

p. 98 **left bottom** http://spielverlagerung.de/2011/12/26/eine-weihnachtsgeschichte-fritz-walter-die-todeself-und-der-zweite-weltkrieg

p. 98 **right bottom** http://de.wikipedia.org/wiki/Todeself

p 100 **top** Wikipedia/© Photo RMN

p. 100 **bottom** Deutsches Historisches Museum, Berlin

p. 101 Bundesarchiv

p. 102 **left** http://www.emmemm.de

p. 103 **right** Wikipedia/Max Montecinos

p. 106 **right** bpk/Hans Hubmann

p. 107 **left** ullstein bild – Yavuz Arslan

p. 107 **right** ullstein bild – Sven Simon

p. 111 ullstein bild

p. 113 http://www.spartacup.schoolnet.co.uk/Fbritishladiep.htm

p. 115 **top** ullstein bild – Public Address

p. 115 **bottom** ullstein bild – ddp

p. 116 **top** ullstein bild – CARO/Rupert Oberhäuser

p. 116 **bottom** ullstein bild – ddp

p. 120 **top left** ullstein bild – Yavuz Arslan

p. 120 **top right** ullstein bild – Sven Simon

p. 120 **centre** *Rom: Die Olympischen Spiele 1960 mit Sieger Tabelle* by Joh. Jacobs & Co., Berlin: Erich-Zwirner, 1960. Printed by Elsnerdruck/ Courtesy Eric Chaim Kline Bookseller

p. 120 **bottom** Deutsches Historisches Museum

p. 121 ullstein bild – Heritage Images/Land of Lost Content

p. 122 **top left** http://www.zhc-grubenlampe.org/?Sponsoring:Werbung_am_Mann

p. 122 **top right** http://portal.krefeld-pinguine.de/index.php?option=com_content&view=article&id=105&Itemid=60&lang=de

p. 122 **bottom** ullstein bild – Werner OTTO

p. 123 **top left** foto: h.festag

p. 123 **top right** ullstein bild – Teutopress

p. 126 ullstein bild – Public Address

p. 127 ullstein bild – Reuters

p. 128 ullstein bild – ddp

p. 129 ullstein bild – Boness/IPON

p. 131 ullstein bild – Reuters

p. 132 ullstein bild – AP

p. 134 ullstein bild – Reuters/© Arnd Wiegmann

p. 135 ullstein bild – Reuters/© Christian Hartmann

p. 137 **top** Thomas280784 (aus de.wikipedia.org)

p. 137 **bottom** http://bathroomreader.com/tag/strange/

p. 138 **top** ullstein bild – CARO/Andreas Riedmiller

p. 138 **bottom** ullstein bild – imagebroker.net/J.W.Alker

p. 139 **top left** ullstein bild – CARO/Frank Sorge

p. 139 **top right** ullstein bild – Kreth

p. 139 **bottom** ullstein bild – AP/Tina Fineberg

p. 141 **top** ullstein bild – imagebroker.net/Thomas Frey

p. 141 **bottom** ullstein bild – Bullstein bild – Reuters/KAI PFAFFENBACHoness/IPON

p. 143 **top left** ullstein bild – Public Address

p. 143 **top right** ullstein bild – Werek

p. 143 **bottom** ullstein bild – Camera 4 Fotoagentur
p. 144 **left** ullstein bild – Team 2 Sportphoto
p. 144 **right** ullstein bild – imagebroker.net/Michael Weber
p. 145 http://hannani42.yoo7.com/t38571-topic
p. 146 ullstein bild – Sven Simon
p. 147 ullstein bild – Horstmüller
p. 148 **left** ullstein bild – Claus Bergmann
p. 148 **right** ullstein bild – imagebroker.net/Jochen Tack
p. 150 **top** ullstein bild – CARO/Marc Meyerbroeker
p. 150 **centre** ullstein bild – Sven Simon
p. 150 **bottom** ullstein bild – Pressefoto Ulmer
p. 151 **left** http://juniordesignerer.deviantart.com/art/
the-Thrilla-in-Manila-264177464
p. 151 **right** ullstein bild – United Archives/91040
p. 152 **left** ullstein bild – AP
p. 152 **right** ullstein bild – Reuters
p. 153 **left** ullstein bild – sinopictures/CNS
p. 153 **right** ullstein bild – Uli Winkler
p. 155 **top** ullstein bild – Günter Peters
p. 155 **bottom** Thomas Dietrich
p. 156 ullstein bild – Public Address
p. 157 **top** Gert Kähler
p. 157 **bottom** Johanna Kähler
p. 159 ullstein bild – Giribas
p. 160–161 © Olympiastadion Berlin GmbH
p. 181 **top right/left** gmp Archive
p. 181 **bottom** gmp Architekten
p. 182 gmp Architekten
p. 183–187 Marcus Bredt
p. 189 **top right/left** gmp Archive
p. 189 **bottom** gmp Architekten
p. 190 gmp Architekten
p. 191–195 Marcus Bredt
p. 197 Baukunstarchiv, Akademie der Künste, Berlin
p. 198 Auer + Weber + Assoziierte
p. 199 Meisterwerke der Kunst. Architektur II Hgg. zur
Förderung des Kunstunterrichts vom Landesinstitut für
Erziehung und Unterricht Stuttgart mit Unterstützung
des Ministeriums für Kultus, Jugend und Sport Baden-
Württemberg, 1999
p. 200 RKW Architektur+Städtebau
p. 201 Foster + Partners, Norman Robert Foster
p. 202 gmp Architekten

p. 203 Courtesy CSAC Archive, Parma, Italien
p. 204 Karl Krämer (Hg.), Bauten der Olympischen Spiele
1972 München, Stuttgart 1969
p. 205 Renzo Piano Building Workshop
p. 206 A:AI Archiv für Architektur und Ingenieurbaukunst
NRW
p. 207 schlaich bergermann und partner
p. 208 Schulitz + Partner Architekten BDA
p. 209 Zaha Hadid Architects
p. 210 Schuster Architekten Düsseldorf
p. 211 Otto Ernst Schweizer, Die architektonische
Großform. Karlsruhe 1957
p. 212 Souto Moura – Arquitectos, Lda.
p. 213 Tange Associates
p. 216–217 Multivision Hamburg
p. 218–219 Multivision Hamburg
p. 220–221 a&o buero
p. 222–223 a&o buero
p. 224–225 a&o buero

Though every effort was made to ascertain authorship and
provenance for all illustrations used, this was not possible
in some instances. All legitimate claims will be settled.

BIBLIOGRAPHY

Sport in antiquity
_Karl-Wilhelm Weeber, *Die unheiligen Spiele. Das antike Olympia zwischen Legende und Wirklichkeit*. Zurich/Munich: Artemis & Winkler 1991, p. 11
_Xenophanes, "Elegy", cited from Ulrich Sinn, *Das antike Olympia*. Munich: H.C. Beck, 2004, p. 26
_Lewis Mumford, *Die Stadt. Geschichte und Ausblick*. Munich: Deutscher Taschenbuch Verlag, 1979, p. 271 (originally published 1961 as *The City in History: its Origins, its Transformations and its Prospects*)

Physical education and sport in the 19th century
_Wilhelm Busch: source http://gutenberg.spiegel.de/buch/4111
_Peter Ustinov: source http://www.zitate.de/kategorie/Sport

"Citius, altius, fortius": the modern Olympic Games
_Pierre de Coubertin, "Nouveaux Programmes", in: Deutsche Olympische Gesellschaft (ed.), *Olympisches Lesebuch*. Hanover: Hermann Schroedel Verlag, et al. 1971, p. 15
_Peter Martin, "'Rassenkampf' im Sport", in: Peter Martin/Christine Alonzo (ed.), *Zwischen Charleston und Stechschritt. Schwarze im Nationalsozialismup*. Munich/Hamburg: Dölling und Galitz, 2004, p. 332
_Franz Miller et al.: *So kämpfte und siegte die Jugend der Welt. XI Olympiade Berlin 1938*. Munich: Knorr & Hirth, 1936
_Günter Behnisch, "Das Dach über der Landschaft", in: *Architekten Behnisch + Partner: Arbeiten aus den Jahren 1952–1987*. Hatje Cantz Verlag 1989, p. 43

Sport and politics
_"Stell Dir vor: Während du zuhause Deinen Truthahn gegessen hast, plauderte ich da draußen mit den Männern, die ich ein paar Stunden vorher noch zu töten versucht hatte" ["Just imagine: while you were sitting at home eating turkey, I was having a chat out there with those men that I was still trying to kill a few hours previously"]: Source http://werwiewo.wordpresp.com/2010/12/22/das-weihnachtswunder-von-1914/

_Odd Nansen: Source http://www.zeit.de/online/2006/40/fussball_kz/seite-2
_Josef Goebbels: Source http://de.wikipedia.org/wiki/Sportpalastrede
_Herbert Zimmermann, 1954: Source http://web.ard.de/special/helden1954/pages/2463.php?ch=1
_Declan Hill: *The Fix: Soccer and Organized Crime*, Ontario 2010, p. 233 ff
_Johannes Müller, *Die Leibesübungen. Ihre biologisch-anatomischen Grundlagen, Physiologie und Hygiene sowie Erste Hilfe bei Unfällen*. Leipzig: Teubner Verlag, 1926
_Bertold Brecht, "Die Krise des Sports", cited from: Deutsche Olympische Gesellschaft (ed.), *Olympisches Lesebuch*. Hanover: Hermann Schroedel Verlag, et al. 1971, p. 25

Sport and commerce
_Oliver Hassencamp: Source http://www.sportwissenschaften.info/dbquotations/seite-Kommerz-and.html
_Advertising for ZHC Grubenlampe: Source http://www.zhc-grubenlampe.org/?Sponsoring:Werbung_am_Mann
_Sie möchten bei den Krefeld Pinguinen werben? [You want to advertise with the Krefeld Pinguine?] Source http://portal.krefeld-pinguine.de/index.php?option=com_content&view=article&id=105&Itemid=60&lang=de
_Gunter Gebauer, *Sport in der Gesellschaft des Spektakels*. Sankt Augustin: Academia Verlag, 2002
_Markus Lamprecht and Hanspeter Stamm, *Sport zwischen Kultur Kult und Kommerz*. Zurich: Seismo Verlag, 2002

Being a winner too
_ Source: http://www.rp-online.de/sport/fussball/die-groessten-fussball-katastrophen-1.1513277
_The "Thrilla in Manila": Source http://de.wikipedia.org/wiki/Thrilla_in_Manila
_The biggest spectator events: Source http://sportbild.bild.de/SPORT/sportmix/2011/02/02/die-10-groessten-sport-events-der-welt/millionen-vor-dem-tv.html
_Spectator choreographies: Source http://www.fussball-kultur.org/fussball-kulturpreis/fanpreis-2011/preistraeger-2011.html

_FC St. Pauli – Freude schöner Fußballzauber [Joy, oh
football – game so precious]: Source http://www.
festgestaltung.de/fangesaenge/st_pauli1
_The Berlin Olympic Stadium as an example of a venue:
Source http://www.olympiastadion-berlin.de/special-
business-eventp.html

Quotations
_Gustav Le Bon, *Psychologie der Massen*. Stuttgart: Kröner
Verlag, 1982
_Étienne-Louis Boullée, *Abhandlung über die Kunst*.
Zurich and Munich: Artemis, 1987
_Elias Canetti, *Crowds and Power*. New York: Farrar, Straus
and Giroux, 1984, p. 15-30
_Johann Wolfgang von Goethe, *Italienische Reise*, Munich:
Stiebner Verlag 1999
_Peter Sloterdijk, *Die Verachtung der Massen. Versuch über
Kulturkämpfe in der modernen Gesellschaft*. Frankfurt am
Main: Suhrkamp Verlag, 2000

"Rahn has to shoot from a distance.

Rahn shoots!

Goal! Goal! Goal! Goal! (short pause)

Goal for Germany!

Left-footed shot from Rahn. Schäfer crossed into the middle. Schäfer won out against Boszik. 3 : 2 for Germany! Call me mad! Call me crazy!"

(Radio Reporter Herbert Zimmermann 1954)

Above left: The title page of a Hamburg newspaper dated 5 July 1954. From today's perspective, the outcome of a horserace may not appear quite so important. On the other hand, Mercedes' double victory was undoubtedly very important, but was somewhat overshadowed by the football euphoria at winning the World Cup.
Above right: After having won the 1954 World Cup: the team process triumphantly through Munich.

THE "MIRACLE OF BERN"

The victory of the German team at the 1954 World Cup final in Switzerland against the *unbeatable* Hungarians has been the subject of many interpretations. Nine years after the defeat in World War II, at a time when, on the one hand, the *economic miracle* was just gathering pace, while on the other hand ruins everywhere served as a reminder of the war, the event was described as the *rebirth* of a nation. Here the *David* versus *Goliath* perspective is decisive: Hungary was unbeatable. Germany was still ostracised. In the final Germany trailed by 0 : 2 and fought its way back – the symbolism is clear. The range of responses which the victory awoke in people is apparent from the following quotes – the language of the recent past was still very familiar to some of them …

"That was the Miracle of Bern. A miracle of comradeship and the united offensive."
BILD 5/7/1954

In turn, Peco Bauwens, then President of the German Football Association, said in a speech in celebration of the German victory in the Löwenbräukeller (beer cellar) in Munich:

"When other people dance around the pitch before the game with their flags then it is not acceptable that our people should be banned from carrying our proud German flag. We will not accept this. Our team presented them with the bill for this. (…) This victory has shown that there can no longer be any slurs on the sport and the German people if we are to be treated sincerely."

And once again from the tabloid newspaper *Bild* an article titled *Poor Little Football Wife*:

"The wife makes sacrifices in silence. Not only does she keep the sweaty training kit and the eternally dirty sport shoes clean. (…) The womenfolk also adjust their daily routine to the training times of their husbands, catering to his diet wishes in the kitchen. They occasionally swallow a harsh word for the sake of his mood, his joy in competition."
BILD 3/7/1954

The 2006 "summer fairy-tale" in Essen-Rüttenscheid … but even fairy-tales eventually come to end.

SUMMER FAIRY-TALE

The football World Cup in Germany in 2006 had a completely different function to the victory in 1954. Germany was now a transformed country – economically powerful, peaceful, re-united and thus apparently freed from the consequences of World War II. Germany was a normal country.

The task was therefore – as in the case of the 1972 Olympic Games in Munich – to present a picture of a peaceful Germany to the numerous foreign fans. It was something akin to a political assignment. This was achieved in a largely undirected manner – from virtually one day to the next it became popular again to display the German flag, in every imaginable (and some unimaginable) ways. Something was achieved that Germans themselves had not considered possible in this form: a peaceful celebration.

A number of special ingredients were required for this: the good weather (imagine four weeks of rain!). The German team's style of play, who were suddenly no longer *clod footed*, no longer "Teutonic tanks". And the fact that Germany was knocked out in the semi-final – at precisely the right point in time.

"The Chancellor also Screams for Germany."

Franz Josef Wagner, commentator:

"I think that we are all homesick, pure homesickness, homesick for each other. Homesick for one's wife, one's child, one's family, homesick for one's country. We now have a country that is so beautiful that one is reduced to tears. The country of castles, of the four seasons, the country of Luther. The UNO has chosen Beethoven as its hymn, Schiller wrote the text. We have forgotten our Germany. Now it reveals itself again, as exciting as a woman. I believe one has to love one's country like a woman. What kind of country do we love. First of all, a country is a landscape. There is a church in the landscape, in front of which a stream rushes by. I see leaves and small branches and trout, which one can fish. (…) It is a landscape of gently rolling hills, the evening sun comes late. The people peacefully fold their hands. They are hands which have worked, which have grasped wet mud, have sorted out the rotten leaves. I love these hands, they are Germany."

BILD 14/06/2006

"WHAT A GAME"

A British journalist experienced the opening game between Germany and Costa Rica:
"I fell in love with the World Cup in the Allianz Arena, Munich. (…) It is a heady feeling, being present at an event that the entire world is watching. The air itself seems coloured and distinct. There are invisible lines going out from the event to streets and houses around the world.

The game itself? (…) The game was perfection. Lots of goals. Skill. And spirit. It started early: in the sixth minute, Philipp Lahm, a German defender who looked so young that it seemed as though the ballboy had wandered onto the pitch by accident, suddenly cut past a defender and blasted a shot in the corner of the Costa Rican goal. I rose with the rest of the Stands and we roared.

It was over. All over. How could Costa Rica, tiny Costa Rica, playing in the opening match in Germany, against the powerful Germans, now down 1-0, outplayed in the first few minutes, ever hope to come back from that goal? Someone must have forgotten to tell Paulo Wanchope, the tall, athletic Costa Rican striker, because a few minutes later, he ran through the worryingly weak German defence to equalize 1-1. The game went back and forth, all the time played at a frantic pace. All the time the crowd, German and Costa Rican, cheered and roared at every piece of skill and magic. All the time we were caught, 66,000 of us, in the spirit that not one of us, not a single one of us, wanted to be anywhere else for that moment. What a game. What a time to be alive.

For men like me, whose fathers and older male relatives had served so long and hard against the Nazis, it had been a worrying thought to go into a Stadium with so many Germans shouting in unison and waving flags. I know that is not a politically correct thing to say, but it was true. As I approached the Stadium with the flags everywhere, hackles that I didn't even know I had rose on the back of my neck. To see tens of thousands of Germans, many dressed in identical soccer uniforms, all chanting and singing; it had too many resonances from too long ago. But after ten minutes, I realized I was wrong. Not at this wonderful tournament, staged in a glorious June where the sun shone bright and it seemed like the whole world was watching. Not when all of Germany came out, charming and hospitable. Not when some of the dreadful ghosts of the past were laid to rest.

After the game came the street party along the boulevards of central Munich. In the cobbled courtyards, steeped in history, Iranian and American fans waved to one another. They were not the only ones: fans from almost every part of the world sang and partied together. The marvellous, wonderful Germans offered around bottles of beer. The Costa Ricans staged an impromptu salsa party. The Mexicans jumped up and down, arms around one another, arms around anyone else, and we danced and sang until our throats ached. When it was over, I staggered through the train Station and saw that the floor was covered with hundreds of sleeping fans. I saw three young German teenagers dressed in lederhosen and green felt hats, asleep leaning against the wall. I saw no violence, no fights, no racist shouts, no thefts, no pickpockets, no stealing. I may have been lucky, but it was a wonderful, international party."

DECLAN HILL, THE FIX:
SOCCER AND ORGANIZED CRIME

SPORT FREE FROM POLITICS?
THE OLYMPIC BOYCOTTS

From the beginning, international sporting events have had a political aspect – this was also the case in antiquity, but above all since the beginning of the Olympic Games in modern times. They did not always result in the boycott of an entire country, but there have been boycott threats since nationalists attempted to prevent a German sportsman participating in Athens in 1896 – unsuccessfully – because Coubertin was a Frenchman. The most important boycotts:

1952 Helsinki: Taiwan, at this time still Nationalist China, did not participate in the games as the People's Republic of China was also invited.

1956 Melbourne: Egypt, Lebanon and Iraq announce their boycott due to the Israeli-Egyptian War in the same year. The Netherlands, Spain and Switzerland do not attend due to the crushing of the Hungarian national uprising by the soviets. The People's Republic of China cancelled due to the participation of Taiwan.

1968 Mexico City: South Africa is accepted onto the IOC, resulting in 40 African states threatening boycott – South Africa is excluded once again. A number of black Americans boycott the games in support of the Black Power movement.

1972 Munich: Rhodesia (today's Zimbabwe) is invited to participate in the games, resulting in 40 African states threatening boycott. Rhodesia's invitation is withdrawn again.

1976 Montreal: Canada recognises the People's Republic of China, whereupon *Nationalist China*, due to participate under the name *Taiwan*, leaves the games. Due to a rugby game played by the New Zealand team in apartheid South Africa 22 African states refuse to participate.

1980 Moscow: Due to the Soviet Union's invasion of Afghanistan the USA and 65 further countries boycott the games, including Germany.

1984 Los Angeles: In a *counter-boycott* the USSR and 13 further countries withdraw from the games "due to fears for the safety of its athletes in light of the anti-soviet and anti-communist activities in the USA."

1988 Seoul: North Korea and five further states – including the Seychelles – do not participate because North Korea does not feel it has been fairly treated.

COMPETITION OF THE SYSTEMS OR: THE "GREAT POWER OF THE OLYMPIC IDEA" (A. BRUNDAGE)

The sporting relations between the Federal Republic of Germany, as part of the Western Alliance, and the German Democratic Republic, as part of the Warsaw Pact, represent a special chapter in the mixing of sport and politics: the war between the political systems was battled out on the cinder track, the victory of the faster runner, jumper or thrower was interpreted as the victory of the superior political system. This inevitably culminated in disputes over participation in the Olympic Games – inevitably, as it is the sporting event with the greatest worldwide propaganda value.

The starting point was that the Federal Republic formed a National Olympic Committee (NOC) virtually at its founding and was immediately accepted onto the International Olympic Committee (IOC) as the representative for the whole of Germany – personal contacts clearly played a major role in this. The GDR also established an NOC, however it failed to be accepted onto the IOC; the FRG's claim to sole representation also extended to sport. In contrast, the President of the IOC, Avery Brundage, advocated an all-German team.

This competed for the first time in 1956, following long negotiations, under the black-red-gold flag with Olympic rings. The common anthem was Beethoven's *Ode to Joy*.

In 1955 the NOC of the GDR was *provisionally* accepted onto the IOC; in Rome in 1960 and Tokyo in 1964 there was once again an all-German team, which was selected on the basis of elimination heats. In 1968, seven years after the building of the wall, two separate German teams competed, but still under a common flag and with the same anthem. Ironically, two independent teams competed for the first time at the 1972 Olympic Games in Munich; the GDR had established its position, and according to the number of medals, proved itself to be the superior system.

Entry of the all-German Olympic team at
the 1956 Games in Melbourne.

WOMEN
AND SPORT

Women of the British Ladies Football Club, 1895.

WOMEN AND SPORT

Today, the fact that women want to and are able to participate in sports goes without saying. However, depending on the social and cultural character of a state, this was not always the case. Two aspects need to be distinguished: women's sporting activities in themselves and their public presentation in front of spectators. The first was generally tolerated, the second not – which reflects a *masculine* perspective and a masculine moral conception.

In the development of gymnastics and sport in the 19th century to today's mass spectacle women have always been discriminated against: sport was and would continue to be presented as a danger to health and unaesthetic. However, the reasons given are only a pretext – at heart it has always been about *gender*, the moral danger posed to men by being exposed to a naked female calf or tight clothing or even a pair of trousers. That this contains a reversal of responsibility is obvious; one could have excluded the men because they allow themselves to become aroused by the women …

The first Olympic Games of modern times took place without the participation of female athletes, however in the same year, 1896, women members of the Arbeiterturnerbund (Workers' Gymnastics Federation) were accorded the same voting rights. The previous year the first public women's football match took place in England. The public reporting is faced with a problem – for women's competitions the use of the sportswomen's first name alone is preferred, so as not to cause difficulties for the families.

In 1928 the first light athletics competitions for women were held at the Olympic Games.

A taboo to this day is the freely mixed team – a woman is not allowed to compete with men. The only exception is horseback riding.

"LOOKS UGLY ON WOMEN"

Baron de Coubertin coined the slogan: "Olympic Games are a paragon of male athleticism, and the applause of the women is their reward."

"Sprints longer than 100 m are not at all recommended for women. In any event, one does not select the 100 m, even though this is desirable, but 150 m, in order to prevent confusion with the men's 100 m sprint."
JOHANNES MÜLLER, DIE LEIBESÜBUNGEN, 1926

"Competition distorts the female countenance, it gives the charming feminine movement a hard, masculine tone. It put pay to grace, in a word: it looks ugly on women. Competition befits the man, it is foreign to the female nature."
KARL RITTER VON HALT, THE LATER PRESIDENT OF THE NATIONAL OLYMPIC COMMITTEE IN THE 1920S

Fanny Blankers-Koen, mother of two, won four gold medals in London in 1948 and was nicknamed the *flying housewife:*

"I like being in the kitchen as much as on the sports ground."

Warning for women rowers: *"(...) with the woman's weak pelvic floor (forced respiration) can lead to an abdominal ptosis and a lowering of the inner genital organs."*
PROF. NOACK 1962

"The female anatomy is not suited for football shirt advertising. It distorts the advert."
GERMAN FOOTBALL ASSOCIATION, 1978

"The women's national football team are already world champions, and I see no reason why men cannot achieve the same as women."
ANGELA MERKEL, GERMAN CHANCELLOR

"My new favourite sport is curling! At last a great, intelligent, typical women's sport, don't you think? Permanently bent over and for the most part with scrubber and kettle in the hand."
HARALD SCHMIDT, ENTERTAINER

"I know very well why today's society ladies play sport: because their husbands' erotic interest has declined. Without being too polite – the more they play sport, the more these men's interest will decline."
BERTOLT BRECHT, "THE CRISIS OF SPORT"

FOR EXAMPLE BOXING

An icon of German women's boxing – the multiple World Champion, Regina Halmich.

Without a doubt, the women's sport discipline that has struggled the longest with acceptance problems is boxing. The fight *man against man* could hardly be conducted *woman against woman*, as this would jeopardise a domain of male dominance: namely the fight as a special, gender-specific characteristic of men – despite all the amazons.

In actual fact women's boxing has been around since the 19th century, albeit not as a recognised sport but as a fairground attraction, sometimes even held against men. Above all it was practised in England, with its sport and betting mania, in contrast, public women's boxing was banned in Germany until 1918. It was only in 1996 that amateur women's boxing was included in the statutes of the German Boxing Association, from 2012 it is an Olympic discipline.

This raises the question as to when synchronised swimming, after all an Olympic discipline, will be (re)-opened for men. In fact it used to be an exclusively male discipline, at the end of the 19th century, before they were ousted by the women. Today there are male synchronised swimmers at the national level, however they are excluded from the Olympic Games.

Boxing match between Julia Sahin and Hollie Dunaway, 2007.

"I ALSO TAKE A LOOK AT THE MEN"

In the meantime, the development of women's sport has taken a curious turn: if male opposition in its time was at least partly based on a rejection of the exposed calf or waving hair as *immodest*, that is the specifically sexual, then today a reverse development can be observed – those women who, for social or religious reasons wish to conceal their body or hair, above all those from the Islamic culture, are now *de facto* excluded from the majority of sports, even when they are permitted to play them in their own country. There are now regulations – written as well as unwritten – which don't define how much the woman can reveal but how much she must reveal. A well known example is the clothing regulation for the 2004 Olympic Games in Athens, which defined the maximum size of the shorts. Whether women want to present themselves in this manner obviously plays no role in this context. The old advertising slogan *sex sells*, namely selling things with attractive images of women, also appears to apply in sport. However, this is a male perspective.

And in beach volleyball, the sport with the tight women's shorts, the men wear loose clothing.

Beach volleyball in Essen which – as is well known – "lies on the waterfront".

But, and that is the beauty of sport – sexist or not, regulations or not: the thrill is genuine.

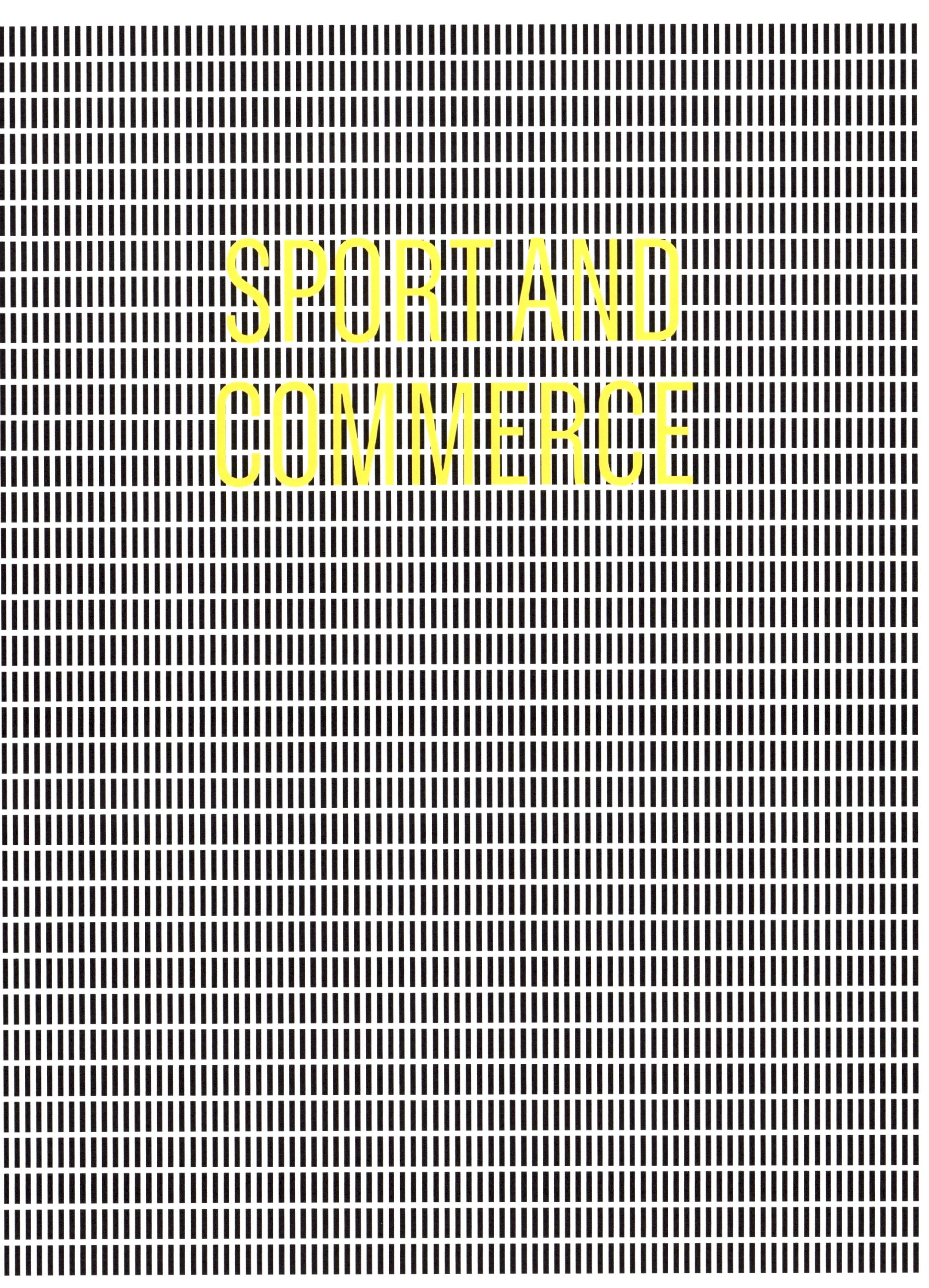

SPORT AND
COMMERCE

SPORT AND COMMERCE

The sponsor and his advertising space – no tennis court or football club of the lower leagues manages without them. The sponsor gives money and in turn wants to place his company's logo. Sport costs money, from the jersey to the upkeep of the stadium – more money than can be obtained from membership fees and public funds.

Conversely, the world of commerce understands very well that, as a rule, sport is well received by the public as an advertising medium (with the exception of doping scandals) and is therefore largely risk-free. And when sport is also shown on television, it has a multiplication effect that can hardly be matched by other media.

Today, elite sports in particular cannot exist without commercial backing: men and women who want to achieve top performances have to train on a full-time basis and they need a professional support team and facilities, from the trainer to the training camp. To be able to do this it is necessary to have financial support; the sportsman's *wages* depend on the popularity of his sporting discipline: a football player or Formula One driver earns several times that which can be expected by an Olympic pentathlon athlete or a hockey team.

However, whenever money comes into play – literally – corruption is not far off: it affects officials who fight for a position, advertisers who fight for the best possible promotion of their product, their town or nation, and finally the athletes themselves who fight for victory and hence the best possible financial reward.

"You need to know that sport is business, that fun is business, and that the combination of fun and sport is one of the best businesses."
(NIKOLAUS BRENDER,
STUTTGARTER ZEITUNG, 5/8/2008)

SPORT AND ADVERTISING

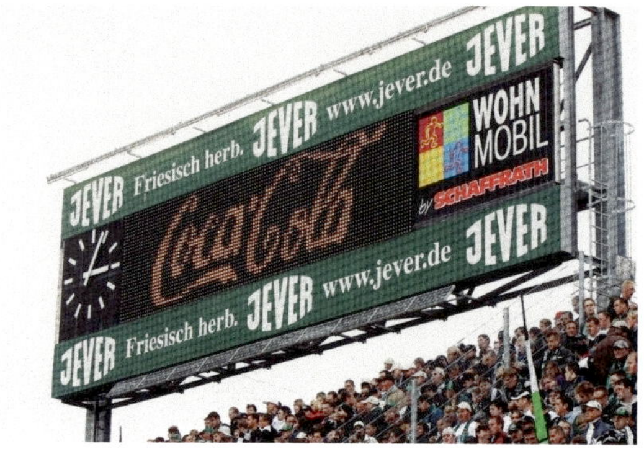

The intention of the display board is "really" to show the results.

In the process, sportswomen and men themselves become moving advertising hoardings: here you can see no less than seven stickers for certain products – but you can't see everything. In any case, it is hard to make out what the connection is between a car and a bi-athlete.

SPORT AND ADVERTISING

You could call it a *win/win* situation: many people are interested in sport. They like to watch it on television or live as a spectator, even if they themselves are not actively involved in sport. Many associate sport with terms like *healthy, active, young*, all of which are positive. This means that sport is an ideal place for advertising of any type, from direct advertising spots during the commercial breaks through to the sponsorship of big events costing millions; according to a recent study, only eight percent of spectators are against sponsoring.

The most popular events are the World Cup and the European Football Championships, as well as the Olympic Games and Bundesliga football matches. The former certainly reach audiences of over a billion.

At the publicly-owned television stations, surreptitious advertising during programmes is still frowned upon – with the exception of sports programmes where this rule is not applied. In justification one might say that sportsmen and women as *advertising hoardings* can hardly be called surreptitious – they are much too conspicuous for that. The comedian and writer Oliver Hassencamp put it this way: "The cross that a top athlete must bear should be wide – to provide enough advertising space."

One inevitable consequence of sport's dependence on advertising and the funds it can generate is the orientation of events and forms of contest towards television viewers, rather than towards participants. And even less orientation towards the sportsmen and women themselves.

"Ahead of the others" when you drink the coffee of a certain brand – that is what advertising is trying to suggest: if you buy this or that product, you'll be ahead of the others …

Early forms of advertising: today, advertising for a cigarette brand would hardly be possible, but if it were it would probably not show an anonymous footballer, but a famous star.

WITH A WIDE CHEST

Just how much money is involved is revealed when we look at the names of the Bundesliga club stadiums and of those of the sponsors – whose names are placed most conspicuously on the jerseys – and consider the income from jersey sponsoring.

Not that advertising in sport is new: see the English Cup Final between Tottenham Hotspur and Burnley in 1962.

BUNDESLIGA FOOTBALL JERSEY SPONSORS IN 2011/12:

CLUB	NAME OF STADIUM	JERSEY	EUROS PER YEAR FOR JERSEY SPONSORING
Bayern München	Allianz-Arena	Telekom	up to 25 million
VfL Wolfsburg	Volkswagen Arena	VW	up to 20 million
Schalke 04	Veltins-Arena	Gazprom	12.5 million
Borussia Dortmund	Signal Iduna Park	Evonik Industries	8 million
Werder Bremen	Weser-Stadion	Targo Bank	up to 10 million
Hamburger SV	Imtech Arena	Emirates	up to 7.5 million
VfB Stuttgart	Mercedes-Benz Arena	GAZi	6 million
Hertha BSC	Olympiastadion	Deutsche Bahn	4.5 million
Borussia M'Gladbach	Borussia-Park	Postbank	4 million
1. FC Köln	RheinEnergieStadion	Rewe Group	4 million
Hannover 96	AWD-Arena	TUI	3 million
1. FC Nürnberg	Easycredit-Stadion	AREVA	3 million
1. FC Kaiserslautern	Fritz-Walter-Stadion	Allgäuer Latschenkiefer	4.5 million
FC Augsburg	SGL-Arena	AL-KO	1 million
FSV Mainz 05	Coface Arena	Enteva	2.8 million
TSG 1899 Hoffenheim	WIRSOL Rhein-Neckar-Arena	Suntech	not disclosed
SC Freiburg	MAGE SOLAR Stadion	Ehrmann	2.5 million

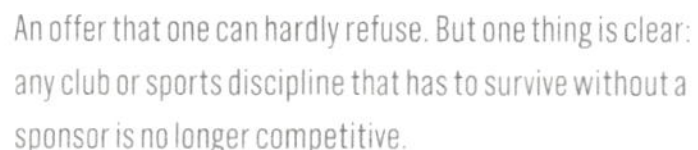

An offer that one can hardly refuse. But one thing is clear: any club or sports discipline that has to survive without a sponsor is no longer competitive.

This offer from the internet shows how advertising options are conveyed.

ADVERTISING FOR ZHC PIT LAMP

In 1973, the producer of an alcoholic beverage had the logo of his company displayed on a player's chest for the first time – and caused a scandal. The scandal soon subsided, because clubs quickly recognised the financial advantage. Today, over 100 million Euros of income is generated by jersey advertising in the top league alone. But the phenomenon is not restricted to football; today, no sports discipline manages without advertising. Here are two examples of how a handball club, the Zwickau club Grubenlampe (Pit Lamp) and an ice hockey club try to market themselves on the internet:

"Advertising on the player
You have the opportunity to advertise directly on the jerseys and tracksuits – at all matches – championships, cup and friendly matches, and competitions. What this achieves: your company, your logo, your advertising is always seen by the viewers and spectators. But not only that. You achieve additional promotional effects through the pictures of the games in the regional press and on our website. With exposure in a higher league there is an even greater effect. Don't hesitate and secure the best advertising space the Club has available.
We are happy to advise!"

SOURCE: HTTP://WWW.ZHC-GRUBENLAMPE.ORG

The manufacturer of a herbal alcoholic beverage was the first to introduce jersey advertising in football.

"You want to advertise with the Krefeld Penguins?
Do you want to see your advertising on the jerseys, the boards, in the programme or on the display board? Here is information on how to advertise with the Krefeld Penguins. You can send your email here to enquire about the exact terms and conditions, and prices (…) or give us a ring: (…)."

SOURCE: HTTP://PORTAL.KREFELD-PINGUINE.DE

Atlanta is the city where Coca-Cola was developed and where the corporation's head office is located to this day. Hardly surprising then that people talked about the Coca-Cola Games at the time.

Fizzy pop for everyone – sports officials at a press conference (1989).

THE COCA-COLA GAMES

The 100-year jubilee of the modern Olympic Games took place in 1996. There was a general assumption that Athens would be selected for the Jubilee Games, as it would reconnect the ancient era with the first modern Games and the end of the 20th century.

Instead, Atlanta was selected. Atlanta is the main seat of Coca-Cola, which had invested heavily in the city's application and in the operation of the Games. These became the Games with the most uninhibited and most conspicuous private-company advertising. These were also the Games with the slogan "Atlanta Can't Organize Games" – a sarcastic interpretation of the abbreviation ACOG which stands for "Atlanta Committee for the Olympic Games".

On Coca-Cola's website one can read:
"Large sporting events such as the Olympic Games attract people all over the world and inspire them to practice sport themselves. For this reason, worldwide support of these events is very important for the Coca-Cola organisation.
In addition to refreshing beverages we are primarily contributing a wide range of services, experience and finance to our partnerships. This benefits not only the organisers, athletes and fans, but also sport as a whole. For example, the International Olympic Committee invests a substantial part of the income from sponsors in promoting sport and physical exercise around the globe." [1]

The central organisation of German sport, the Deutsche Olympische Sportbund, has no compunction in writing: *"New Coke song for the 2012 Olympic Games. (…) This month, Coca-Cola Germany has started the competition 'Your move makes the beat' on the Coke Channel on myVideo.de. In order to take part you just upload a short video that shows you practicing sport and which focuses on the special sound of sport. The best ideas will be used to compile the Coke Song for the 2012 Olympic Games."* [2]

The question as to why an organisation that is committed to the Olympic idea engages so directly with a single company is not asked.

What is true for the IOC also applies to FIFA, the international governing body of football. The ranking list of national teams published by FIFA is called *FIFA/Coca-Cola world ranking list*. When one considers the close connection between a company and *non-commercial* sports organisations, one may ask what the influence is of one on the other. Who pays decides?

1 Source: http://www.coca-cola-gmbh.de/nachhaltigkeit/gemeinwohl/sportfoerderung/index.html

2 Source: http://www.dosb.de/de/olympia/olympische-news/detail/news/neuer_coke_song_zu_den_olympischen_spielen_2012

LET'S HAVE A LOOK – SPORT AND TELEVISION

LET'S HAVE A LOOK –
SPORT AND TELEVISION

*"**Sports programmes** on television offer sport as a show, interlaced with advertising spots. Advertising is the core of sport for the spectators. It is the centre around which sporting events are arranged."*
GUNTER GEBAUER, SPORTS SCIENTIST, 2002

The calculation is simple: the number of people watching a sports event on television is a multiple of the spectators actually at the event (although the people in the stadium are indispensable because their clothing, mood and enthusiasm are an essential part of the broadcast). At the semi-final of the 2006 FIFA World Cup between Germany and Italy there were about 80,000 people in the stadium but 29 million Germans watched the match on the television, not counting those spectators viewing on a public screen, or those in other countries such as Italy.

Every year the prices paid by the television stations to the sporting associations go up in order to retain the broadcasting rights; these expenses are then recovered from advertising revenue. This explains the link between the advertising straplines and stickers and the broadcast – the latter secures the former and the former turns the latter into a worthwhile investment. It is quite possible that sport benefits from this, but the whole thing has precious little to do with its essence. Although sportswomen and men profit from the income, some of which is astronomical, they have to pay the price of going through life as living advertising hoardings …

But the publicly-owned television channels, for which advertising outside sports events is precisely regulated by law, are turning into permanent advertising broadcasts even after 8 p.m. when advertising spots are prohibited.

THE BUNDESLIGA RIGHTS

It's the first thing that happens after any game, and it's mandatory at every press conference: the interviewee is placed before a wall covered with the logos of the advertisers.

In 1963, the Bundesliga was established as the top league in German football. The broadcasting of news and match reports was considered part of the mandate of publicly-owned broadcasting stations. However, it all changed at an exponential rate …

PERIOD	PURCHASER	BROADCASTER	PRICE PER SEASON
1965–1969	ARD/ZDF	ARD/ZDF	0,33 million €
1969–1974	ARD/ZDF	ARD/ZDF	1,33 million €
1674–1978	ARD/ZDF	ARD/ZDF	2,25 million €
1978–1983	ARD/ZDF	ARD/ZDF	3,45 million €
1983–1988	ARD/ZDF	ARD/ZDF	4,10 million €
1988–1991	Ufa	RTL	20,30 million €
1991–1994	Ufa	RTL + Premiere	40,90 million €
1994–1999	ISPR	Sat.1 + Premiere	112,50 million €
1999–2000	ISPR/Ufa	Sat.1 + Premiere	169 million €
2000–2001	Kirch-Gruppe	Sat.1 + Premiere	355 million €
2001–2002	Kirch-Gruppe	Sat.1 + Premiere	328 million €
2002–2003	Kirch-Sport	Sat.1 + Premiere	290 million €
2003–2004	Infront (Günter Netzer)	ARD + DSF + Premiere	291 million €
2004–2006	ARD/DSF/Premiere	ARD + DSF + Premiere	300 million €
2006–2009	ARD/DSF/Arena	ARD + DSF + Arena	420 million €
2009–2013	ARD/DSF/Sky/Telekom	ARD + ZDF + DSF + Sky+ LigaTotal (IPTV)	412 million €

Source: http://www.soccer-warriors.de/2010/08/09/entwicklung-der-tv-gelder-fuer-die-deutsche-bundesliga

SELLING THE GAMES

What is true for Bundesliga matches and football at European and world level also applies to the Olympic Games. Although initially the participants were amateurs, they were under increasing pressure to become professionals as the competition between states to win contests grew stronger. Professionalism covered all areas: the athletes, the sports buildings, the media effectiveness of the events – and hence also the commercialisation. While the longstanding IOC President Avery Brundage had intended to manage completely without financial participation from the outside, the 1984 Games in Los Angeles, which were financed through private commercial enterprise, showed that a lot of money could be made from them; the question therefore arose as to who was entitled to that money.

Consequently, as a result of commercialisation – which was driven particularly under IOC President Juan Antonio Samaranch (1980–2001) – television exerts greater influence over the contests and advertising companies exert greater influence over television. The construction of stadiums, positioning of cameras, size and position of banner ads, forms of competition and broadcasting times: everything is negotiated as in a mutual business partnership.

A special twist in the tale is the fact that although the IOC does not finance the Games (that is the responsibility of the respective cities or states), it controls all rights – and hence revenue – from the broadcasting.

SUMMER OLYMPIC GAMES	COSTS OF WORLDWIDE TELEVISION RIGHTS IN MILLION US$	COSTS OF EUROPEAN TELEVISION RIGHTS IN MILLION US$
1960 Rome	1.0	0.27
1964 Tokyo	5.0	–
1968 Mexico City	9.5	1.0
1972 Munich	17.8	1.8
1976 Montreal	34.8	4.6
1980 Moscow	88.0	5.7
1984 Los Angeles	287.6	22.0
1988 Seoul	407.1	30.2
1992 Barcelona	635.4	94.5
1996 Atlanta	925.0	240.0
2000 Sydney	1331.0	350.0
2004 Athens	1500.0	394.0
2008 Peking	1700.0	443.0

CHOREOGRAPHY
OF THE TELEVISION MASSES

Sports associations, particularly those that have to worry about their existence because their sport is not televised (and hence does not attract television revenue and only little advertising revenue for its associations, clubs and sportsmen and women), try to obtain a share of the market by organising attractive events and shows that are suitable for television. And we are not talking here about new and trendy sports disciplines, but about the modification of traditional events. Here are some examples to make the point.

It remains a mystery why there is "a perfect cross-country track in the snow" along the banks of the River Rhine at Düsseldorf, especially since there definitely isn't any snow.

WINTER SPORTS

Biathlon inside Schalke's Veltins Arena:

– an open air event is relocated into an indoor venue

"Tour de Ski" cross-country event:

– several races are combined into one complete event

Sprint contests as part of cross-country races:

– short duration, high tension (included, although quite the opposite
of the cross-country skiing discipline)

Pursuit contests and mass starts in cross-country races, Nordic combined and biathlon events:

– increased suspense through direct comparison

Parallel slalom:

– made twice as attractive

Of course, "Give us back our game" is a naive demand – "our game" has long since changed, with the result that we only appreciate a game that is free from advertising and played by non-professionals if it is played on the green in the park.

SUMMER SPORTS

Bundesliga:
– originally the nine matches all took place on a Saturday at 15:30 hours; now these matches are spread over three days and five different viewing times
Modern pentathlon:
– organised so that some of the disciplines take place together
"Golden League sports festivals":
– attempt to increase the excitement by organising series of events (overall winner)
Track and field:
– the restart after a false start is no longer permitted so that races take place on time and it is easier to plan the whole programme schedule

It is now almost a given that the design of stadiums is primarily suited to television reporting rather than the respective sport or spectator comfort. This includes exact details of the building, the height and position of advertising banners, daylight angles and shadow effects which are included in the specifications and have to be accommodated by the designers. This is quite apart from the obligatory two questions to players and trainers who are filmed in front of an advertising hoarding that is quickly put up for the purpose. A stadium must be suitable for television reporting. It may also be suitable for spectator viewing.

By the way: spectators, too, try to display their banners, posters or choreographed movements so that they make it on to the television.

"IF YOU SUPPORT ME FOR MOSCOW, I'LL SUPPORT YOU FOR QATAR"

"IF YOU SUPPORT ME FOR MOSCOW, I'LL SUPPORT YOU FOR QATAR"

"Corruption has become endemic in sport and seriously compromises the integrity of Olympic sports." It is safe to assume that the Canadian Richard Pound, Vice President of the International Olympic Committee (IOC) for many years, knows what he is talking about. For a long time now there have been more or less proven rumours about FIFA President Josef Blatter, and FIFA and IOC members, that they are susceptible to corruption. If this were not the case, there would hardly be a need for the Ethics Commission which has now been established at the IOC.

Without going into further detail: international governing bodies, particularly FIFA and the IOC, deal with billions when awarding the right to host events and the associated rights. But their members are amateurs who are often connected with each other through personal relationships. In itself that is not reprehensible, but it makes them vulnerable. Information about cases of corruption rarely reaches the public because the sports federations are in charge of their own jurisdiction.

The last case, which is difficult to explain with rational criteria, was the simultaneous award of the football World Cups to Russia (2018) and Qatar (2022 – in the middle of summer!). For the event in Qatar, the organisers are now thinking about mechanical cooling in the stadiums.

Nobody can really object to the award of a World Football Championship to Russia (other than some democracy fanatics) – so does that mean we can wave Qatar through at the same time? Why the countries for these two Championships had to be selected at the same time remains a mystery.

Jubilation at the change of office – Sepp Blatter takes over as FIFA President from João Havelange in 1998, who himself does not appear to be very enthusiastic.

ETHICS MOVES IN –
VIA THE COMMISSION

The IOC's Ethics Commission was established for the first time in 1998 when it became known that members of the organisation had been bribed for the selection of the venue for the next Winter Games; as a result, six members were excluded, four resigned and ten were officially warned.

In 2011, the Commission investigated accusations against João Havelange (long-standing President of FIFA), Issa Hayatou (President of the Confederation of African Football) and Lamine Diack (President of the International Association of Athletics Federations). According to the findings of a Swiss Court, a sports rights agency had paid 9.5 million US Dollars for the acquisition of television rights. The punishment for the officials: a reprimand, a warning, a voluntary resignation – Havelange is 95 years old. The court had found that payments to numerous officials between 1989 and 2001 totalled 138 million Francs.

According to an announcement by Josef Blatter, the files, which apparently include names of additional implicated persons, were supposed to be made public on 17 December 2011. That was postponed for an unspecified period.

However, Blatter asserted that it is "our strong will to disclose the file as soon as possible and thereby to finally bring the past to a closure". A new Governance Commission is intended to "focus on the future rather than dealing with the past"…

IF YOU HIT ME, I'LL HIT YOU

WARNER ACCUSES BLATTER OF BRIBERY

(SPIEGEL, 30/12/2011)

Jack Warner *had announced a tsunami of sports politics on several occasions; now the former Vice President of FIFA could act on this. Warner has raised serious accusations against his former boss Joseph Blatter. He claims that Blatter had bribed him in order to secure the vote for election as FIFA President.*

HAMBURG – A single Dollar is getting FIFA boss Joseph S. Blatter into difficulties. It seems that the tsunami that had been announced at the re-election of Blatter as boss of the International Football Federation is gradually gaining momentum. The former Vice President of FIFA, Jack Warner, whose own vest is far from spotless, has claimed in a personal statement that he had bought the regional TV rights for the 1998 World Cup from the Federation for one Dollar – in consideration for supporting Blatter in his *brutal* presidential election campaign against the erstwhile UEFA President Lennart Johansson (Sweden). Warner further claims that, as President of CONCACAF (Confederation of North, Central American and Caribbean Association Football), he ensured that the CONCACAF delegates would support Blatter in the elections to become the boss of FIFA. But it does not stop there: Warner is supposed to have received further perks in the form of television contracts at peppercorn prices in return for support for Blatter's re-election.

"Blatter has sold the TV rights for 2002 and 2006 to me, not to the Caribbean Football Union (CFU). There is no doubt that this has happened because of my work for his re-election", Warner said in his statement. With the contracts for 2010 and 2014 it is supposed to have been a similar story, albeit with the CFU as *vehicle*.

Warner had announced a tsunami on several occasions

The new controversy has a particularly intriguing background: in mid-2011, Warner had been suspended by the FIFA Ethics Commission due to suspected corruption; soon after he announced his retirement from the International Federation. In a probably unique mud-slinging match, Warner and Blatter's original rival candidate for this year's presidential elections, Mohamed Bin Hammam from Qatar, had been accused of having bribed members of the CFU with 28,000 Euros. Warner and Bin Hammam vigorously denied the accusations. However, Bin Hammam, the former President of the Asian Football Confederation, eventually withdrew his candidature and was later banned for life. Blatter won the ballot without a rival candidate with 186 of the 203 votes.

Very soon after his dismissal, Warner had announced that he would kick off a *football tsunami*

– without however acting on his threats. Now he seems set to start his revenge campaign against Blatter and FIFA. In October 2011, Warner had already claimed that he and Bin Hammam had been used by Blatter to offer gifts to officials entitled to vote before the 1998 and 2002 FIFA elections. One of these officials is supposed to have been the Vice President of the Ethics Commission, Petrus Damaseb.

As usual, FIFA's comments on the new accusations were brief. The *new information would be investigated* but no further comments would be made.

The suspended member of the FIFA Executive Committee, Jack Warner, in conversation with journalists in Zurich; he himself was stripped of his post on the grounds of suspected bribery.

MEMBERS OF THE
FIFA EXECUTIVE COMMITTEE

POSITION	NAME	MEMBER COUNTRY
President	Joseph S. Blatter	Switzerland
Senior Vice President	Julio H. Grondona	Argentina
Vice President	Issa Hayatou	Cameroon
Vice President	Chung Mong-Joon	South Korea
Vice President	Jack A. Warner	Trinidad and Tobago
Vice President	Angel María Villar Llona	Spain
Vice President	Michel Platini	France
Vice President	Reynald Temarii	Tahiti
Vice President	Geoff Thompson	England
Member	Michel D'Hooghe	Belgium
Member	Ricardo Terra Teixeira	Brazil
Member	Mohamed Bin Hammam	Qatar
Member	Senes Erzik	Turkey
Member	Chuck Blazer	USA
Member	Worawi Makudi	Thailand
Member	Nicolás Leoz	Paraguay
Member	Junji Ogura	Japan
Member	Amos Adamu	Nigeria
Member	Marios Lefkaritis	Cyprus
Member	Jacques Anouma	Ivory Coast
Member	Franz Beckenbauer	Germany
Member	Rafael Salguero	Guatemala
Member	Hany Abo Rida	Egypt
Member	Witali Mutko	Russia

Source: http://de.wikipedia.org/wiki/FIFA-Exekutivkomitee

At the 2011 Annual Congress in Zurich, Sepp Blatter appeals to FIFA members to support him in finding a solution to the internal problems, without external help.

SPORT MOVING AWAY FROM SPORT

An open-air sports discipline such as
biathlon takes place in an enclosed hall
– 50,000 spectators, and the athletes,
are excited. The next step would be to
only have a virtual competition.

SPORT MOVING AWAY
FROM SPORT

At one time, sport was a movement involving running, jumping, throwing
as well as contests between men and between women in a natural environ-
ment; it had developed from man's natural movements. It was not until spectators turned sport into a spectacle that certain facilities had to be created
for these spectators, and hence for sport – items like stadiums, arenas, venues: initially people performed swimming in rivers or lakes; then the indoor swimming pool evolved with a standardised 50-metre pool.

The latter already represents a move away from the natural process, the
natural movement. Today, sporting activities are even further removed
from the natural processes, in two ways. On the one hand, through financial mechanisms, television – with its millions of viewers – has made sport
dependent on this funding and is imposing completely new requirements
regarding events and how they can be broadcast: on punctuality, on carrying out the event in spite of potential bad weather, on visual quality.

On the other hand, more abstract activities are gaining ground in sport
itself: we run on a mechanical running track. We cycle on a stationary exercise bike. We go skiing on Lüneburg Heath throughout the year. Or we
perform movements in tune with virtual images.

And we celebrate *summer fairy-tales* (a term used by Germans celebrating
the unexpected success of the German team) not in the stadium but at public places where large display screens are the trigger for collective emotions.

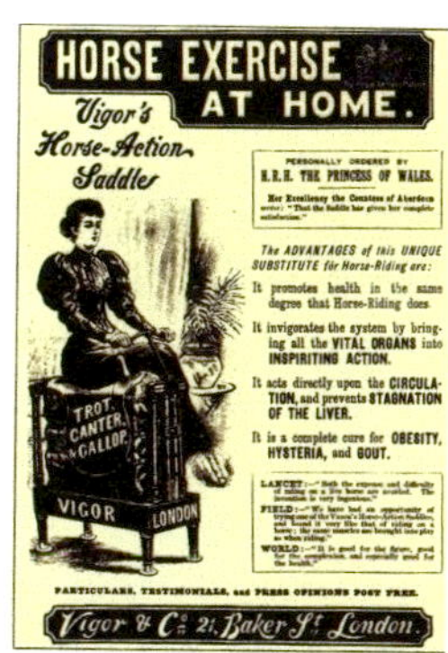

Afterall, when the technology allowed,
there was always sport "replacement"
for your home sweet home: here an
excerise horse to ride.

ARTIFICIAL SNOW
AND MOUNTAINS

As climate change causes temperatures to rise, snowfall in the mountains becomes a question of survival for those communities that live from winter tourism. Many sports disciplines depend on snow, which is less and less reliably available. The solution is to create snow artificially, using *snow cannons*. That makes it possible for world championship and world cup events to take place even though the crocuses are already out next to the track. Artificial snow is now so ubiquitous and common that ski racers, to name but one example, prefer to ski on that rather than on non-artificially treated snow.

In 2007 there were about 3,100 snow cannons in Europe which used up one million litres of water and 260,000 megawatt hours of electricity. Therefore these snow cannons contributed not insignificantly to global warming through their energy consumption.

The sporting value of events such as the sprint contests of cross-country skiers on the banks of the river Rhine in Düsseldorf or of bi-athletes in a venue in Gelsenkirchen is quite limited anyway (one might also argue that sprint races, which were only introduced for the sake of television, do not really have a place in cross-country racing).

Snow cannons at work. Somehow one gets the feeling that fresh air and natural weather are just unnecessary nuisances.

Climate change, which is one of the causes of the ever-reducing snowfall, is accelerated by the high energy input required for snow production.

Admittedly, an indoor swimming pool is also an artificial sports facility. But that skiing should be available all year round in Dubai, of all places, doesn't really make sense.

Surely there is fun to be had: all-year skiing facility in Bispingen. Lüneburger Heide (2007).

THE GENUINE "ALPINE FEEL"

In the Alps, the chances of finding reliable snow in winter are reducing because of climate change; on the other hand, there are now six indoor venues in Germany that offer skiing facilities all the year round: Jever Ski Hall in Neuss, the Alpincenter in Bottrop, the Snow Funpark in Wittenburg, the Snowtropolis in Senftenberg (Brandenburg) and the Snow Dome in Bispingen (Lüneburger Heide). There, people can ski on artificial snow and artificial mountains all the year round. At a venue in Oberhof/Thüringen, there are facilities for cross-country and biathlon only. According to the website of a venue in the Dutch Landgraaf and those of ten other European indoor venues, you can experience the genuine *Alpine feel*.

At these venues the attraction seems to be not so much the downhill run but rather the easy accessibility and the combination of a low-risk mountain with facilities for birthday parties and skiing courses including bars and restaurants: a winter Disneyland.

SPORT AND WII

By now sport has made its way into our living rooms. Games consoles such as Wii by Nintendo (since 2006) or Playstation 3 by Sony (since 2007) have a new type of control system via which it is possible for people's movements to appear as digital images on a screen of a television set, i.e. when somebody makes a paddling motion, boats are moved on the screen (if you have the right game). A contest between several people can be simulated using several controllers.

An onlooker who cannot see the television screen watches a scene of one or several people moving in a senseless and usually hectic way. But, these movements can also be considered a sporting activity and the outcome of the contest is by no means arbitrary, but depends on the individual's speed and control.

The loneliness of a long-distance poser is very well expressed here: he can only practice sport when he has watched a television screen beforehand.

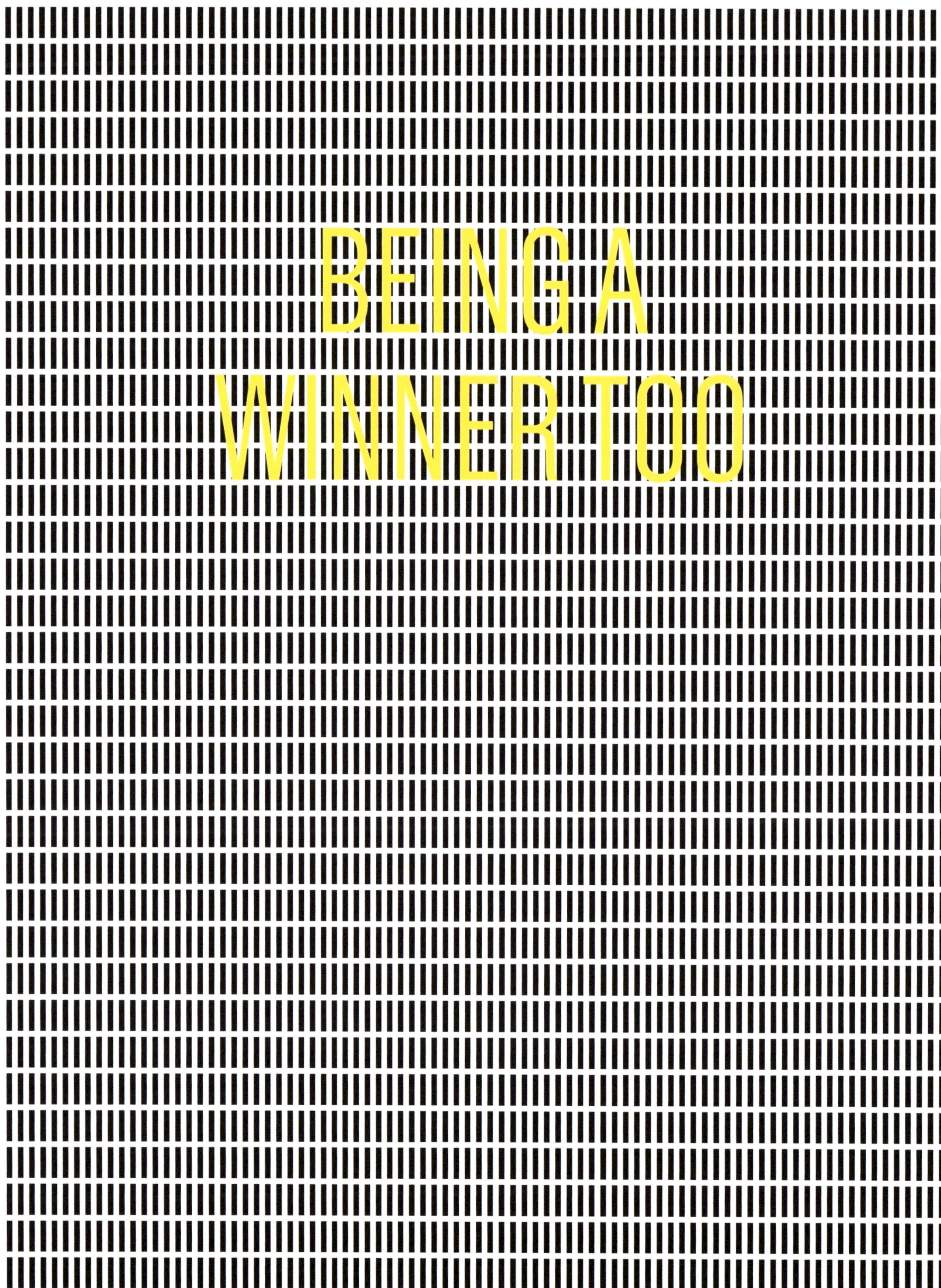

BEING A
WINNER TOO

BEING A WINNER TOO

Competition in sport as a sublimation of the fight for survival always has violent undertones; in sports competitions based on religious motivation in particular, the notion of death was an important psychological element. The rules of a sports discipline determine what type of violence is permitted and what is not – the latter is sanctioned with penalty points, red cards, disqualification or similar: a foul committed in the penalty area is punished with a penalty, a punch below the belt with a points deduction. Players committing fouls in ancient Greece were whipped.

Violence amongst sportsmen during the contest is one thing, violence amongst sports spectators is quite another: it has nothing to do with specific rules (except those of general civility) and is related to emotional involvement in sport. Watching sport without feverishly supporting one side or the other makes sport an abstract *choreography*, the sequence of which (other than in ballet) is not predetermined; that may be interesting, even beautiful, but has nothing to do with sport as a competition and the spectator's emotional engagement. These spectators identify with a club, a player, a team, a city or a nation – they transfer this identification to the contestants or teams and hope that they might win – and that means that they are winners too.

ULTRAS, FANS AND HOOLIGANS: US AGAINST THEM

When, in a town of 580,000 residents, 300,000 turn out in their cars to celebrate a championship, it is true to say: football moves.

ULTRAS, FANS AND HOOLIGANS:
US AGAINST THEM

Us against them – that is the heart of spectator emotion. What it means however, is that each element of the contest as well as the spectator behaviour – that of both the home and away supporters – has an emotional impact. Typical reactions are the booing of a player who has moved to a different club (betrayal), the collective roar when a player of the spectators' team has been fouled (menace), whistling at the referee (attempt to influence the *impartial* agent in one's favour). The most important however is still the vocal encouragement of one's own side – a ritual that was, and is, important in many war-like confrontations (battle cry) in order to overcome one's fear with an audible or visible collective action, such as the waving of flags.

Football, surely, is one of the sports that evokes the strongest emotion in spectators, including – at the extreme – violent confrontations between supporters of different sides. Those amongst them who consciously involve or even provoke physical violence as a form of confrontation are called hooligans – in contrast to normal fans. It is however not possible to distinguish these terms very clearly: in certain situations the fan may become a hooligan, while the hooligan may behave peacefully. Ultras are fanatical, organised supporters of a club who are often critical of the club management and who are often responsible for collective action in the stadium; this may include the choreography of fan songs, confetti showers, large banners and the display of emblems. Their influence in the stadium and club grows on the basis of their effective collective organisation.

Lions can be sad too, if only because they are abused as a silly mascot.

HOOLIGANS: "FROM BANKERS TO DOCTORS AND THE UNEMPLOYED – EVERYONE IS THERE"

Seventy-five people dead, 1,000 injured in Port Said, Egypt, in early 2012; 39 people dead at the final match of the European Cup Winners' Cup at the Heysel Stadium in Brussels in 1985 (the match took place in spite of this, with a 90-minute delay); up to 150 hooligans battle 300 policemen inside the Berlin Olympic Stadium in 2010: violence and riots are a recurring feature in the context of football matches – and surprisingly only in that context. So far, the attempts at finding an explanation have been less than convincing – in Port Said there were supposed to have been political reasons, in Germany one often hears that "these were not fans, but hooligans", which actually doesn't explain anything; intellectuals often like to blame the supposedly low IQ of spectators at mass events (the *dumb mass*), as if there were not also bankers who conspired to create a scrap after the match:

"The fight gives you an adrenalin rush, which is addictive. And it is an incredible feeling of power if you can defeat your adversary. And at the weekend you can finally let your hair down, and get over the week's frustrations. From bankers to doctors and the unemployed – everyone is there. (...) We are well organised. (...) There are group emails from the boss, we have pre-paid mobile sim cards which are discarded after a while. Then we get into the car or the train and meet up at the matches. On principle we go to all matches. Throughout Germany, even to Austria. We follow a certain code in our fights: you don't kick anyone once they're on the ground."

THE BIGGEST CATASTROPHES

The biggest catastrophes in the world's stadiums all have different causes – gaps in the safety provisions, spectator transgressions, accidents as triggers. And yet, it is astonishing how much these catastrophes are suppressed from the collective conscience. Here is a reminder of incidents over the last 66 years.

9 March 1946 Thirty-three people are killed during a mass panic on the occasion of the English FA Cup match between Bolton Wanderers and Stoke City at Burnden Park.

30 May 1964 318 people die in the national stadium at Lima after the referee does not allow a late goal by Peru against Argentina. (After the uproar a mass panic broke out.)

23 June 1968 In the Argentinian capital Buenos Aires, 74 people are crushed in front of the closed stadium gates as they try to leave the stadium after the River Plate against Boca Juniors derby.

2 January 1971 Sixty-six fans are crushed to death in Glasgow's Ibrox Stadium at the derby between Rangers and Celtic, as thousands of Rangers supporters stream back into the stadium following the late equaliser by their team, and clash with the other spectators leaving the arena.

17 February 1974 In the Egyptian capital Cairo, 49 people die because fans pushing into the Zamalek Stadium cause the collapse of a wall.

8 February 1981 In the Greek city of Piraeus, thousands of fans push to the exits shortly before the end of the match – 24 spectators are crushed to death.

20 October 1982 In Moscow, 340 people die as Spartak fans push back into the stadium after a late goal in the UEFA Cup match against Dutch FC Haarlem.

18 November 1982 Drunken youths in the Pascual Guerrero Stadium in Cali, Columbia, urinate from the higher tiers onto the fans sitting below. The ensuing confrontation leaves 24 dead.

11 May 1985 A discarded cigarette sets the main grandstand of the Valley Parade Stadium on fire during the English Third Division match between Bradford City and Lincoln City – 56 died.

29 May 1985 At the European Cup Winners' Cup Final between Liverpool and Juventus Turin, 39 people die in Brussels' Heysel Stadium as hooligans trigger a mass panic.

"Catastrophe in the Heysel Stadium in Brussels before the final match of the European Cup Winners' Cup (Juventus Turin v. Liverpool FC, 1 : 0) …

12 March 1988 A hailstorm in the national stadium of Katmandu (Nepal) starts a panic. Because the exits are locked, the spectators of the match between Nepal and Bangladesh cannot escape. Between 71 and 93 people die according to varying reports.

15 April 1989 At the Hillsborough Football Stadium in Sheffield (Great Britain), a panic breaks out at the FA Cup semi-final between Liverpool and Nottingham Forest. Ninety-five people die. One spectator remains in a coma until his death in March 1993. Up to 200 people are seriously injured during the incident.

14 January 1991 Rioting by football fans during a friendly match in the South African city of Orkney results in at least 42 dead and many injured. Many people are trampled to death and others die of their injuries.

5 May 1992 In the Furiani Stadium at Bastia, Corsica, a grandstand collapses during the Cup semi-final between SC Bastia and Olympique Marseille. Fifteen people die.

16 October 1996 Prior to kick-off of the World Cup qualifier between Guatemala and Costa Rica, the stadium in Guatemala city, with its space for 45,000 spectators, is already filled beyond capacity. In spite of that, more football fans try to get in. Eighty-four people are trampled to death, about 150 are injured.

11 April 2001 Thousands of fans push to the entrances of the Ellis Park Stadium in Johannesburg (South Africa) which is already filled to its capacity of 60,000 spectators. According to eyewitnesses, the police use tear-gas against the crowd. Fourty-three people die and 160 are injured during the mass panic.

... English hooligans stormed the pitch before the match and attacked the Italian fans. There were 39 dead and over 400 people injured."

10 May 2001 At a football match in Accra (Ghana) angry fans throw plastic seats onto the pitch. When the police respond with tear-gas grenades, a mass panic ensues. But the gates of the arena, which holds 70,000 people, are locked. A total of 126 spectators are trampled to death as they try to escape.

3 June 2007 Twelve football fans are trampled to death in Chililabombwe (Zambia) during the international match between Zambia and the Congo.

19 September 2008 During riots at a match in Butembo in the east of the Democratic Republic of Congo, 13 people die and 54 are injured.

29 March 2009 During a mass panic before the World Cup qualifying match between Ivory Coast and Malawi, 19 people lose their lives and 132 people are injured.

1 February 2012 70 people lose their lives during a serious affray following the match between Al-Masri and Al-Ahly, Cairo, in Port Said. Thousands more are injured.

SOURCE: RHEINISCHE POST

"Hansa Hooligans" show up with their own banner
(here at the match between FC St. Pauli and Hansa Rostock in 2009).

A closed-circuit television system in a modern stadium: Big Brother is watching you. In football this seems to be quite normal – this was a "friendly" match (2006).

19 NOVEMBER 2011:
HANSA ROSTOCK VERSUS FC ST. PAULI

Increasingly, there are complaints in Germany about hooligan violence in stadiums. Clubs are penalised for insufficient security measures – via the German Football Association's own jurisdiction; the perpetrators themselves are pursued under the general law enforcement procedures, if they can be caught.

Deployment of the police for securing the peaceful completion of football matches is paid for by the public rather than the clubs. The extent of the measures is demonstrated – as an extreme example – by the Second Division game between Hansa Rostock and FC St. Pauli in 2011; their respective fan groups are considered to be hostile to each other. Prior to the match the police and representatives of the two fan groups and the clubs' *fan liaison officers* discussed various measures.

Two special Deutsche Bahn trains started in Hamburg-Altona. The fans had to pass through a security lock and were searched for weapons, pyro-technology and gas bottles. Under special Federal police powers it was not permitted to carry such items in the trains to and from Rostock on that day only(!). Also prohibited: flags with staffs which could be used as batons. In Rostock the 1,600 fans were received by the police and shepherded to a locked holding compound. From there they were ferried by bus to the *guest block* in the stadium which had been cordoned off including a wide safety corridor. Video monitoring was used, as were sniffer dogs for explosives. Several hundred policemen controlled the transport. Body searches, cage detention and being forced into a *guest block*: only football-crazy people submit to such a procedure.

However, all this effort came to nothing. The match had to be interrupted because of rioting: rockets were fired from the Rostock fan camp into the guest block. The President of Hansa Rostock asked the public for help concerning the problems with the home fans. The German Football Association penalised Hansa with a spectator-free home match and FC St. Pauli with a fine of 8,000 Euros.

IT IS ALSO POSSIBLE WITHOUT

List of Olympic sports disciplines where no violent confrontations have occurred:

Summer: Badminton, Basketball, Archery, Fencing, Football (women), Weightlifting, Golf, Handball, Hockey, Judo, Canoeing, Track and field, Modern pentathlon, Cycling, Equestrian disciplines, Wrestling, Rowing, Rugby, Shooting, Swimming, Sailing, Taekwondo, Tennis, Table tennis, Triathlon, Gymnastics, Volleyball

Winter: Bobsleigh, Skeleton, Curling, Figure skating, Speed skating, Luge, Alpine skiing, Freestyle skiing, Nordic skiing, Snowboarding

MASS FASCINATION

MASS FASCINATION

Why do about 300,000 spectators go to the Bundesliga football stadiums week after week, come rain or snow, in spite of the fact that they can watch the matches more cheaply at home via pay-TV (or for free in the case of international matches)? What motivates some people to pay horrendous amounts of money to watch a final here, or some other sporting event there? Is there really anything that you can see better from the back row at Centre Court in Wimbledon, at Hockenheim for Formula One, the Maracanã Stadium in Rio de Janeiro – what can you see that you wouldn't be able to follow better from the comfort of your own home, including slow motion replays and commentaries? Nothing.

And yet many of these events are fully booked. Also intellectuals, poets and scientists are enthusiastic about football; clearly the explanation that these are primitive rituals or a case of enjoying violence does not stand up. Components of this fascination are the excitement and tension between preferably evenly matched adversaries, the identification with one side, probably also the wish to melt into a larger whole for which the term *mass* is used, rather pejoratively. This explanation however is not sufficient; it is more likely that very deeply seated instincts are involved.

THE "THRILLA IN MANILA"

1st October 1975: a heavyweight boxing match takes place at Manila in the Philippines. There are about 25,000 spectators at the venue, while the number of worldwide spectators is estimated at 300 million. How can it be that two men measure their strength to certain rules and so many people want to see it?

It was undoubtedly not just about this boxing match. Muhammad Ali, formerly Cassius Clay, fascinated people with his elegant technique, his big mouth and his history: in 1964 he became World Heavyweight Champion for the first time; however, he was stripped of the title because he objected against military service in the US army. He did not regain his boxing licence until 1970 and fought Joe Frazier for the World Champion title, and lost. Though Frazier was also black, he was considered the *good black* in the eyes of the white American population, while Ali was considered the baddie because of his objection to military service. After a second fight with Frazier, which Ali won, Frazier challenged Ali, who had by now become World Champion, to the *Thrilla* match.

So the public's huge interest, especially in the USA, was only superficially about the question as to who was the better boxer; subliminally there were many levels on which it was possible to identify with one or the other of the boxers – including racism.

By the way: Muhammad Ali won the fight by a narrow margin. It was a battle to the last. After the fight, Ali said: "We came to Manila as young champions, and we left as old men."

*"It's gonna be a thrilla
and a chilla
and a killa
when I get the gorilla
in Manila"*

THE BIGGEST
SPECTATOR EVENTS

It is not possible to record the spectator numbers of televised sports events; the number of television sets would have to be taken into account, as well as the number of people on earth in order to arrive at an accurate result. Here are some telling figures:

The Super Bowl, the final game in US baseball, was supposed to have attracted up to 800 million viewers; the match is broadcast in 180 countries.

An average of 593 million spectators watched the opening ceremony of the 2008 Olympic Games in Beijing.

In 2010 an average of 329 million TV viewers watched the live broadcast of Spain's 1 : 0 victory over Holland in the World Cup Final in South Africa.

178 million watched the live broadcast of Usain Bolt's 100-metre victory in Beijing in 2008.

166 million viewers watched the final of the UEFA European Cup between Spain and Germany in 2008.

56 million watched the football Champions' League final in 2004; five years later, the number had increased to 109 million.

SOURCE: HTTP://SPORTBILD.BILD.DE

National stadium, Beijing.

The large stadium in Pyongyang, North Korea, during the opening ceremony of the World Festival of Youth and Students (1989).

THE LARGEST SPORTS FACILITIES

SPECTATOR NUMBERS	NAME	CITY	COUNTRY	OPENING DATE	TYPE
220.000	Strahov Stadium	Prague	CZE	1926	Various events
150.000	May First Stadium	Pyongyang	PRK	1989	Various events
120.000	Yuba Bharati Krirangan	Kolkata	IND	1984	Football
109.901	Michigan Stadium	Ann Arbor	USA	1927	American football
107.282	Beaver Stadium	University Park	USA	1960	American football
105.064	Aztec Stadium	Mexiko City	MEX	1966	Football
102.455	Neyland Stadium	Knoxville	USA	1921	American football
102.329	Ohio Stadium	Columbus	USA	1922	American football
101.821	Bryant-Denny Stadium	Tuscaloosa	USA	1929	American football
100.200	Bukit Jalil National Stadium	Kuala Lumpur	MAS	1998	Football
100.119	Texas Memorial Stadium	Austin	USA	1924	American football
100.000	Melbourne Cricket Ground	Melbourne	AUS	1853	Australian football, Cricket
99.354	Camp Nou	Barcelona	ESP	1957	Football
96.000	Maracanã Stadium	Rio de Janeiro	BRA	1950	Football
94.700	FNB Stadium	Johannesburg	RSA	1989	Football
93.607	Memorial Coliseum	Los Angeles	USA	1923	American football
93.000	Ranji Stadium	Kolkata	IND	1894	Cricket
92.746	Sanford Stadium	Athens	USA	1929	American football
92.400	Tiger Stadium	Baton Rouge	USA	1924	American football
92.200	Cotton Bowl Stadium	Dallas	USA	1932	American football
91.704	FedEx Field	Landover	USA	1997	American football
91.136	Rose Bowl Stadium	Pasadena	USA	1922	American football
91.000	Beijing National Stadium	Beijing	CHN	2008	Various events

Source http://de.wikipedia.org/wiki/Liste_der_größten_Stadien_der_Welt

SPECTATOR BALLET

One might think that cheerleading as entertainment during the break is a little strange: should it not be the game itself that rouses the spectators?

SPECTATOR BALLET

Spectator ballet – the term actually does not refer to gracious movement by masses of people in tutus. But when the *wave* ripples through – whenever nothing is happening in the match but the mood is good – when people jump up and down in unison, when choreographies are rehearsed by a minority and are then accepted and carried out by the majority, when reciprocal chants break out between opposite grandstands, i.e. whenever the issue is not victory or defeat but when it is about having fun, about being part of it, then you can talk about spectator ballet or choreography. How much of it has been organised in each case, and how much arises spontaneously, is an open question. The important point is: the spectators become actors, co-players in a secondary event to the main event which actually becomes more prominent than the sporting event (which may not be all that exciting). In the USA, where there are cheerleaders, this is particularly prevalent: originally created to cheer the team and fill in the breaks, cheerleading has now become a sports event in its own right with State and World Championships.

Mexican wave at Leverkusen Stadium during the Women's World Cup match Japan v. Mexico.

THE MEXICAN WAVE

In addition to the shouting of rhythmic slogans, for example *Ha-Es-Fow* (English phonetics for HSV = Hamburger Sportverein), with the emphasis on the last syllable in order to drive the team forward, the Mexican wave is the best-known element of spectator participation at sports events. It is created by spectators getting up and throwing their arms in the air in quick sequence.

What looks like a spontaneous idea, and in Germany was perceived as the invention of Mexican spectators at the 1986 Football World Cup, probably has its origin in the cheerleader world of the USA. The Dresden traffic researcher Dirk Helbing has now scientifically investigated the phenomenon's origin and spread: he arrives at the conclusion that 35 people are enough to initiate a wave in a stadium with 50,000 spectators, that as a rule the wave moves clockwise with a width of 6 to 12 metres and a speed of 12 metres per second.

However, it is not necessary to know these facts to perform the Mexican wave.

SPECTATOR CHOREOGRAPHY

Pre-planned and rehearsed spectator choreographies are particularly popular at sports events that promise to be exciting, that attract many spectators and that are highly emotional, i.e. above all, at team sports events.

One may ask whether the term *choreography* is actually appropriate for such displays, since it is normally reserved for artistic presentations. But when considering that the word originally refers to the recording of the chorus movements in ancient Greek theatre, it appears quite appropriate. After all, the chorus reacts to the action on stage. The first three choreographies, which received an award from the German Academy for Football Culture (yes, it really exists!) in 2011, provide evidence of the diversity of spectator reactions:

St. Paul sweatshirt: "Kneel down, you vassals. St. Pauli is visiting"

Unfortunately, the box for about 30 super fans of football who don't like bubbly but prefer beer and curry sausage has now been dismantled.

FC ST. PAULI – "JOY, OH FOOTBALL – GAME SO PRECIOUS"

Everybody will (and should) love and support their club, but for many years now FC St. Pauli – from that part of Hamburg with the same name – has had a reputation for being especially creative when it comes to off-pitch activities. Two examples: for several years an advertising agency had its own box – self-built as a counter-design to the boxes of those who come more for corporate reasons than for supporting the team. It had 30 seats, each with its own beer tap and a screen at the back of the seat in front, and an electric railway that would bring curry sausage directly to the seat.

Many clubs have created fan songs by changing the lyrics of well-known songs. But only FC St. Pauli has dared tackle Beethoven's *Ode to Joy*, and even laced it with a sense of irony – because the song was created at a time when the team was not exactly known for its sophisticated football:

"Joy, oh football – game so precious / Played by our Sankt Pauli
Wonder goals and magic passes / Football heroes all are thee
One-touch passes and step-over / Heroes of Elysium
Joy, oh football – game so precious / Played by our Sankt Pauli."

"We love you, we love you, we love you, and where you play we follow, we follow, we follow 'cause we support Sankt Pauli – Sankt Pauli, Sankt Pauli and that's the way we like it – we like it, we like it."

"Aux Armes! Aux Armes! Nous sommes Sankt Pauli! Et nous allons gagner! Allez braun-weiß! Allez braun-weiß! LaLaLaLaLaLaLaLaLa."

"Que Sera, Sera, What ever will be, will be, The Champions of Germany, FC Sankt Pauli."

"Police everywhere – justice nowhere": who says that the mass doesn't have a sense of irony?

PAPAL MASSES, POP CONCERTS

Pope Benedict XVI visits Berlin and holds a mass in the stadium (2011).

PAPAL MASSES, POP CONCERTS

Sport and its spectators: part of a religious ceremony, a religious experience in ancient Greece (and in other cultures). The stadium or arena: a round bowl which is the architectural expression of the shared experience, and which provides the backdrop. The Mexican wave and other choreographies as outward expressions of shared feelings and the sense of belonging to a community: it all seems to indicate that a stadium is not only suitable for sporting events, but also for other community-based events.

That is not to say however that football and other types of sport are a religion, just as a rock concert in a stadium has no religious background at all. But nevertheless, similar community-forming elements to those enacted in a mass – such as singing along, waving lighters together in the dark – help to create an experience of community.

The joint prayer or hymn sung by all during a papal mass in a stadium is not quite the same as "You'll never walk alone" before a football match. But the fervour, the shared joint experience, can nevertheless evoke the same power of feeling in each individual.

© Olympiastadion Berlin GmbH

© Olympiastadion Berlin GmbH

THE BERLIN OLYMPIC STADIUM AS AN EXAMPLE OF A VENUE

The extent to which a stadium (although perceived as a sports arena only) can be used as a facility for general events can be seen on the website of the Berlin Olympic Stadium:

WE OFFER YOU THE FACILITIES FOR YOUR EVENT!

Hidden behind the historic façade of the Berlin Olympic Stadium are numerous multi-faceted locations. The four-storey atrium that is a unique feature of worldwide fame, the underground warm-up area or the VIP Driveway South are just some of the facilities which can be individually configured and arranged according to your wishes.

EVENTS IN 2012 POSSIBILITIES OF AN EXCEPTIONAL LOCATION

Make 2012 your very special year and organise your event, together with our Special & Business Events Team, in the exclusive VIP area of the Berlin Olympic Stadium. Stage the launch of your strategy or kick-off meeting with us. Use the background of UEFA EURO 2012 and the Summer Olympic Games for your summer party. And why not book your preferred date now for your 2012 Christmas Party.

Have a look yourself and explore the Berlin Olympic Stadium as your next event location.

Feel honoured!

The panorama windows of the Hall of Honour grant you breathtaking views. But there is more to it than meets the eye: the Hall of Honour is the perfect location for prestigious events or your gala dinner. The Hall can be decorated according to your wishes and the type of event.

During sporting events and concerts the Hall of Honour is reserved for national or international performing artists, members of the government or presidents and high-ranking politicians. On the days when no event is taking place, the Hall of Honour is your perfect venue in an exclusive and historic setting. Enjoy the setting sun and the rising Olympic spirit over a glass of wine.

Four ways to celebrate

Welcome to the Atrium with its four lounge areas: the Coubertin, Olympia, Jesse-Owens and Players lounges. You won't have to go searching for a comparable location – it doesn't exist. The open

Business lounge on the gallery of the Olympic Stadium, Berlin.

© Olympiastadion Berlin GmbH

ensemble of rooms with its interconnecting futuristic staircase will leave you stunned and invites you to take a look around, just relax or rest in awe. This facility is unique and is suitable for parties or all other events without strict, formal settings. If that's not a reason to celebrate!

Tactically clever

The place reserved for the top athletes just before they enter the stadium. Here, the coaches give the last instructions to their players. The perfect opportunity to prepare your team for the coming season. You can be the coach who briefs his top salesmen on your latest product or project, and explain the new tactical moves. This is where important tactical decisions are made so that your opponent won't stand a chance!

The dressing rooms offer a great variety of event set-ups. You can perfectly stage workshops or small group presentations. Let your guests feel that they are special and important to you as you take a seat in the dressing room in order to give instructions on the tactics board or show a video on the TV screens.

Give a pep talk in front of classic rows of seating, hold a creative meeting in a circular arrangement or use the dressing rooms for what they are designed for: as changing rooms before setting foot on the "holy turf".

Aim for the home strait

Why not celebrate where Usain Bolt achieved two world records, and make your event a unique experience on the blue track of the Berlin Olympic Stadium.

Enjoy the breathtaking backdrop with your guests under the open sky and avail yourself of the numerous combination options we can offer with our range of facilities."

SOURCE: HTTP://WWW.OLYMPIASTADION-BERLIN.DE/SPECIAL-BUSINESS-EVENTS.HTML

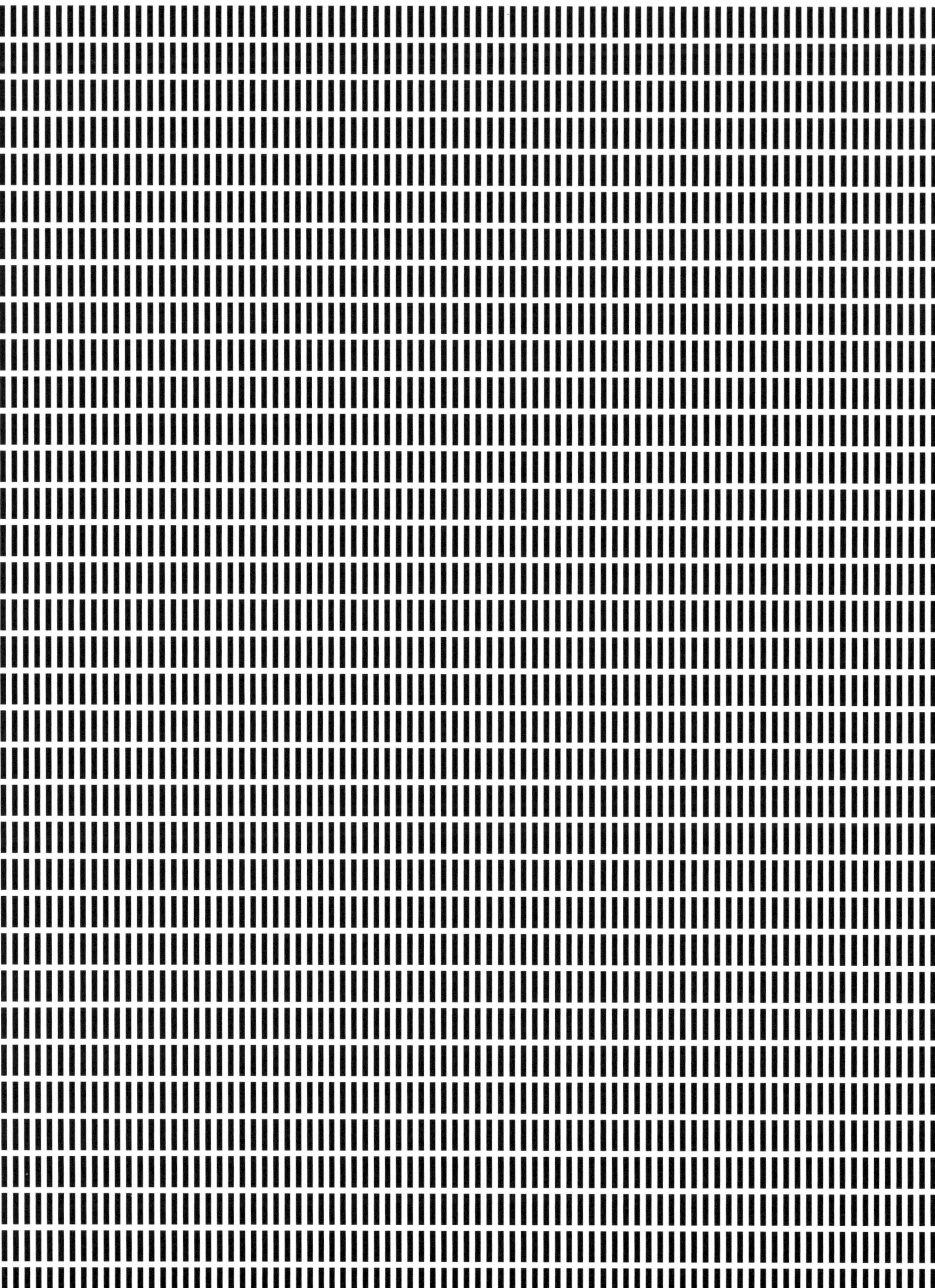

QUOTATIONS

GUSTAVE
LE BON

The substitution of the unconscious action of crowds for the conscious activity of individuals is one of the principal characteristics of the present age.

(…)

Reason is an attribute of humanity of too recent date and still too imperfect to reveal to us the laws of the unconscious, and still more to take its place. The part played by the unconscious in all our acts is immense, and that played by reason very small.

(…)

Thousands of isolated individuals may acquire at certain moments, and under the influence of certain violent emotions – such, for example, as a great national event – the characteristics of a psychological crowd.

(…)

The disappearance of the conscious personality, the predominance of the unconscious personality, the turning by means of suggestion and contagion of feelings and ideas in an identical direction, the tendency to immediately transform the suggested ideas into acts are the principal characteristics of the individual forming part of a crowd.

(…)

The individual forming part of a crowd acquires (…) a sentiment of invincible power which allows him to yield to instincts which, had he been alone, he would perforce have kept under restraint. He will be the less disposed to check himself from the consideration that, a crowd being anonymous, and in consequence irresponsible, the sentiment of responsibility which always controls individuals disappears entirely.

(…)

In crowds the foolish, ignorant, and envious persons are freed from the sense of their insignificance and powerlessness, and are possessed instead by the notion of brutal and temporary but immense strength.

(…)

Whether the feelings exhibited by a crowd be good or bad, they present the double character of being very simple and very exaggerated.

(…)

Little adapted to reasoning, crowds, on the contrary, are quick to act.

(…)

Being in doubt as to what constitutes truth or error, and having, on the other hand, a clear notion of its strength, a crowd is as disposed to give authoritative effect to its inspirations as it is intolerant.

(…)

Crowds being only capable of thinking in images are only to be impressed by images. It is only images that terrify or attract them and become motives of action.

(…)

The crowd demands a god before everything else.

GUSTAVE LE BON, PSYCHOLOGIE DES FOULES (THE CROWD: A STUDY OF THE POPULAR MIND), 1895

ETIENNE-LOUIS BOULLEE

The coliseum in Rome is one of the most beautiful monuments in Italy. Its structure creates a majestic and striking unity. Its embellishment, however, seems to me to be bad architecture that only moderately fulfills its purpose. I have therefore taken it upon myself to find a suitable framework for a noble design. This would mean solving one of the most exciting tasks in architecture.

(…)

It is namely not always fear of punishment that holds one in check and hinders people from doing bad things. One must offer the people strong enticements that steer them away from that which is bad. What could, however, be the nature of such a temptation? National games. Yes, national games. This is because everything that offers its services to our senses is transferred to our souls. This is a principle that the games of a nation should follow. Should one proceed accordingly, one has, without a doubt, an effective means of forming and maintaining sound customs.

(…)

National games are noble and impressive. The soul of the citizen is raised and purified under the watch of all. Why should one not make use of such a means, which hardly requires victims and which, through the stimulus of entertainment, restores sound customs? The plan for a round structure, which I present here, is intended to elevate moral and political qualities.

(…)

One imagines 300,000 people gathered in an amphitheatre arrangement where no one can hide from the gaze of the crowd. A unique effect is caused by this situation: the beauty of the astonishing spectacle is based on the spectators themselves. They become the spectacle.

(…)

Indeed, what would be more enthralling than to see this wonderful arena filled with glowing youth who tried to excel in all forms of physical exercise, for example in races, in which their entire physical skill may unfold and display their willingness to defend the Fatherland in military rallies.

ÉTIENNE-LOUIS BOULLÉE, ESSAI SUR L'ART (ESSAY ON ART), CA. 1791

ELIAS
CANETTI

The Fear of being Touched

There is nothing that man fears more than the touch of the unknown. (…) Man always tends to avoid physical contact with anything strange.

(…)

All the distances which men create round themselves are dictated by this fear. They shut themselves in houses which no-one may enter, and only there feel some measure of security.

(…)

The repugnance to being touched remains with us when we go about among people. (…) Even when we are standing next to them and are able to watch and examine them closely, we avoid actual contact if we can. If we do not avoid it, it is because we feel attracted to someone; and then it is we who make the approach.

(…)

It is only in a crowd that man can become free of this fear of being touched. That is the only situation in which the fear changes into its opposite. The crowd he needs is the dense crowd, in which body is pressed to body; a crowd, too, whose psychical constitution is also dense, or compact, so that he no longer notices who it is that presses against him. (…) The man pressed against him is the same as himself. He feels him as he feels himself. Suddenly it is as though everything were happening in one and the same body.

(…)

The more fiercely people press together, the more certain they feel that they do not fear each other. This reversal of the fear of being touched belongs to the nature of crowds. The feeling of relief is most striking where the density of the crowd is greatest.

The Open and the Closed Crowd

The crowd, suddenly there where there was nothing before, is a mysterious and universal phenomenon. A few people may have been standing together – five, ten or twelve, not more; nothing has been announced, nothing is expected. Suddenly everywhere is black with people and more come streaming from all sides as though streets had only one direction. (…) they have a goal which is there before they can find words for it. This goal is the blackest spot where most people are gathered.

(…) the urge to grow is the first and supreme attribute of the crowd. (…) The natural crowd is the open crowd; there are no limits whatever to its growth; it does not recognize houses, doors or locks and those who shut themselves in are suspect. Open is to be understood here in the fullest sense of the word; it means open everywhere and in any direction. (…)

In contrast to the open crowd which can grow indefinitely (…) there is the closed crowd.

(…)

The closed crowd renounces growth and puts the stress on permanence. The first thing to be noticed about it is that it has a boundary. It establishes itself by accepting its limitation. It creates a space for itself which it will fill. (…) The entrances to this space are limited in number, and only these entrances can be used; the boundary is respected

(…)

The boundary prevents disorderly increase, but it also makes it more difficult for the crowd to disperse and so postpones its dissolution. In this way the crowd sacrifices its chance of growth, but gains in staying power. (…) It is the expectation of reassembly which enables its members to accept each dispersal. The building is waiting for them; it exists for their sake and, so long as it is there, they will be able to meet in the same manner. The space is theirs, even during the ebb, and in its emptiness it reminds them of the flood.

The Crowd as a Ring

An arena contains a crowd which is doubly closed.

(…)

The arena is well demarcated from the outside world. It is usually visible from far off

(…)

Outside, facing the city, the arena displays a lifeless wall; inside is a wall of people. The spectators turn their backs to the city. They have been lifted out of its structure of walls and streets and, for the duration of their time in the arena, they do not care about anything which happens there; they have left behind all their associations, rules and habits. Their remaining together in large numbers for a stated period of time is secure and their excitement has been promised them. But only under one definite condition: the discharge must take place inside the arena.

The seats are arranged in tiers around the arena, so that everyone can see what is happening below. The consequence of this is that the crowd is seated opposite itself. Every spectator has a thousand in front of him, a thousand heads. As long as he is there, all the others are there too; whatever excites him, excites them; and he sees it. They are seated some distance away from him, so that the differing details which make individuals of them are blurred; they all look alike and they all behave in a similar manner and he notices in them only the things which he himself is full of. Their visible excitement increases his own.

There is no break in the crowd which sits like this, exhibiting itself to itself. It forms a closed ring from which nothing can escape. (…) this crowd is doubly closed, to the world outside and in itself.

The Discharge

The most important occurrence within the crowd is the discharge. Before this the crowd does not actually exist; it is the discharge which creates it. This is the moment when all who belong to the crowd get rid of their differences and feel equal.

These differences are mainly imposed from outside; they are distinctions of rank, status and property. (…) In every sphere of life, firmly established hierarchies prevent him touching anyone more exalted than himself, or descending, except in appearance, to anyone lower. In different societies the distances are differently balanced against each other. (…) Man petrifies and darkens in the distances he has created. (…) He forgets that it is self-inflicted, and longs for liberation. But how, alone, can he free himself? Whatever he does, and however determined he is, he will always find himself among others who thwart his efforts. So long as they hold fast to their distances, he can never come any nearer to them.

Only together can men free themselves from their burdens of distance; and this, precisely, is what happens in a crowd. During the discharge distinctions are thrown off and all feel equal.

(…) It is for the sake of this blessed moment, when no-one is greater or better than another, that people become a crowd.

But the moment of discharge, so desired and so happy, contains its own danger. It is based on an illusion; the people who suddenly feel equal have not really become equal; nor will they feel equal for ever. (…)

But the crowd, as such, disintegrates. It has a presentiment of this and fears it. It can only go on existing if the process of discharge is continued (…)

Destructiveness

The destructiveness of the crowd is often mentioned as its most conspicuous quality, and there is no denying the fact that it can be observed everywhere, in the most diverse countries and civilizations. (…)

The crowd particularly likes destroying houses and objects: breakable objects like window panes, mirrors, pictures and crockery; and people tend to think that it is the fragility of these objects which stimulates the destructiveness of the crowd. (…)

The destruction of representational images is the destruction of a hierarchy which is no longer recognized. (…) In this act the discharge accomplishes itself. (…)

The more usual kind of (…) destruction (…) is simply an attack on all boundaries. Windows and doors belong to houses; they are the most vulnerable part of the exterior and, once they are smashed, the house has lost its individuality; anyone may enter it and nothing and no-one is protected any more. (…)

Of all means of destruction the most impressive is fire (…)

The Eruption

The open crowd is the true crowd, the crowd abandoning itself freely to its natural urge for growth. An open crowd has no clear feeling or idea of the size it may attain (…) Men might have gone on disregarding it if the enormous increase of population in modern times and the rapid growth of cities, had not more and more often given rise to its formation.

(…)

The closed crowds of the past (…) had turned into familiar institutions. (…) All ceremonies and rules pertaining to such institutions are basically intent on capturing the crowd; they prefer a church-full secure to the whole world insecure. The regularity of church-going and the precise and familiar repetition of certain rites safeguard for the crowd something like a domesticated experience of itself. These performances and their recurrence at fixed times supplant needs for something harsher and more violent.

(…)

All the rebellions against traditional ceremonial recounted in the history of religions have been directed against the confinement of the crowd (…)

I designate as eruption the sudden transition from a closed into an open crowd. This is a frequent occurrence, and one should not understand it as something referring only to space. A crowd quite often seems to overflow from some well-guarded space into the squares and streets of a town where it can move about freely, exposed to everything and attracting everyone.

(...)

Since the French Revolution these eruptions have taken on a form which we feel to be modern. (...) The history of the last 150 years has culminated in a spate of such eruptions; they have engulfed even wars, for all wars are now mass wars. The crowd is no longer content with pious promises and conditionals. It wants to experience for itself the strongest possible feeling of its own animal force and passion and, as means to this end, it will use whatever social pretexts and demands offer themselves.(...)

Panic

Panic (...) is a disintegration of the crowd. (...) The more people were bound together by the performance and the more closed the form of the theatre which contained them, the more violent the disintegration. (...)

However little crowd feeling there may have been in the audience, awareness of a fire brings it suddenly to a head. The common unmistakable danger creates a common fear. For a short time the audience becomes something like a real crowd. (...) An active crowd-fear (...) is the common collective experience of all animals who live together in herds and whose joint safety depends on their speed. (...)

Only one or two persons can get through each exit at a time and thus the energy of flight turns into an energy of struggle to push others back. Only one man at a time can pass between the rows of seats and each seat is neatly separated from the rest. Each man has his place and sits or stands by himself. (...)

The sudden command to flee which the fire gives is immediately countered by the impossibility of any common movement. Each man sees the door through which he must pass; and he sees himself alone in it, sharply cut off from all the others. It is the frame of a picture which very soon dominates him. Thus the crowd, a moment ago at its apex, must disintegrate violently, and the transmutation shows itself in violent individual action: everyone shoves, hits and kicks in all directions. (...)

Panic is a disintegration of the crowd within *the crowd. The individual breaks away and wants to escape from it because the crowd, as a whole, is endangered. But, because he is physically still stuck in it, he must attack it. To abandon himself to it now would be his ruin, because it itself is threatened by ruin. In such a moment a man cannot insist too strongly on his separateness (...)*

The Attributes of the Crowd

(...)

1. The crowd always wants to grow. There are no natural boundaries to its growth. Where such boundaries have been artificially created e.g. in all institutions which are used for the preservation of closed crowds – an eruption of the crowd is always possible and will, in fact, happen from time to time.

(...)

2. Within the crowd there is equality. This is absolute and indisputable and never questioned by the crowd itself. It is of fundamental importance and one might even define a crowd as a state of absolute equality. (...)

3. The crowd loves density. *It can never feel too dense. Nothing must stand between its parts or divide them; everything must be the crowd itself. The feeling of density is strongest in the moment of discharge. (…)*

4. The crowd needs a direction. *It is in movement and it moves towards a goal. The direction, which is common to all its members, strengthens the feeling of equality. A goal outside the individual members and common to all of them drives underground all the private differing goals which are fatal to the crowd as such. (…) A crowd exists so long as it has an unattained goal. (…)*

Another distinction is that between rhythmic *and* stagnating *crowds. This refers to the next two attributes, equality and density; and to both of them simultaneously.*

The stagnating *crowd lives for its discharge. But it feels certain of this and puts it off. It desires a relatively long period of density to prepare for the moment of discharge. (…) The process here starts not with equality, but with density; and equality then becomes the main goal of the crowd, which in the end it reaches. Every shout, every utterance in common is a valid expression of this equality.*

(…)

In the rhythmic *crowd, on the other hand (for example the crowd of the dance), density and equality coincide from the beginning. Everything here depends on movement. All the physical stimuli involved function in a predetermined manner and are passed on from one dancer to another. Density is embodied in the formal recurrence of retreat and approach (…) And thus, by the skilful enactment of density and equality, a crowd feeling is engendered. These rhythmic formations spring up very quickly and it is only physical exhaustion which bring them to an end. The next pair of concepts – the* slow *and the* quick *crowd – refer exclusively to the nature of the goal. The conspicuous crowds which are the ones usually mentioned and which form such an essential part of modern life – the political, sporting and war like crowds we see daily – are all* quick *crowds. Very different from these are the religious crowds whose goal is a heaven, or crowds formed of pilgrims. Their goal is distant, the way to it long, and the true formation of the crowd is relegated to a far off country or to another world.*

(…)

This is a mere indication of the nature of these forms. We shall have to consider them more closely. (…)

EXTRACT FROM ELIAS CANETTI, "CROWDS AND POWER", 1960

JOHANN WOLFGANG VON GOETHE

The amphitheatre is thus the first outstanding monument of the Antique that I see and it is so well preserved! As I entered, but even more as I walked around its edge above, it seemed strange to me to see at once something so great and, actually, to see nothing. It does not wish to be seen empty, but full of people (…) For such an amphitheatre is built so that the people may be impressed by themselves, to be at their best.

The general need to satisfy that is the architect's basic task here. He prepares such a crater with art, as simple as possible, so that its jewel becomes the people themselves. When they saw themselves like this together, they had to be amazed by themselves, for they were otherwise only used to seeing themselves all walking around together at the same time, in crowds without structure and with little discipline. The multi-headed, many-minded, back-and-forth-swaying and confused animal is unified into a single, noble body, destined to unity, linked like a figure brought to life by a single spirit. The simplicity of the oval is tangible for all eyes in the most agreeable manner, with every head serving as a measure to how awesome the entirety is.

JOHANN WOLFGANG VON GOETHE, ITALIAN JOURNEY, VERONA,
16 SEPTEMBER 1786

PETER SLOTERDIJK

It is Canetti's merit to have formulated a defining theory of this stage of modernisation in which the crowd, if capable of congregation, appeared before itself and for itself and belonged to the key scenarios of the modern psycho-political space.

(…)

For the most part, current masses no longer come together as congregations or spontaneous crowds; they have entered a regime in which their character is no longer expressed in the physical act of coming together, but in the participation in mass media programmes.

(…)

The spontaneous crowd has become a mass that is part of a programme, which – as per definition – is no longer bound to the act of physical congregation in a shared location. In it one becomes mass as an individual. Now one is mass without seeing the others. In consequence, today's societies – one might say post-modern societies – no longer use their own physical experience as the primary yardstick for their orientation, but see themselves through the spectacles of mass media symbols, discourses, modes, programmes and prominent personalities.

PETER SLOTERDIJK, DIE VERACHTUNG DER MASSEN, 2000

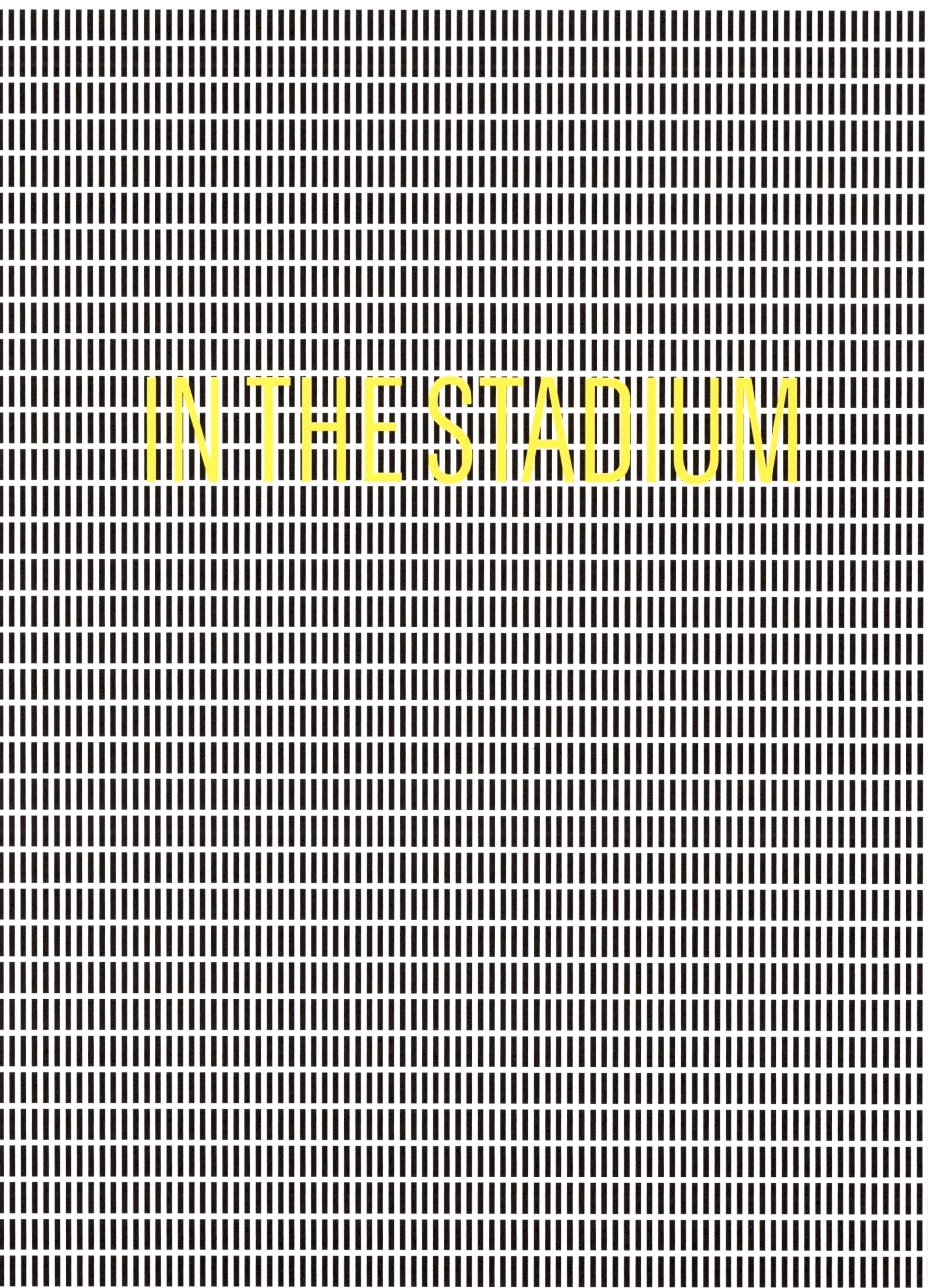

IN THE STADIUM

VON GERKAN, MARG AND PARTNERS BUILD FOR UEFA EURO 2012

WARSAW

The national stadium was built on the existing dilapidated earth-wall stadium that had not been used since 1988.

NATIONAL STADIUM, WARSAW, POLAND, 2012

For Poland, the national stadium in Warsaw is an icon. It was constructed in 1955 on the rubble of the destroyed city, opposite Warsaw's old city centre on the far side of the Vistula River, and was inaugurated as Decade Stadium on the occasion of the 11th anniversary of the founding of the Polish Committee for National Liberation, which had taken place in Moscow. (Stadion Dziesięciolecia, architects: Jerzy Hryniewiecki, Zbigniew Ihnatowicz and Jerzy Sołtan).

In 1940, German occupying forces had locked the Warsaw Jews into a ghetto and then murderously put down the desperate uprising in 1943. In 1944, the old city was destroyed and the uprising of the Polish Home Army was quashed by the German onslaught of bombs and grenades, while the Red Army was waiting on the opposite bank of the Vistula River where the stadium was later to be built.

In 1968, during the harvest festival and in front of 100,000 people, the philosopher Ryszard Siwiec set fire to himself in protest against the invasion of Czechoslovakia by Warsaw Pact forces.

In 1983, Pope John Paul II (Karol Józef Wojtyła) celebrated a triumphant mass with 100,000 faithful.

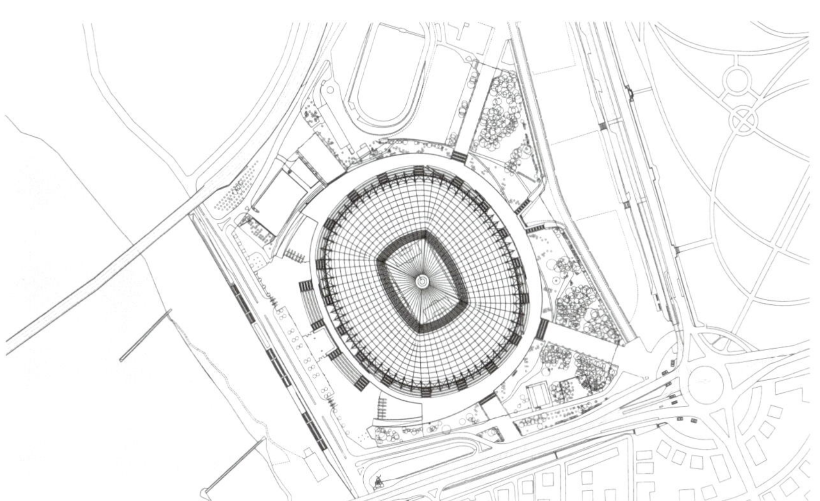

Site plan

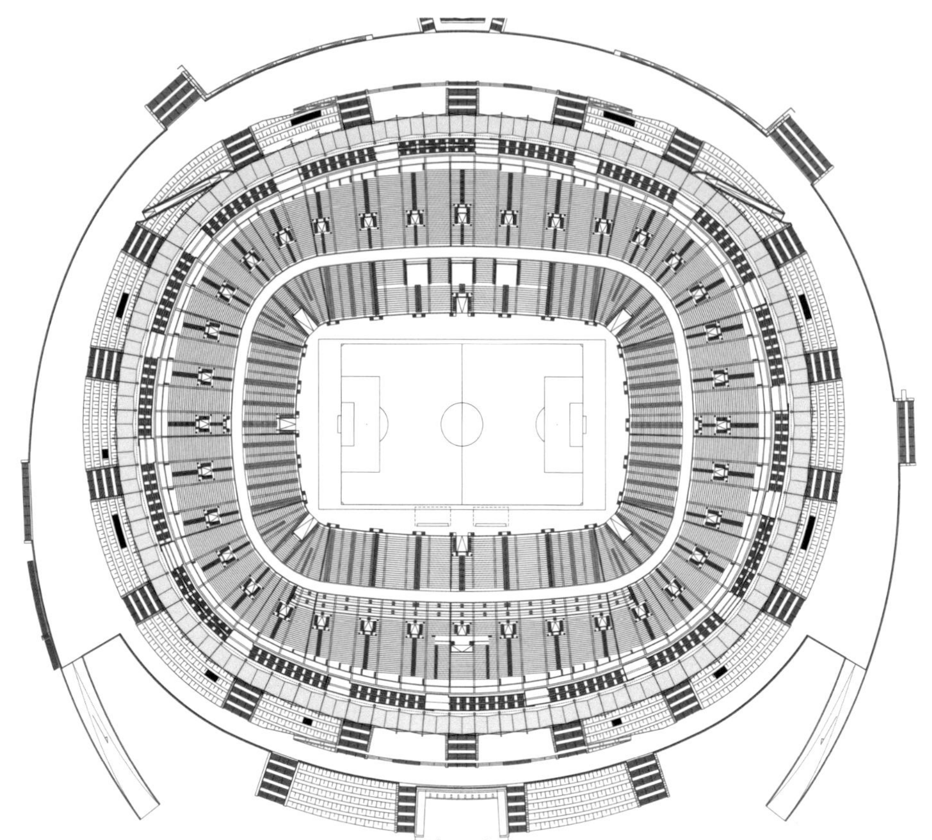

Floorplan level 5

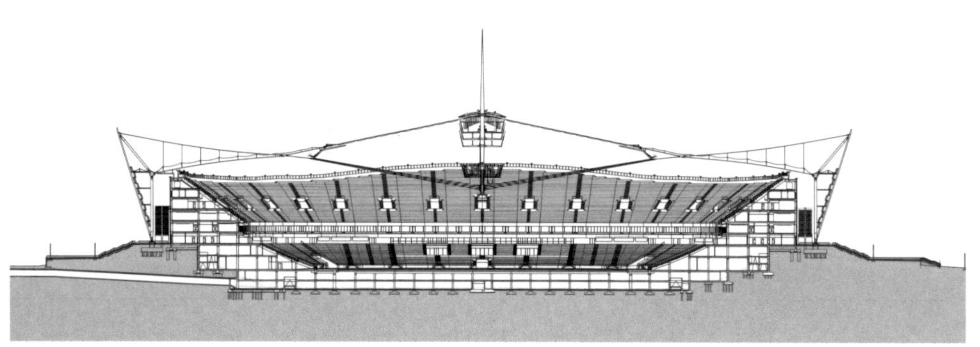

Longitudinal section

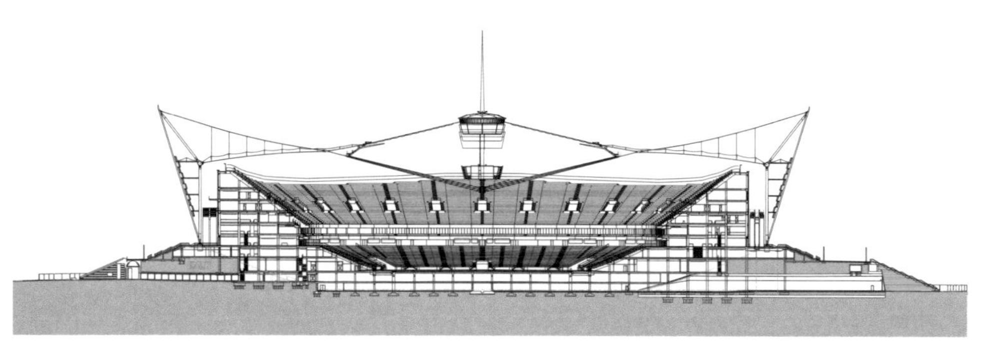

Cross-section

The new Polish national stadium was to be built in the same place, but also had to preserve the memory of its history. For this reason the architects decided, in agreement with their Polish colleagues, to construct the stadium above the grandstand banks on top of the previous stadium, which had to be retained. The grandstand banks themselves – including the retained tunnel entrances and sculptures – were not touched and, with their oval form, determine the geometric layout of the new structure.

The football arena for the opening game of the 2012 European Football Championship rises up on this historic base like a crown above the Vistula plains. Similar to a traditional wicker basket with red and white expanded metal ribbons woven into it, it presents itself as in illuminated landmark opposite the rebuilt Warsaw inner city, which has been declared a World Cultural Heritage site …

The national stadium has been designed as a multi-purpose arena for a diverse range of uses, and features a removable textile roof above the pitch. The translucent roof membranes are supported from a lightweight filigree steel-cable construction covering both the grandstands and the central portion which is retractable to the middle. The lightweight cable structure is based on the minimalist principle of a spoke-wheel design with a rim as the outer compression ring and a hub as the inner tensile ring.

The fixed outer grandstand roof has a hub of bundled cables as a tensile ring, whereas the retractable inner roof above the pitch is supported by a 70-metre high central needle which is held by four cable bundles and which floats above the pitch like a column suspended in mid-air. It also carries the video screens and the folding roof storage housing and, from the outside, stands out as a landmark at the centre of the arena.

The illumination of red/white and transparent sheathed outer tensile bars and the floodlighting of the roof membranes ensure that the national stadium radiates in the national colours. In this way the building's outward appearance is light and open.

Designed as a multi-purpose arena, the stadium offers space for 55,000 spectators.

KIEV

OLYMPIC STADIUM, KIEV, UKRAINE, 2012

Kiev – the capital of Ukraine – is considered the legendary place of origin in Russia. The national stadium in the midst of the historic inner city changed its name in tune with the history of the city.

Construction on the stadium started here in 1914 and in 1923, following the Ukrainian War of Independence, it was rebuilt for the Ukrainian Soviet Socialist Republic and named after Leon Trotsky. Stalin forced the leader of the revolution into exile and he was ultimately murdered in 1929, in Mexico. The stadium was then called the Red Stadium. It was rebuilt again in 1936 in the same place and named *Republican Stanislav Kosior Stadium* after the new Ukrainian party boss; then after his downfall in 1938 its name was changed to *Nikita Sergeyevich Khrushchev*, and after his demise, *Stalin Stadium*; after Stalin's death and conversion in 1953 it again became the *Khrushchev Stadium*, and when he was removed from power in 1962 it became the *Olympic Stadium*. At that time it had been extended to accommodate 100,000 spectators, including an upper grandstand tier and floodlighting for the Olympic football games held in the Soviet Union.

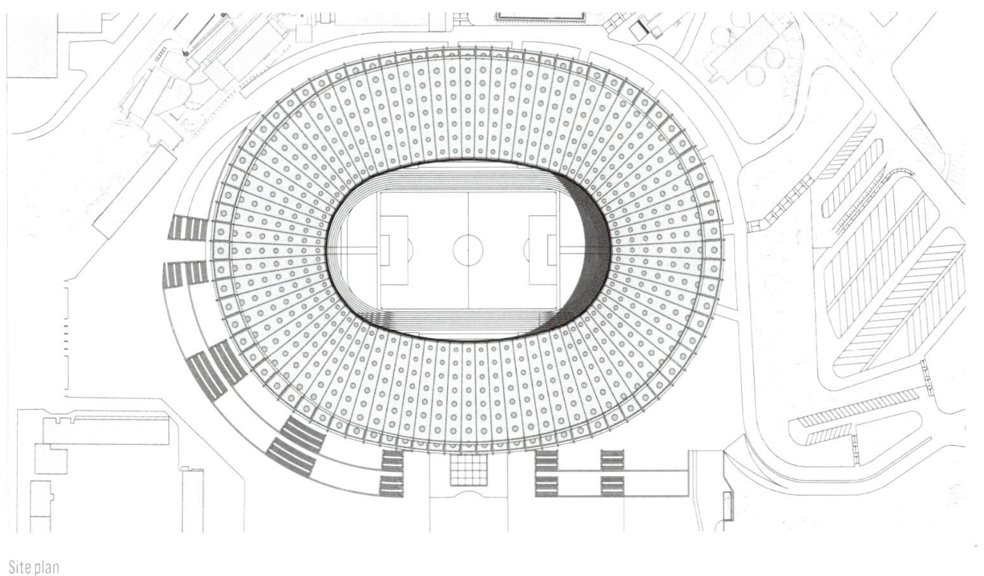

Site plan

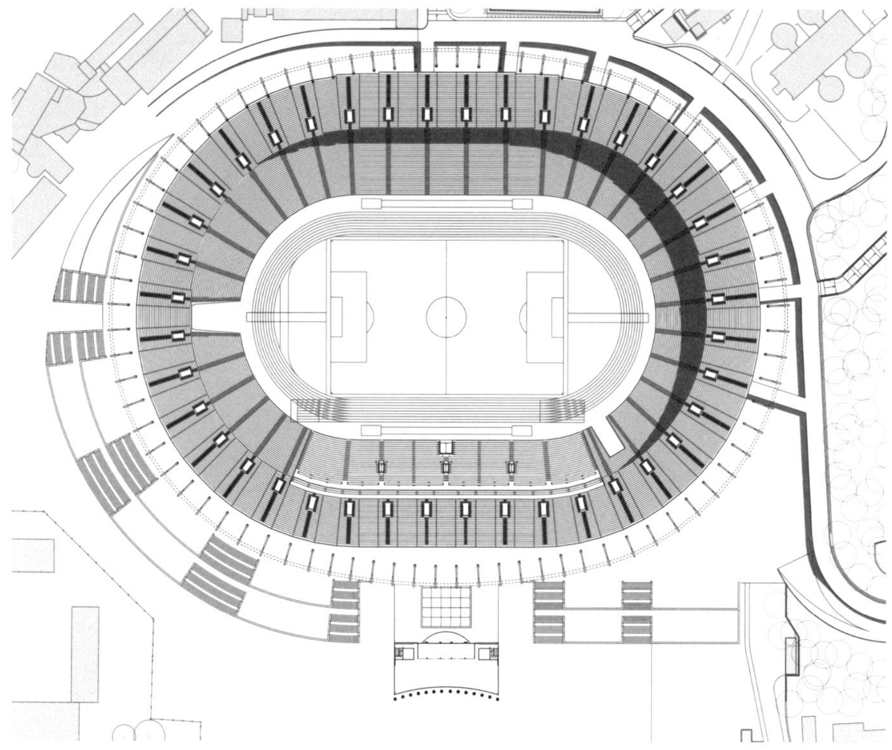

Top view stand

Longitudinal section

Cross-section

The stadium stands on a plinth structure that arises from the location on a slope and that had been reconstructed in a different guise.

The conversion and roofing-over of the Olympic Stadium for the final game of UEFA EURO 2012 required that the running tracks and the upper tiers of the grandstands be retained. The elegant wide-span construction was considered a historic monument and was not suitable for carrying additional loads required by the extension (similar to the Berlin Olympic Stadium).

For this reason, the architects von Gerkan, Marg and Partners designed an outer ring of columns, in the rhythm of the existing grandstand structure, with its own foundations for the lightweight spoke-wheel roof construction. The lower compression ring and the upper, outer compression ring are curved, with different radii, and act as rims for the spokes from the inner tensile ring, above supports with different kinking, so that they would be sufficiently bent on the long sides to be able to sustain the radial tensile forces.

The new design respects the historic fabric with its important filigree pre-stressed concrete upper tier – the frame of the new roof structure was detached and placed clear of the existing bowl.

The membrane roof with its radial stays that lead from the outer compression rings to the inner tension rings.

This change in form, and the bracing tensile support for the huge roof membrane provided by the rings of the peaking air-supports, characterises the unmistakable architectural appearance with its elegant aesthetic. The star-shaped reinforcements needed for distributing the tension in the roof membrane all round the air-support rings make the roof appear like a star-studded sky.

View over the roof construction towards Kiev.

Left: The bowl is being encased in a filigree glass facade, which acts almost as a kind of showcase, and will be duly illuminated with appropriate lighting.

Following Pages: The interior gains an individual, unmistakable identity with a roof structure incorporating air-supports and domes of light.

STADIUMS OF THE
MEMBERS
OF THE AKADEMIE
DER KÜNSTE,
BERLIN

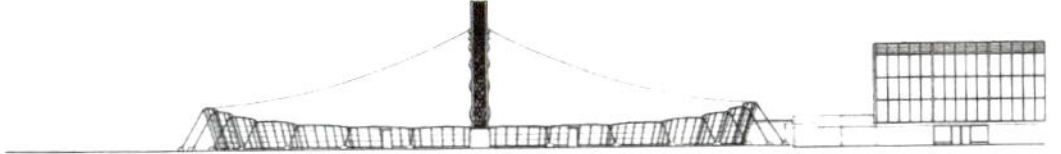 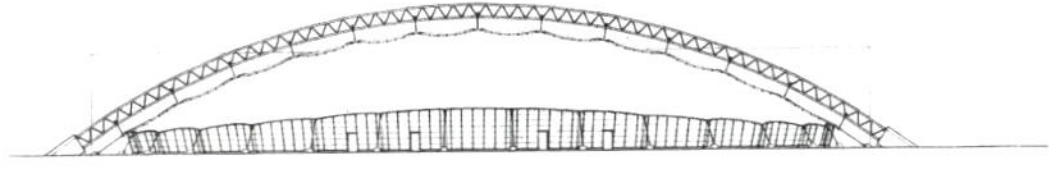

Kurt Ackermann

SKATING TENT IN THE MUNICH OLYMPIC PARK

Year of completion 1983
Design Kurt Ackermann,
Ackermann und Partner,
Architekten BDA
Structural engineers Jörg
Schlaich, schlaich bergermann
und partner   Client Münchner
Olympiapark GmbH
Construction period
1982–1983   Seating 120–140

Around ten years after the Olympic Games in Munich a further arena was to be erected in the Olympic Park suitable for all year ice skating. This was a difficult task as the characteristic architecture of the Olympic buildings, with the integration of the landscape and tent roof, established a strong precedent. The architects of the new arena sensitively incorporated them into the overall site while developing an independent design.

They devised a tent construction in the form of a lightweight plane load-bearing structure. The floating quality of ice skating is mirrored in the character of the pre-stretched cable-net construction which conveys an impression of lightness as well as providing an optimal solution for large span widths in terms of both function and construction. A polyester support fabric, PVC coated on both sides, was selected. The light membrane was applied to a timber grating mounted on a cable net. Thanks to the saddle-type suspension, the top two ridge cables form 12 oval openings. They are covered with crystal clear polycarbonate plates mounted onto the ridge cables, with clearance ensuring a natural ventilation of the arena.

Professor Dr. techn. h. c. **Kurt Ackermann** Born on 2/3/1928 in Insingen über Rothenburg ob der Tauber, lives in Herrsching am Ammersee
Since 1984 member of the Akademie der Künste, Berlin, Architecture Section

1946–1948 Apprenticeship and journeyman's exam as mason and carpenter | 1949–1954 Architectural studies at the Oskar-von-Miller Polytechnic and the Technical University (TU) Munich | since 1953 Freelance architect in Munich, since 1993 partnership with Peter Ackermann | 1970–1980 On the Committee of Patrons of Bauen + Wohnen | 1974–1993 Full professor and Director of the Institute for Design and Construction, University of Stuttgart | 1971 and 1980 Guest Professor for Design, TU Vienna | 1976–1984 Specialist advisor to the German Research Association (DFG) | 1995 Guest Professor TU Munich

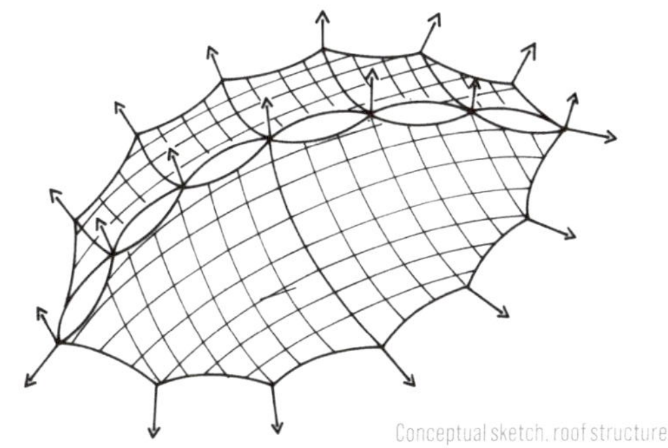

Conceptual sketch, roof structure

Year of completion 2010   Architect/Design Fritz Auer,
Auer+Weber+Assoziierte Statik   Structural engineers ISP Scholz
Client Stadtwerke München Services GmbH, Munich
Construction period 2007–2010   Seating Restaurant: approx. 500
Olympic Hall: approx. 14,000

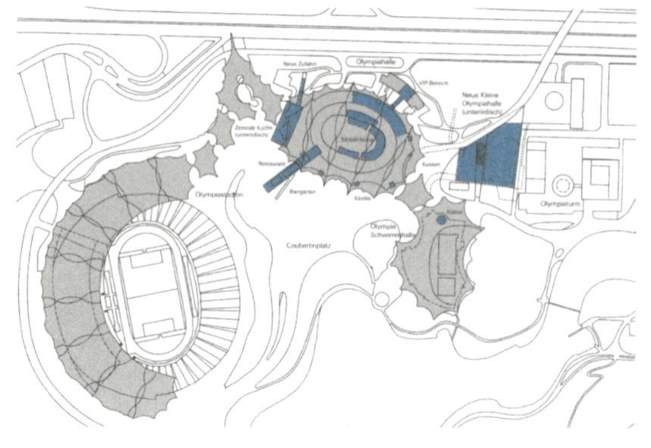

Site plan

Fritz Auer

CONVERSION AND EXTENSION OF THE OLYMPIC HALL IN THE MUNICH OLYMPIC PARK

Prof. **Fritz Auer**

Born on 24/6/1933 in Tübingen, lives in Stuttgart
Since 1993 member of the Akademie der Künste,
Berlin, Architecture Section

1953–1962 Study at the Technical University Stutt-
gart, awarded Degree | 1958 and 1959 Stipend for
the Cranbrook Academy of Arts, Bloomfield
Hills, Michigan, USA, Master of Architecture |
1960 Collaboration with Behnisch und Lambart,
Stuttgart | 1965 Collaboration with Yamasaki +
Associates, Birmingham, Michigan, USA and
Jäger und Müller, Stuttgart | 1966–1979 Partner in
the architects Behnisch & Partner | since 1980 Of-
fice partnership Auer + Weber | 1985–1992 Profes-
sor for Building Construction and Design, Munich
University of Applied Sciences | 1993–2001 Pro-
fessor for Design, Stuttgart State Academy of Art
and Design | 2006 Auer+Weber+Assoziierte

From the MTV Music Awards ceremony to horse-
riding tournaments – the Olympic Hall in Munich, site of the gymnastics and handball games
in 1972, hosted a wide variety of events in subse-
quent years as a multi-purpose hall. Almost thir-
ty years after the games it was looking a little

worse for wear as a result of the provisional measures which detracted from the light aesthetics of
its appearance. As a consequence, the architects
Auer+Weber+Assoziierte – partners in the original design of the Olympic Park – undertook a
fundamental redesign and refurbishment.

The redesign provided a new restaurant with
beer garden as well as a series of permanently in-
stalled kiosks in the entrance area of the arena.
The technical and gastronomic supply and disposal facilities were centralised. In the hall itself
the VIP area was modernised so that either individual sponsor rooms or large connected areas
could be rented. The seats in the section of the
grandstand accessible from this area were converted into comfortable *business* seats. The former bowling alley restaurant was converted into
a *Backstage Club* which could be used to host a
disco, cabaret or VIP hospitality events.

On the east side of the Olympic Hall a *New
Small Olympic Hall* was built below ground – the
respect for the park's architecture, which remains formative to this day, can be clearly felt.

Year of completion 1972 Architect/Design Behnisch & Partner
Partners Structural engineers Leonhardt und Andrä, Jörg Schlaich;
Roof Frei Otto Landscape design Günther Grzimek
Client Olympia-Baugesellschaft, München
Construction period 1968–1972 Seating 77,000

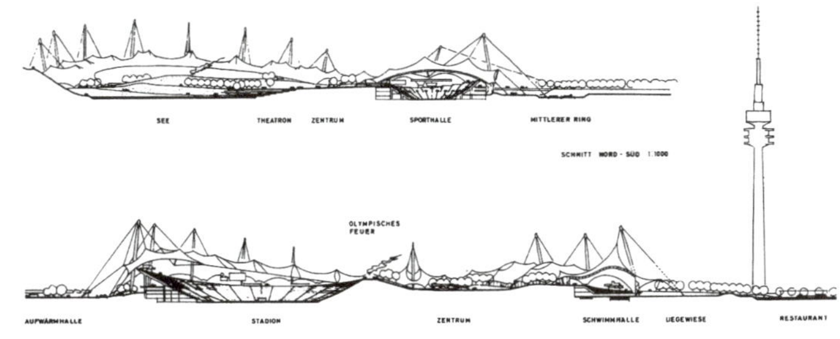

Top: Section, Noth-South
Bottom: Section, East-West

Günter Behnisch

MUNICH OLYMPIC STADIUM

The tent roof became the great symbol of the 1972 Olympic Games: it represented lightness, buoyancy, play, the provisional, and under no circumstances deployment, axis, alignment to something – everyone could read this from it. However, the roof only represented one side of this great architectural idea. The other consisted in the design of the entire site as a large park.

In contrast to all previous buildings for an Olympic Games which was growing ever larger, the design did not consist of individual sporting sites but a park landscape which combined all sporting facilities in one large complex. The original site, which was largely level ground, was fashioned with hills and hollows which were used for spectator terraces, an open-air theatre and a lake. A public park was created which was not merely symbolic of the high-performance sport of specialists, but to this day is open to all, facilitating a diverse range of activities from tobogganing in winter to bathing in summer.

"The avoidance of monumentality and the playful landscaping have provided the people of Munich with a sport park characterised by grace and urbanity." (Peter M. Bode, architecture critic)

Prof. Dr. h. c. **Günter Behnisch**
Born on 12/6/1922 in Lockwitz near Dresden, died on 12/7/2010
1982–1993 member of the Akademie der Künste, Berlin (West), Architecture Department
1993–2010 member of the Akademie der Künste, Berlin, Architecture Section

1939–1947 Military service and captivity in England as a prisoner of war | 1947–1951 Architectural studies at the Technical University Stuttgart | 1951–1952 Work for Rolf Gutbrod | from 1952 Own architect's office, initially with Bruno Lambert in Stuttgart | from 1966 Behnisch & Partner (with Fritz Auer, Winfried Büxel, Erhard Tränkner, Karlheinz Weber and from 1970 Manfred Sabatke; from 1979 with Winfried Büxel, Manfred Sabatke and Erhard Tränker) | 1989 Establishment of a second office in Stuttgart | 1967–1987 Full Professor for Design, Industrial Construction and Planning and Director of the Institute for Building Standardisation, Technical University Darmstadt | from 1989 Büro Innenstadt – later: Behnisch, Behnisch & Partner | 1991 Professor, International Academy of Architecture, Sofia | 1994 Heinrich-Hertz Professor, Technical University Karlsruhe

Year of completion 2011 Architect/Design RKW
Architektur+Städtebau, with RKW Polska und and HPP International
Structural engineers Klaus Bollinger, Bollinger + Grohmann with KBP
Zoltowski Client City of Gdańsk Construction period 2009–2011
Seats 43,608

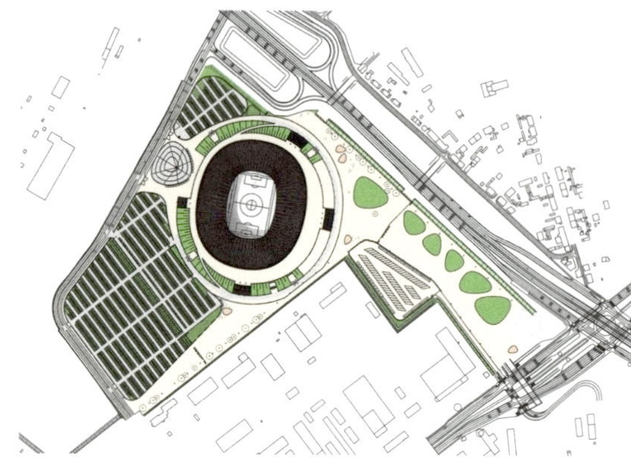

Site plan

Klaus Bollinger

PGE-ARENA GDAŃSK

Gdańsk, Poland

Gdańsk – that is the old Hanseatic city, the city of docks – in the public consciousness since *Solidarność*, including here in Germany, the city on the Baltic's amber coast.

And since the building of the PGE arena for the UEFA EURO 2012 it is also the city whose stadium aspires to bring to life these historical associations through its architecture. The concise form and the range of luminous, radiant gold tones of the outer membrane are reminiscent of irregular pieces of amber, the construction of the membrane, which can be experienced from within, has its roots in engineering construction – ships, airships.

A curved bowl has been built, with stiffening ribs. The supporting structure consists of two components: a total of 82 identical four-chord trusses on the one side, which from the perspective of statics form a single-hipped frame transferring the vertical loads to the ground, and on the other, compression rings in combination with joining elements in the roof which absorb the horizontal forces. The height of the trusses from the base to the surface of the roof is around 38 metres and they extend approximately 50 metres over the terraces. Arranged tangentially to the surface of the roof, the trusses are connected by circumferential steel profiles, which together with the diagonal connecting elements of the roof-surface form a rigid membrane.

Prof. Dr.-Ing. **Klaus Bollinger**
Born on 24/12/1952 in Spalt (Bavaria), lives in Frankfurt am Main
Since 2011 member of the Akademie der Künste, Berlin, Architecture Section

1972–1979 Civil engineering studies, Technical University Darmstadt | 1979/80 Employee of the Ingenieursozietät BGS, Frankfurt am Main | 1980/81 Employee of the engineering company Krebs und Kiefer, Darmstadt | 1981–1984 Research Assistant, Chair for Supporting Structures, Prof. Dr.-Ing. E.h. Stefan Polónyi, University of Dortmund | 1983 Engineering company Bollinger + Grohmann, Darmstadt, later Frankfurt am Main | 1984 Doctorate | 1984–1994 Teaching posts, University of Dortmund, Städelschule Frankfurt am Main | since 1994 Full Professor for Supporting Structures, Institute of Architecture, University of Applied Arts Vienna | 1999–2003 Board of Directors of the Institute of Architecture, University of Applied Arts Vienna, Austria | since 2000 Guest Professor, Städelschule, Frankfurt am Main | 2003–2010 Bollinger Grohmann Offices in Vienna, Paris, Oslo and Melbourne

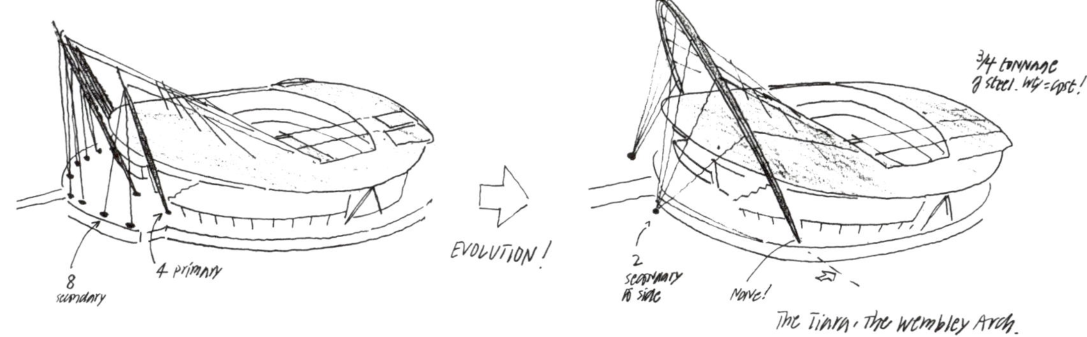

Conceptual sketch, Norman Foster

Norman Foster

WEMBLEY STADIUM

London, Great Britain

Year of completion 2007
Architect/Design Foster +
Partners   Partners HOK
sport architecture
Structural engineers
Mott Stadium Consortium
Client Wembley National
Stadium Ltd.
Construction period 1996–2007
Seating 90,000 for football and
rugby matches, 68,400 to
72,000 for athletics meetings

The old Wembley Stadium was a temple for all sport enthusiasts – not only in England but also in Germany; it gave its name to goals that are still the subject of discussion 50 years later. This stadium, originally built in 1924 and modified numerous times, was the stage for British sport. That was the challenge: to build something on the historical legacy with a comparable symbolic value and meaning in the 21st century.

The result is a 90,000-seat stadium for the Olympic Games 2012, the largest fully covered stadium in the world. The roof is supported by a spectacular, 113 metre-high latticework arch extending across the entire stadium – a new triumphal arch for a new Wembley.

The stadium has been designed above all for football matches, fulfilling this task optimally; the rows of seats extend close to the edge of the pitch. For light athletics events such as the Olympic Games a second stadium floor will be inserted above the first tier of seats providing the necessary ground area for light athletics events – the stadium will then have seating capacity for around 70,000 spectators.

Norman Foster
Lord Foster of Thames Bank
Born on 1/6/1935 in Manchester, lives and works predominately in London
Since 1994 member of the Akademie der Künste, Berlin, Architecture Section

1961 Degree from the Manchester University School of Architecture and City Planning | 1962 Henry Fellowship to Yale University in New Haven, Connecticut, USA, Master's Degree in Architecture | 1963 Team 4 in London (with Wendy Cheeseman – who he married in 1964 – as well as Sue and Richard Rogers) | 1967 Foster Associates with Wendy Foster in London, today worldwide with offices in more than 20 countries | 1968–1983 Collaboration with Buckminster Fuller on numerous projects | Teaching activities and lecture series in Great Britain, USA, Europe, East Asia | Served as the Vice President of the Architectural Association (AA) and as foreign expert at the Royal Institute of British Architects (RIBA)

Year of completion 2010   Architect/Design **Volkwin Marg and Hubert Nienhoff with Robert Hormes, von Gerkan, Marg and Partners**
Partners **Louis Karol architects, Point architects**
Structural engineers   Roof **schlaich bergermann und partner**
Client **City of Cape Town**   Construction period 2007–2010
Seating **68,000**

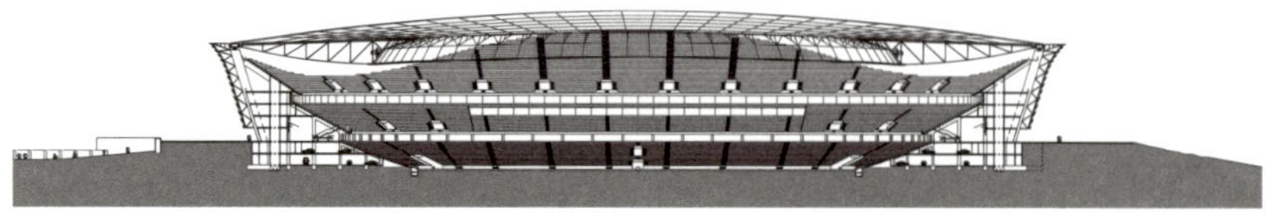

Section

Volkwin Marg

CAPE TOWN STADIUM

Cape Town, South Africa

Since the 2010 World Cup the stadium in Cape Town has become a global icon for the vision of the equality of citizens in a multi-ethnic society – a rare achievement.

The flowing contours of the light-looking circular building, whose translucent outer skin plays with the changing light conditions typical of the location, forms a triad with the horizontals of Table Mountain and the summit of Signal Hill, and has been set into an artificially raised plateau to make it appear lower. In order to accommodate the large number of spectators the seats have been arranged in three sets of terraces, the upper of which swings up and down significantly in accordance with the circular geometry. The suspension roof, hung in the gently undulating outer compression ring, is weighted down with glass cladding to secure it against air suction and has a double curvature in order to conduct the frequent torrential downpours to the outside. The exterior of the 36,000-metre-square roof area is composed of a composite glass for protection against heat and glare; the 16-metre wide inner ring is composed of clear glass in order to admit sunlight to the grass. Including the layer of glass, the lattice construction, supported by cables, has a total weight of 4,500 tons, making it an extremely effective lightweight structure.

Prof. Dr. h. c. **Volkwin Marg**
Born on 15/10/1936 in Königsberg/East Prussia, lives in Hamburg
Since 2010 member of the Akademie der Künste, Berlin, Architecture Section

1964 Degree in architecture at the Technical University Braunschweig | since 1965 Freelance architect, architects' office with Meinhard von Gerkan | 1972 Elected to the Free Academy of the Arts in Hamburg | 1974 Elected to the German Academy for Urban and Regional Spatial Planning | 1975–1979 Vice President, 1979–1983 President of the Association of German Architects (BDA) | 1986 Appointment to the RWTH Aachen University, Department of Architecture, Chair for Urban Planning and Material Studies | 2007 Establishment of the gmp Foundation for the promotion of architectural education

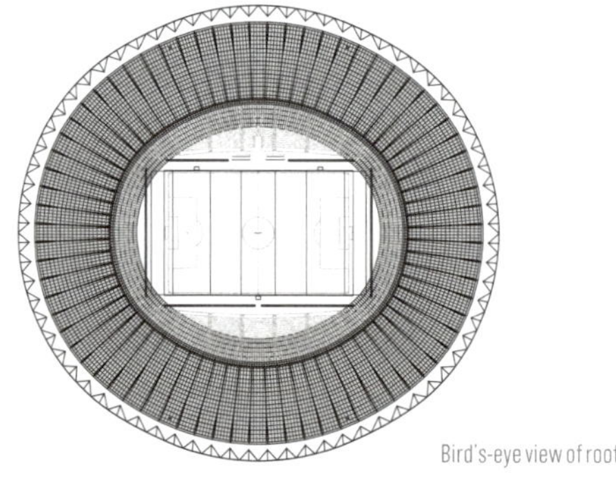

Bird's-eye view of roof

Year of completion **1932**   Architect/Design **Pier Luigi Nervi**
Partner offices **Nebbiosi, Bartoli**   Structural engineer **Pier Luigi Nervi**
Client **City of Florence**   Construction period **1930–1932, 1950–1951**
Seats **47,282**

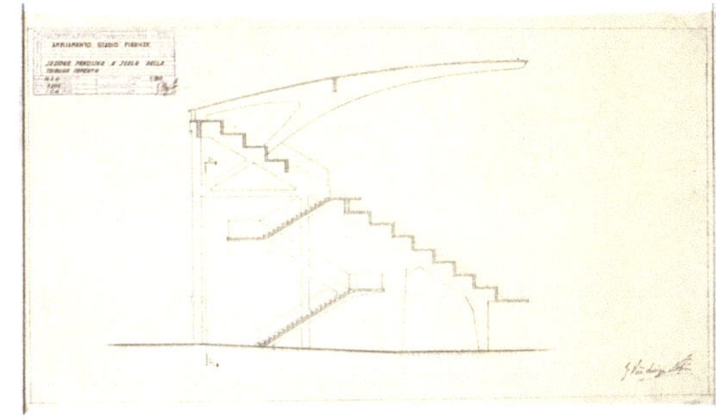

Section through stand

Pier Luigi Nervi

ARTEMIO FRANCHI STADIUM

Florence, Italy

The stadium in Florence is the first in the highly characteristic formal language of the engineer and architect Nervi in which he developed his method of concrete construction, which, despite the supposed *heaviness* of the material, succeeds in generating filigree structures. This is achieved by breaking down the support function of the carrying construction as far as possible: ribs, arches, supports – harder to encase, but incomparably more differentiated. Thus the roofing of the grandstands becomes an abstract pattern with great expressive power – one immediately understands how the construction functions – and at the same time (and as a result) generates an aesthetics conveying a sense of lightness.

Perhaps the most beautiful example of this is the staircase which swings around a 70-metre high *marathon tower*: two opposing arches, one of which is the staircase itself, stiffen each other reciprocally. During the enlargement of the stadium by Nervi in the 1950s additional staircases of this type were built.

Nervi's architecture became a role model for many further stadiums: the purely *functional building* thus received its own formal language.

Prof. Dr. h. c. **Pier Luigi Nervi**
Born on 21/6/1891 in Sondrio/Italy,
died on 9/1/1979
1964–1979 extraordinary member of the
Akademie der Künste, Berlin (West),
Architecture Section

1913 Degree as civil engineer from the University of Bologna | 1913–1923 Architect, design engineer and construction supervisor for the Società per Costruzioni Cementizie | since 1923 Engineering company in Rome with different partners | 1946–1961 Full Professor, University of Rome | 1961/62 Charles Eliot Norton Professor, Harvard University, Cambridge/Massachusetts, USA

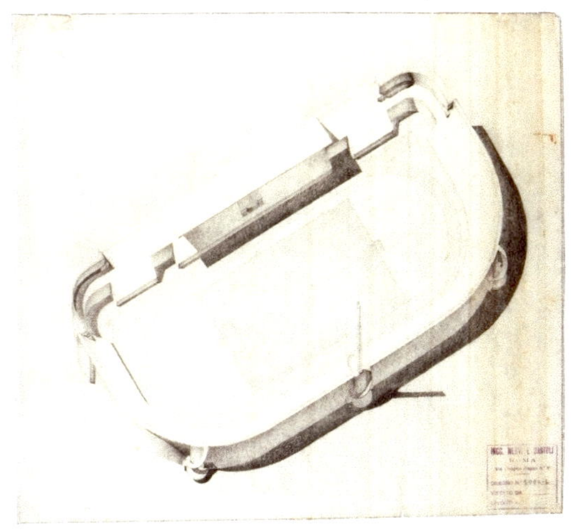

Bird's-eye view

Year of completion 1972 Architect/Design Fritz Auer, Behnisch &
Partner; Frei Otto **Partners** Roof Frei Otto Structural engineers
Leonhardt und Andrä, Jörg Schlaich Client Olympia-
Baugesellschaft, Munich Construction period 1968–1972

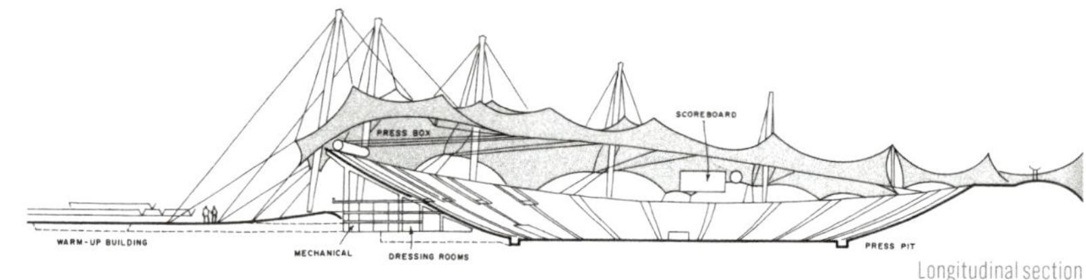

Longitudinal section

Frei Otto

ROOF OF THE MUNICH OLYMPIC STADIUM

The ladies stocking stretched over a number of
wire supports in Behnisch & Partner's competition model was an instrument of persuasion, not
an anticipation of reality. The only precedent was
Frei Otto's pavilion construction for the 1967
World Exhibition in Montreal, but this was only
designed as a temporary construction. Equally
controversial options for the realisation of the
roof were discussed – pre-stressed concrete? A
lattice construction? Wood roofing? Ultimately,
Frei Otto's office was included in the consulta-
tions and his concept proved to be the lightest and
most durable solution: a cable-net construction
composed of numerous, almost regular saddle-
shaped areas edged with cables, suspended at
numerous points from external masts, or inter-
nally supported by means of so-called floating
columns and guyed outwards. The demands this
roof placed on geometrical precision – both in
terms of the layout and the prefabrication – were
completely new. This resulted in the first extensive deployment of computers for such tasks and
a renaissance in the use of cast steel in architecture. The roofing – this too an innovation – was
manufactured from acrylic panels which guar-
anteed the transparency required for television
broadcasts.

Prof. Dr. **Frei Otto**
Born on 31/5/1925 in Siegmar/Saxony,
lives in Leonberg near Stuttgart
1970 –1993 member of the Akademie der Künste,
Berlin (West), Architecture Section
Since 1993 member of the Akademie der Künste,
Berlin, Architecture Section

1943 Began studies at the Technical University
Berlin | 1943–1945 Military service; until end of
1947 prisoner of war in Chartres, France where he
was camp architect | 1948 Studies at the Technical
University Berlin | 1950/51 Study trip to the USA
visiting Wright, Severud, Mendelsohn, Saarinen,
Mies van der Rohe, Neutra, Eames. Study of soci-
ology and town planning at the University of Vir-
ginia, USA | 1952 Chartered Engineer, Technical
University Berlin, work as freelance architect in
Berlin | 1954 Awarded doctorate from the Techni-
cal University Berlin, subject: "The suspended
roof" | 1958–1969 Entwicklungsstätte für den
Leichtbau (Development Workshop for Light-
weight Structures), Atelier Berlin-Zehlendorf |
Since 1969 Atelier Frei Otto, Leonberg/Warm-
bronn | 1964–1991 Professor, University of Stutt-
gart, establishment and direction of the Institute
for Lightweight Structures; awarded emeritus
status in 1991

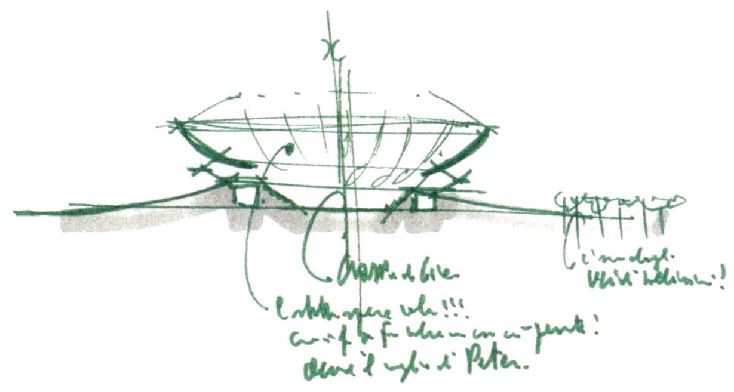

Conceptual sketch, Renzo Piano

Renzo Piano

SAN NICOLA STADIUM

Bari, Italy

Year of completion 1990
Architect/Design Renzo Piano,
Renzo Piano Building Workshop,
architects
Structural engineers
Ove Arup & Partners, M. Milan
Client City of Bari
Construction period 1987–1990
Seats 60,000

A large flower – that was the idea behind the design. Built in the 300,000-inhabitant southern Italian city for the 1990 World Cup, the stadium's spectator terraces are supported by 310 prefabricated concrete elements. 26 *petals* shape the entrance to the upper terraces, thus forming individual sections and solving a safety problem, which following a number of accidents at stadiums was a main consideration of the design. For this reason the upper terrace was also completely separated from the lower terrace.

The prefabricated concrete elements were manufactured on site. Each section rests on four columns which emphasise the elegance and lightness of the construction, providing a feeling of peace and spaciousness for the spectators. As a whole, the structure is designed to echo the gentle hills of Apulia. The stadium was named after the city's patron saint, St. Nicolas.

Prof. Dr. h. c. mult. **Renzo Piano**
Born on 14/9/1937 in Genoa,
lives and works there and in Paris
Since 1993 member of the Akademie der Künste,
Berlin, Architecture Section

1964 Awarded Degree from Milan Polytechnic; during his studies worked in his father's construction company under Franco Albini | 1965–1968 Professor, Milan Polytechnic | 1965–1970 Work for Louis I. Kahn in Philadelphia and Z. S. Makowsky in London, collaboration with Marco Zanuso, acquaintance with Jean Prouvé | 1971 Piano & Rogers with Richard Rogers, London | 1977 Piano & Rice with Peter Rice, Genoa, collaboration up until Rice's death in 1993, since then Renzo Piano Building Workshop with around 150 employees and offices in Paris, Genoa and New York | 2001 Founding of the "Architecture Workshop Foundation" with the Harvard Design School

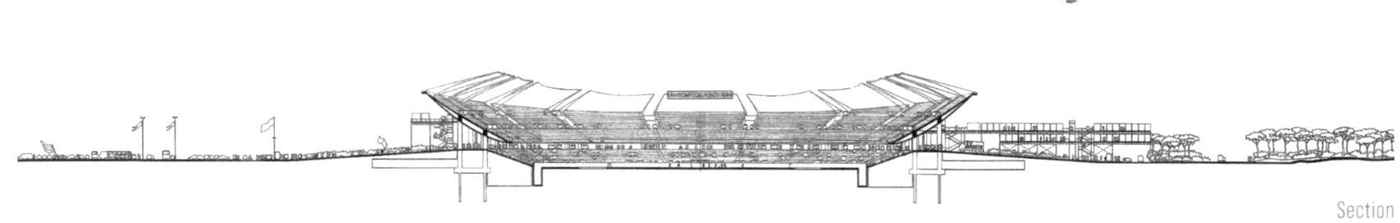

Section

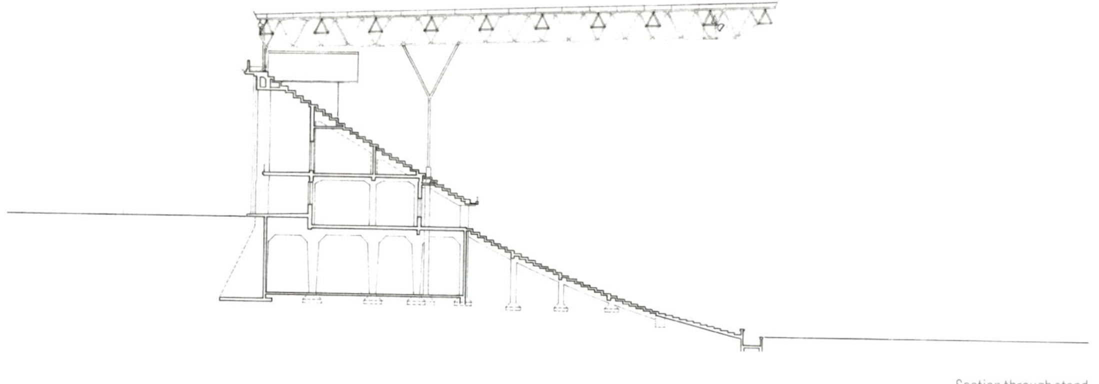

Stefan Polónyi

PARTIAL ROOFING OF THE BERLIN OLYMPIC STADIUM

Year of completion 1972
Architect/Design Friedrich-Wilhelm Krahe, Kurt Dübbers
Structural engineers Stefan Polónyi, Richard von Kalmar
Client City of Berlin
Construction period 1971–1972
Seats 80,000

The task of bringing Werner March's Berlin Olympic Stadium from 1936 into line with the latest technical standards and spectator needs has been raised repeatedly – whenever large sporting events are pending. The last modification for the 2006 World Cup was preceded by a modification for the 1972 World Cup, which also required building a roof for spectators, if only for a section of the terraces. However, the challenge of proceeding with the utmost respect for the original building was also faced back then.

To this end, two areas of around 150 × 58 metres on facing sides of the stadium, whose shape follow the stadium's oval form, were each roofed with a lightweight spatial framework and individually mounted on six four-fold branching supports made of isolated thin steel supports which interfere little with the spectators' field of view. The supports were fixed in the spectator area and at the stadium's crown, the tension bars are anchored at the rear in the circumferential grandstand supports. The roof surface, clad in bent and stretched barrel-shaped acrylic glass plates was translucent.

Prof. em. Dr.-Ing. E. h. mult. Dr. h. c.
Stefan Polónyi
Born on 6/7/1930 in Gyula/Hungary, lives in Cologne
Since 1999 member of the Akademie der Künste, Berlin, Architecture Section

1952 Degree as civil engineer, Technical University Budapest | 1952–1956 Research assistant, Technical University Budapest | Since 1957 Consultant engineer in Cologne | 1965–1972 Full Professor for Structural Engineering, Technical University Berlin; Director, Institute for Structural Analysis | Since 1966 Engineering office in Berlin Test engineer for structural analysis | 1968/69 Senator-elect of the Technical University (TU) Berlin | 1970 Dean, Department of Architecture, TU Berlin | 1973–1995 Full Professor for Supporting Structures, University of Dortmund, co-founder of the Civil Engineering Department; responsible for the course "Constructive Civil Engineering" (awarded emeritus status in 1995) | 1977/78 Senator, University of Dortmund | 1978 Deputy Vice-Chancellor, University of Dortmund | 1983–1987 Dean, Civil Engineering Department, University of Dortmund | 1993 Opened office in Leipzig

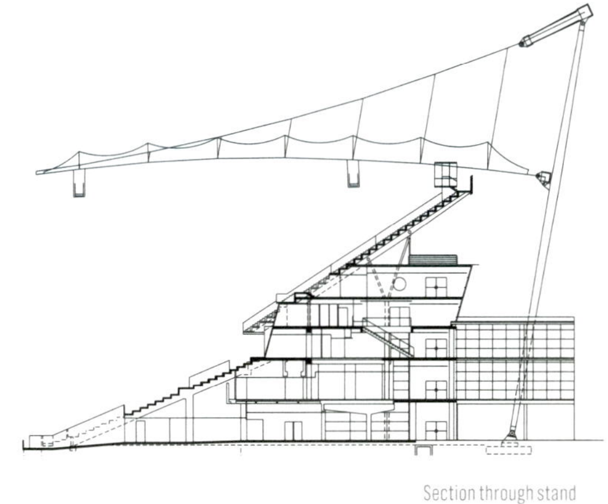

Section through stand

Jörg Schlaich

ROOF OF THE GOTTLIEB DAIMLER STADIUM
Stuttgart

Prof. em. Dr.-Ing. Dr. h. c. mult. **Jörg Schlaich** Born on 17/10/1934 in Stetten/Remstal, lived and worked in Stuttgart until 2009, now in Berlin Since 1999 member of the Akademie der Künste, Berlin, Architecture Section

Year of completion **1993**
Architect/Design
Siegel & Partner
Design stadium roof
Jörg Schlaich und Rudolf Bergermann, schlaich bergermann und partner
Structural engineer
Fischer Friedrich
Client **Landeshauptstadt Stuttgart** Planning and construction period **1991–1993**
Seating **55,000**

1953–1958 Architectural and civil engineering studies at the Technical Universities of Stuttgart and Berlin | 1959–1960 Assistant and lecturer for statics and steel concrete, Case Institute of Technology in Cleveland, Ohio, USA, Master of Science in Civil Engineering | 1960–1962 Further studies on problems of reinforced concrete structures at the University of Stuttgart, Doctorate in Engineering | 1961–1962 Engineer for planning and building inspection, construction company Ludwig Bauer, Stuttgart | 1963–1969 Engineer for construction planning at Leonhardt und Andrä, consultant engineer, Stuttgart; Head engineer for the planning and construction of the cable-net roof over the sports site for the 1972 Olympic Games in Munich | 1970–1979 Partner at Leonhardt und Andrä, consultant engineer, Stuttgart | 1967–1973 Assistant Professor, University of Stuttgart, Institute for Massive Construction | 1974 Professor and Director of the Institute for Massive Construction, later for Design and Construction (today: Institute for Lightweight Structures and Conceptual Design), University of Stuttgart (awarded emeritus status in October 2000) | 1980 Opened office Schlaich + Partner in Stuttgart,

change of name in 1989 to Schlaich Bergermann und Partner (SBP), since 2002 schlaich bergermann und partner (sbp) with offices in Stuttgart, Berlin, New York, São Paulo und Shanghai | 2009 Moved to Berlin

At the time it was the largest membrane roof construction in Europe: the roof of the Neckar Stadium for the 1993 World Athletics Championships; and not only that – it only weighed 13 kilograms per square metre of roofed area – including the steel construction!

That the entire structure was planned and built in just two years was the icing on the cake of an ingenious construction which became a model for many more. It is composed of an internal tension ring connected to two exterior compression rings by means of 40 radial connection cables. The undulating form of the roof, with its high and low points, is a result of the expansion options forming an integral part of the stadium's original design. The roof covering is composed of a PVC-coated polyester membrane held in a double curvature by means of a secondary supporting structure. This construction was selected – this too a special feature – not just for technical or aesthetic reasons, but simply because it was not possible to transfer any additional loads onto or into the grandstand construction. That meant: the new construction must be lightweight, and it must be completely separate from the grandstands.

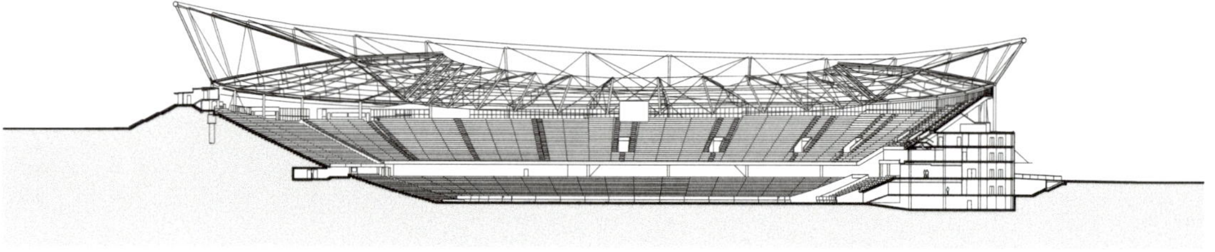

Cross-section

Helmut C. Schulitz

NIEDERSACHSENSTADION (AWD-ARENA)

Hanover

Year of completion **2004**
Architect/Design
Schulitz+Partner
Structural engineers
Roof **RFR** Foundation,
Grandstands **Eilers+Vogel**
Awarding authority **State
Capital Hanover (as awarder of
the works concession)**
Client **Niedersachsenstadion
Projekt- und Betriebsgesell-
schaft mbH & Co. KG, now
Hannover 96 Arena GmbH + Co.
KG** Construction period
2003–2004 Seating **49,000 (of
which 8000 standing, which
can be converted into 4000
seats using Vario seats)**

Stadiums with spectator banks raised from the rubble of the destroyed cities were not uncommon in the post-war period. This was also the case with the Lower Saxony Stadium, as well as the combination of football and light athletic stadium with perimeter track. The stadium in Hanover had already played host to games at the 1972 World Cup and EURO 1988. New demands were raised by the 2006 World Cup: the running track was removed, enabling the spectator terraces to be moved closer together, thus making roofing easier.

In addition to the removal of the running track, the most striking and elegant feature of the AWD Arena is the new roof composed of two concentric spoke-wheel systems supported on articulated steel posts. It reflects the original character of the stadium, whose west grandstand was divided into a lower terrace and an upper covered terrace. The division of the roof into a closed outer and a transparent inner roof resulted in two concentric spoke-wheel systems. The inner roof received a lightweight treatment with cable-tensioned floating columns and a plastic membrane from ethylene tetrafluoroethylene (ETFE). Thanks to its UV transparency, the largest single-layered ETFE roof in the world also avoids the need for frequent grass replacement as usually required in enclosed stadiums.

Prof. **Helmut C. Schulitz**
Born on 17/7/1936 in Bublitz/Pomerania, lives in Braunschweig
Since 2001 member of the Akademie der Künste, Berlin, Architecture Section

1957 Journeyman's exam as mason, Hamburg | 1962 Degree from the Technical University Munich | 1965 Government Architect for the Free State of Bavaria | 1968 Master of Architecture, University of California, Los Angeles | 1969–1970 Assistant Professor, School of Architecture, University of California | 1975–1982 Schulitz+Partner Los Angeles | 1971–1982 Professor, University of California, Los Angeles | 1978–1979 Guest Professor, University of Karlsruhe | 1982–2001 Professor, University of Braunschweig, Director of the Institute for Industrial Construction | 1982 Schulitz+Partner Architekten + Ingenieure Braunschweig | 1987 Guest Professor, Massachusetts Institute of Technology, Cambridge, USA | 1999 Guest Professor, University of Montreal, Canada

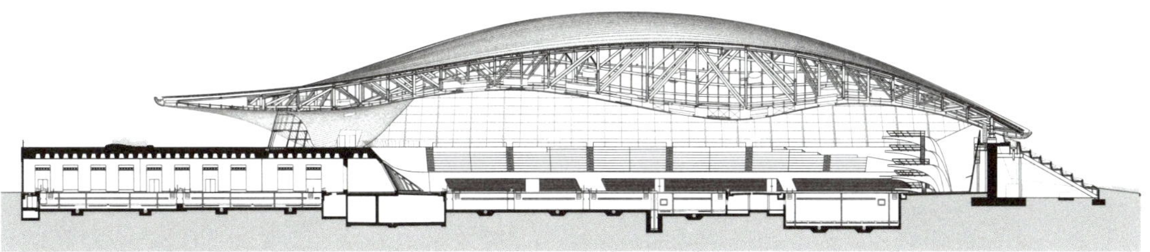

Patrik Schumacher

LONDON AQUATIC CENTRE
Great Britain

Year of completion 2011
Architect/Stadium design
Patrik Schumacher, Zaha Hadid
Architects Partner s+p
architects (sports architects)
Structural engineers Ove Arup &
Partners Client Olympic
Delivery Authority
Construction period 2005–2011
Seating 17,500 Olympic mode,
2000 Legacy mode

Its ground plan resembles a motor boat, its cross-section a wave, inside it houses the new swimming stadium for the 2012 Olympic Games in London. The Aquatic Centre is inspired – as the architects state – by moving water. On the opposite side of a canal, facing Wembley Stadium, its roof forms a flowing wave. With seating for 17,500 spectators during the Games; its interior will be scaled back after their completion to accommodate 2,000.

Despite all the flowing movement, the interior with its three swimming and diving pools is very simple; they are arranged along a single axis. Between the diving pools and the main swimming pool the roof is lowered in a curving motion so that the two sections with their different functions are lent an individual character, while still remaining part of a single connected space.

The immense roof is 160 metres long and supported by a platform at three points. The additional grandstands required for the games are inserted through the opening formed by the wave between the roof and platform; following their dismantling the facade will be closed with glazing.

Prof. Dr. Phil. **Patrik Schumacher**
Born on 30/8/1961 in Bonn, lives in London
Since 2011 member of the Akademie der Künste, Berlin, Architecture Section

from 1980 Study of philosophy and mathematics, later architecture, in Bonn, London and Stuttgart | 1990 Architecture Degree in Stuttgart | 1999 Doctorate in Philosophy, University of Klagenfurt | since 1988 Collaboration with Zaha Hadid | since 1999 Zaha Hadid Architects, London | Director, since 2002 partner in Zaha Hadid Architects, London | Founding Director of the Design Research Laboratory at the Architectural Association School of Architecture (AA), London, since 1996 with Brett Steele | Teaching posts with Zaha Hadid: University of Illinois, Chicago; Columbia University, New York; Yale University, Connecticut; Harvard Graduate School of Design, Massachusetts, as well as in Graz, Amsterdam, Hamburg and Vienna | 1999 Guest Professor, University of Linz | since 2004 Professor, University of Innsbruck, Chair for Experimental Architecture

Year of completion **2003** Architect/Design **Schuster Architekten**
Partner **Atelier Albert Wimmer** Structural engineer **Fischer**
Friedrich Client **SWS – Planungs- und Errichtungsgesellschaft**
Planning and construction period **1999–2003** Seating **16,000**
Temporary enlargement for the 2008 European Championships
Start of construction **2006** Seating **32,000**
Dismantling **Not carried out**

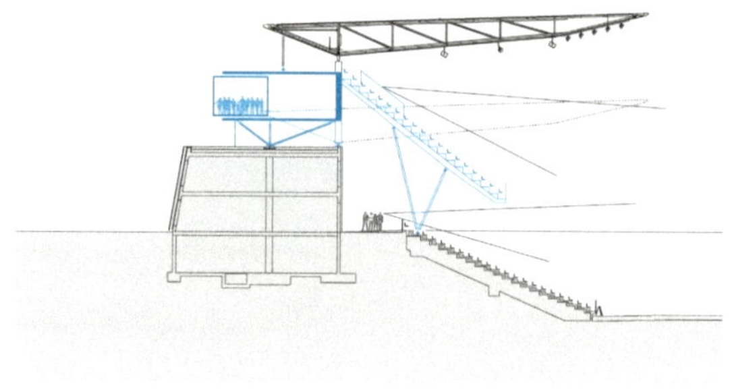

Section through stand

Rolf Schuster

SALZBURG STADIUM/WALS-SIEZENHEIM
(RED BULL ARENA)

Salzburg, Austria

The Baroque palace of Kleßheim, designed by Johann Bernhard Fischer von Erlach around 1700, forms the elegant backdrop for a football stadium with its somewhat profane function. Out of respect for this neighbourhood it was built partially below ground in order to reduce the visible volume.

The resulting building displays clear references to the traditional architecture of the Salzburg countryside: a simple timber barn above which a lightweight roof structure appears to float. The larch wood facade – unusual for a stadium – in combination with the sober roof, gives the stadium both scale and structure.

For the 2008 European Championships a temporary enlargement of the stadium from 16,000 to 32,000 spectators was undertaken. To this end the roof was raised and an additional set of terraces inserted. Unfortunately, the planned dismantling was not carried out so that the stadium's outer appearance no longer corresponds to that originally intended. Following completion a sponsor took over the local football club and altered the interior according to its own conceptions.

Prof. **Rolf Schuster**
Born on 10/03/1953 in Duisburg, lives in Düsseldorf
Since 2008 member of the Akademie der Künste, Berlin, Architecture Section

1971–1975 Architectural studies, University of Applied Sciences Düsseldorf | 1976–1981 Architectural studies, Technical University Darmstadt, Degree | 1982–1986 Research assistant, Building Construction and Design, Architecture Department, University of Kaiserslautern | 1987–1994 Architect's office Mahler Gumpp Schuster, Stuttgart | 1988 Schuster Architekten with Jochen Schuster | 1988/89 Study visit, Villa Massimo, Rome | 1992–1993 Guest Professor, Design, GH University Kassel | 1996–2003 Professor, Integrated Design, University of Wuppertal | since 1998 Schuster Architekten with Jochen Schuster and Olaf Allstedt | 2003 Professor, Institute for Design and Architecture, Technical University Braunschweig

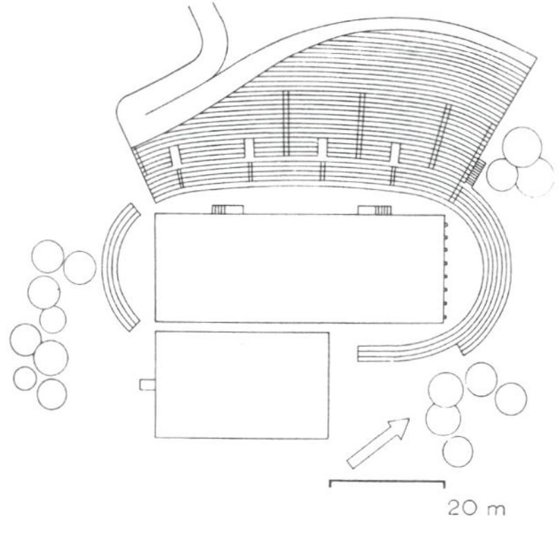 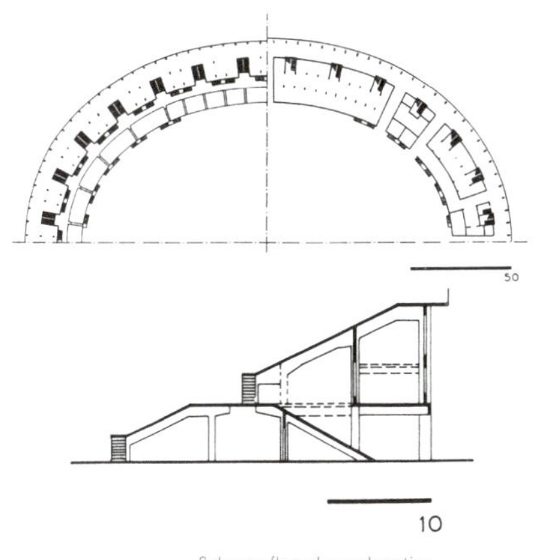

Schema: floorplan and section

Otto Ernst Schweizer

ERNST HAPPEL STADIUM (PRATER STADIUM)
Vienna, Austria

Year of completion 1931
Architect/Stadium design
Otto Ernst Schweizer
Client Stadt Wien
Construction period 1929–1931
Seating 60,000

Plans for a stadium for the city of Vienna, conceived as a *National Stadium*, were drawn up as early as 1915. A foundation stone was laid on the 10th anniversary celebrations of the proclamation of the republic in 1929, without a decision having been made on the final site. The German architect Otto Ernst Schweizer won the ideas competition with the design for an early form of *Sportpark* with swimming pool, cycling track, open-air stage, gymnastics arenas and a sports school. Not all of this was realised, but that which was completed is impressive enough: stadium, cycling track, swimming pool and arena. The stadium was opened on the occasion of the 2nd Workers' Olympics on 11 June 1931. Above all, it was the stadium's organisational structure that was praised, enabling it to be emptied in a short space of time – seven to eight minutes. The stadium was modified a number of times, on the last occasion for the 2008 European Football Championships. To this day it has retained its significance as Austria's largest stadium situated within an extensive landscape park.

The architect had already built the *Urban Stadium* in Nuremberg between 1927 and 1928, for which he received a gold medal in the art competitions at the Olympic Games in Amsterdam.

Prof. Dr. h. c. mult. **Otto Ernst Schweizer**
Born on 27/04/1890 in Schramberg/
Württemberg,
died on 14/11/1965 in Baden-Baden
1955–1965 member of the Akademie der Künste,
Berlin (West), Architecture Department

1906–1912 Training as surveyor | 1914 Architectural studies at the Technical University Stuttgart, then at the Technical University Munich, 1917 Honours Degree | 1925–1929 Senior Municipal Building Surveyor in Nuremberg | 1929 Freelance architect in Nuremberg | 1930–1960 Professor for Municipal Surface Construction, Housing and Settlements, Technical University Karlsruhe | 1937 Member of the Reichsprüfungsamt (Imperial Auditing Office) | Following World War II, member of the Advisory Committee for Reconstruction and liaison officer for the governments of North Baden and North Württemberg | 1948 Member of the Conseil Supérieur d'Architecture et d'Urbanisme (CSAU) deployed by the French military government | 1949 Member of the planning board for the establishment of a provisional government quarter in Bonn | 1950–1954 Urban development consultant for the city of Mannheim

Year of completion 2003   Architect/Design Eduardo Elísio Machado
Souto de Moura, Souto Moura Arquitectos, LDA
Structural engineers Afassociados – Projectos de Engenharia, SA
Client Câmara Municipal de Braga   Construction period 2000–2003
Seats 30,000

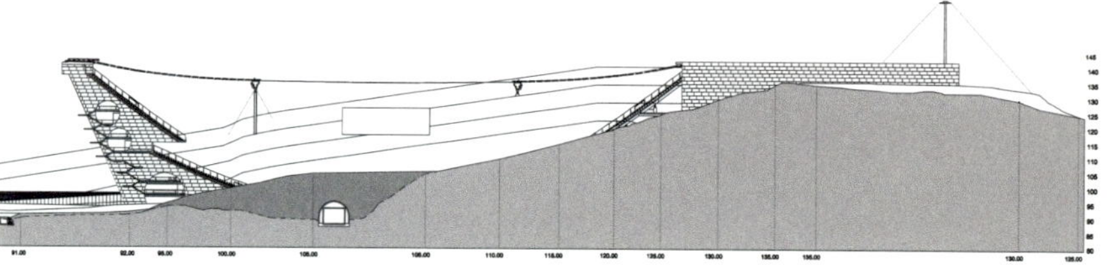

Section

Eduardo Elísio Machado Souto de Moura

BRAGA STADIUM
Portugal

Without doubt, the stadium in Braga is one of the most unusual solutions to this architectural challenge which has given rise to many outstanding, expressive buildings: at first glance it is missing the two sides needed to generate the atmospheric roar of a closed arena. On one of the narrow sides the stadium holding 30,000 spectators is closed by a rock face (with scoreboard), on the other side one has a view of the open landscape from the highest point in the city, the Monte Castro. The arrangement of the grandstands resembles that of the English parliament with *government* and *opposition*, while the actual sporting contest takes place on the grass in between.

The spectator terraces are completely covered. The roofs and grandstands – an original solution – reciprocally support each other (continuing the British metaphor: *government* and *opposition* are dependent on each other); they are connected to each other by over 80 steel cables which make the deep projection to the *rear* possible.

Dr. h. c.

Eduardo Elísio Machado Souto de Moura
Born on 25/7/1952 in Porto, Portugal where he lives
Since 2010 member of the Akademie der Künste, Berlin, Architecture Section

1974 Collaboration with Noé Dinis | 1975–1979 Collaboration with Álvaro Siza | 1980 Degree at the Escola Superior de Belas Artes do Porto (ESBAP) | 1980 Own architect's office | 1981–1991 Assistant Professor at the ESBAP | since 1991 Guest Professor: École Nationale Supérieure d'Architecture de Paris-Belleville (ENSAPB), Harvard University Graduate School of Design, School of Architecture at University College Dublin, ETH Zurich, EPFL Lausanne, international teaching activities

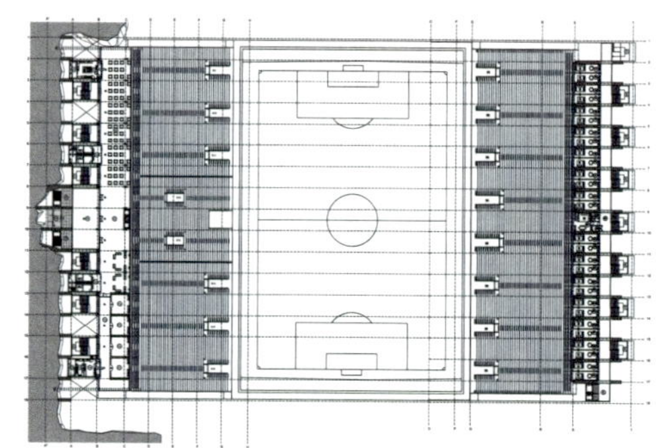

Floorplan of level 1

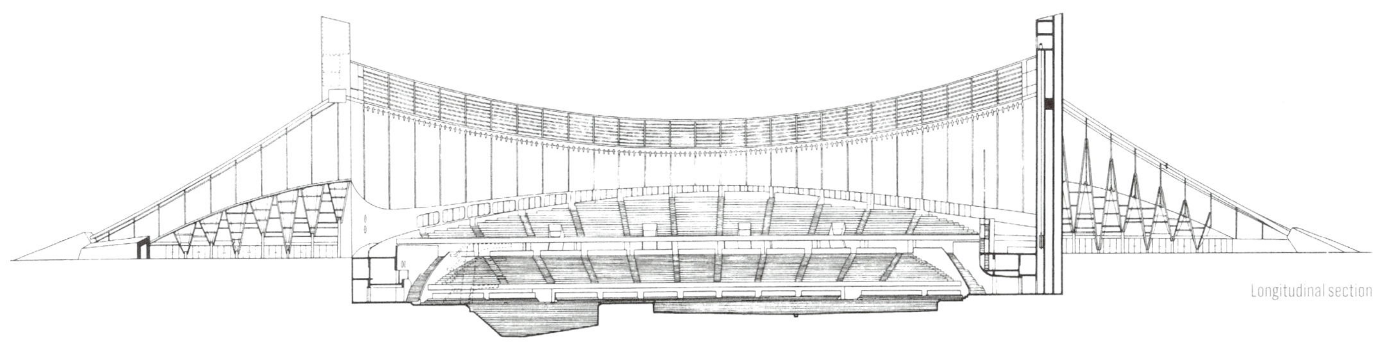

Kenzo Tange

NATIONAL GYMNASIUMS FOR TOKYO OLYMPICS

Tokyo, Japan

Year of completion 1964
Architect/Design
Kenzo Tange & URTEC
Structural engineers
Yoshikatsu Tsuboi Institute
Client Ministry of Building
Construction period 1963–1964
Seating 15,000 first gymnasium,
4000 second gymnasium

The two Olympic gymnasiums that Kenzo Tange designed for the 1964 Games in Tokyo put their stamp on the Games and their appearance like few other Olympic buildings. The concise form of the mussel-like shells open outwards, embracing the public, and in their time the roofs with their suspended steel structures were a technical sensation. In the large gymnasium steel cables are suspended from two massive columns from which the cables supporting the roof-cladding are harnessed at right angles. The opening between the two large main cables is transparent. The small gymnasium is equipped with a single column from which the cables are suspended. The large gymnasium was designed for the swimming and diving competitions, the smaller for the basketball matches.

At the time one speculated as to whether the suspended roofs were to be interpreted as a reference to traditional temple architecture. The association is an obvious one, although the scale is completely different. And the function? A temple of sport?

Prof. Dr. Dr. h. c. mult. **Kenzo Tange**
Born on 4/09/1913 in Imabari/Ehime, Japan, died on 22/03/2005
From 1964 to 1979 extraordinary member of the Academy of the Arts Berlin (West), Architecture Department
From 1979 to 1993 member of the Akademie der Künste, Berlin (West), Architecture Department
From 1993 to 2005 member of the Akademie der Künste, Berlin, Architecture Section

1935–1938 Architectural studies at the University of Tokyo, graduated with the Tatsuno prize | Work in the office of Kunio Mayekawa, a former colleague of Le Corbusier | 1942–1945 Master class for architecture, University of Tokyo | 1946–1961 Kenzo Tange Studio | 1946–1974 Professor for architecture, University of Tokyo | 1956–1958 Professor, University of Kyusyu | 1959 Awarded PhD for a thesis on "The Reorganisation of the City of Tokyo" | 1959/60 Guest Professor, Massachusetts Institute of Technology, Cambridge, USA | 1961–1985 Kenzo Tange & URTEC (urban planners and architects), from 1985 Kenzo Tange Associates | 1972 Guest Professor, Harvard University | from 1977 Honorary Professor in Peru, Argentina, Croatia, Bulgaria, China

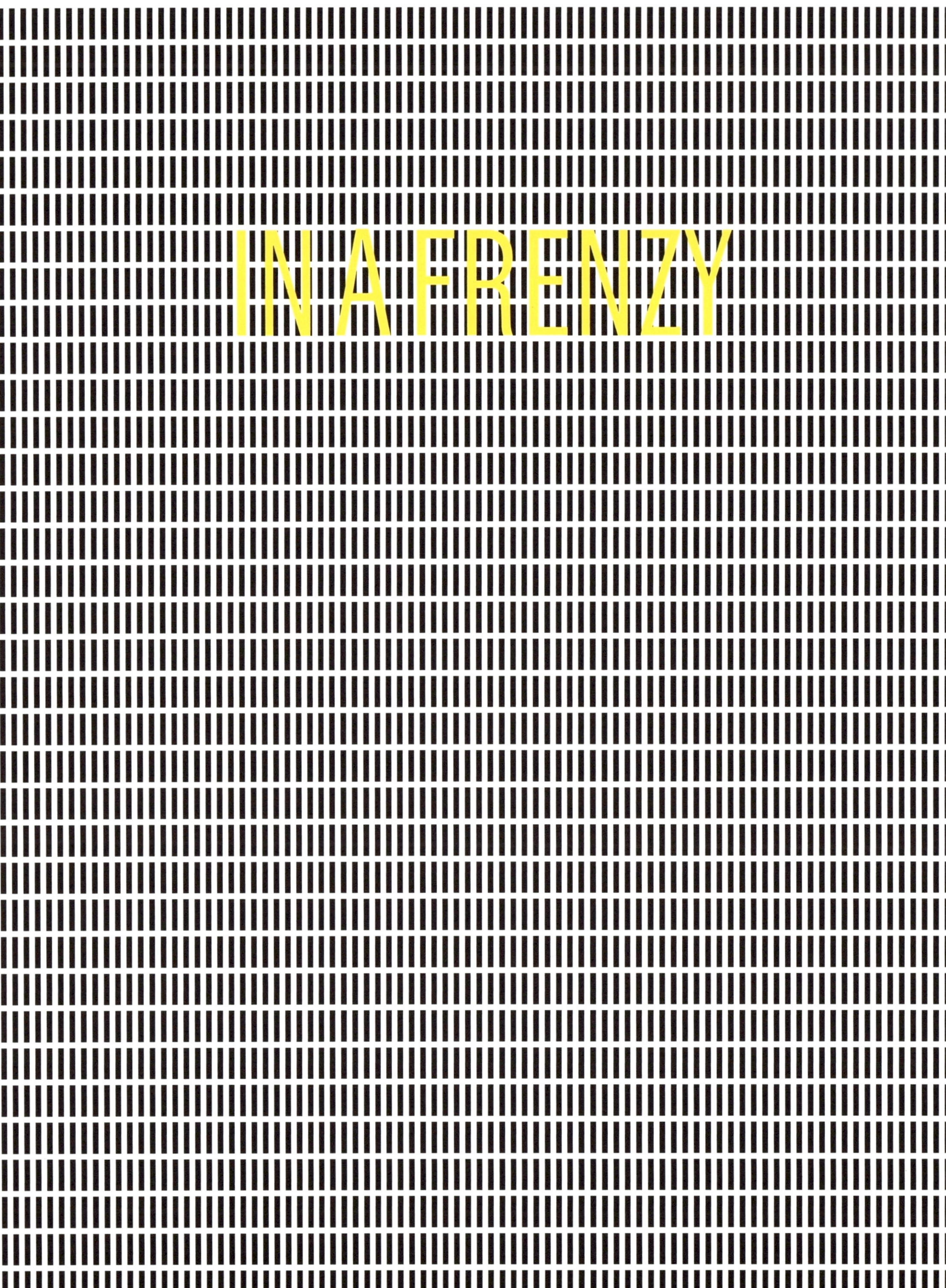
IN A FRENZY

HANNAH LEONIE PRINZLER: IN A FRENZY – A FILM MONTAGE

1 | Impulse and frenzy

Impulsive movement: the most spectacular form of spectator movement in stadiums is the Mexican wave. But there are many other subtle impulses of tension and release that could start just anywhere, then propagate and contribute to the oscillation of emotions in the crowd.

Finally, in a moment of scintillation following victory, the crowd melts into a single whole; time seems to stand still for a moment.

2 | Ornament

When 1,000 people move to exactly the same rhythm the effect is overwhelming. It is difficult not to be affected by the compelling attraction of synchronicity and symmetry with their unique aesthetic appeal. The individual person becomes part of a machine. But its aesthetic beauty also harbours the potential of a brutish force of destruction. In the twinkling of an eye, dancers become soldiers and doves turn into fighter planes.

3 | Structure und chaos

When watching a crowd from a great distance, the fascinating structure of its movement becomes apparent. It almost seems as if there were a higher order controlling the mass and predetermining each individual's actions. In every crowd there is always the potential for break-up, break-out, breakdown and metamorphosis.

On the principle of montage

The installation is based on the musical pattern of a chorus. The images of the film shown on the left-hand screen are repeated on the central, and then the right-hand screen, at intervals of one second. With this device of twofold repetition, it is possible to focus on small movement patterns and make them visible as if looking through a magnifying glass. At the same time, the images create a three-dimensionality which places the viewer in the midst of the action.

Film clips

Olympia – Fest der Völker (1938)
Olympia – Fest der Schönheit (1938)
Leni Riefenstahl;
Alle treiben Sport (1969)
DEFA-Studio für Dokumentarfilme;
Schwärme – Intelligenz der Massen (2009)
Jakob Kneser, a&o buero;
Kategorie C (2008)
Franziska Tenner, A JOUR Film

Film archives

Bundesarchiv Filmarchiv
Progress Film-Verleih
Getty Images
Framepool
Multivision Hamburg
Deutsche Wochenschau GmbH, Hamburg
International Olympic Committee
Norddeutscher Rundfunk

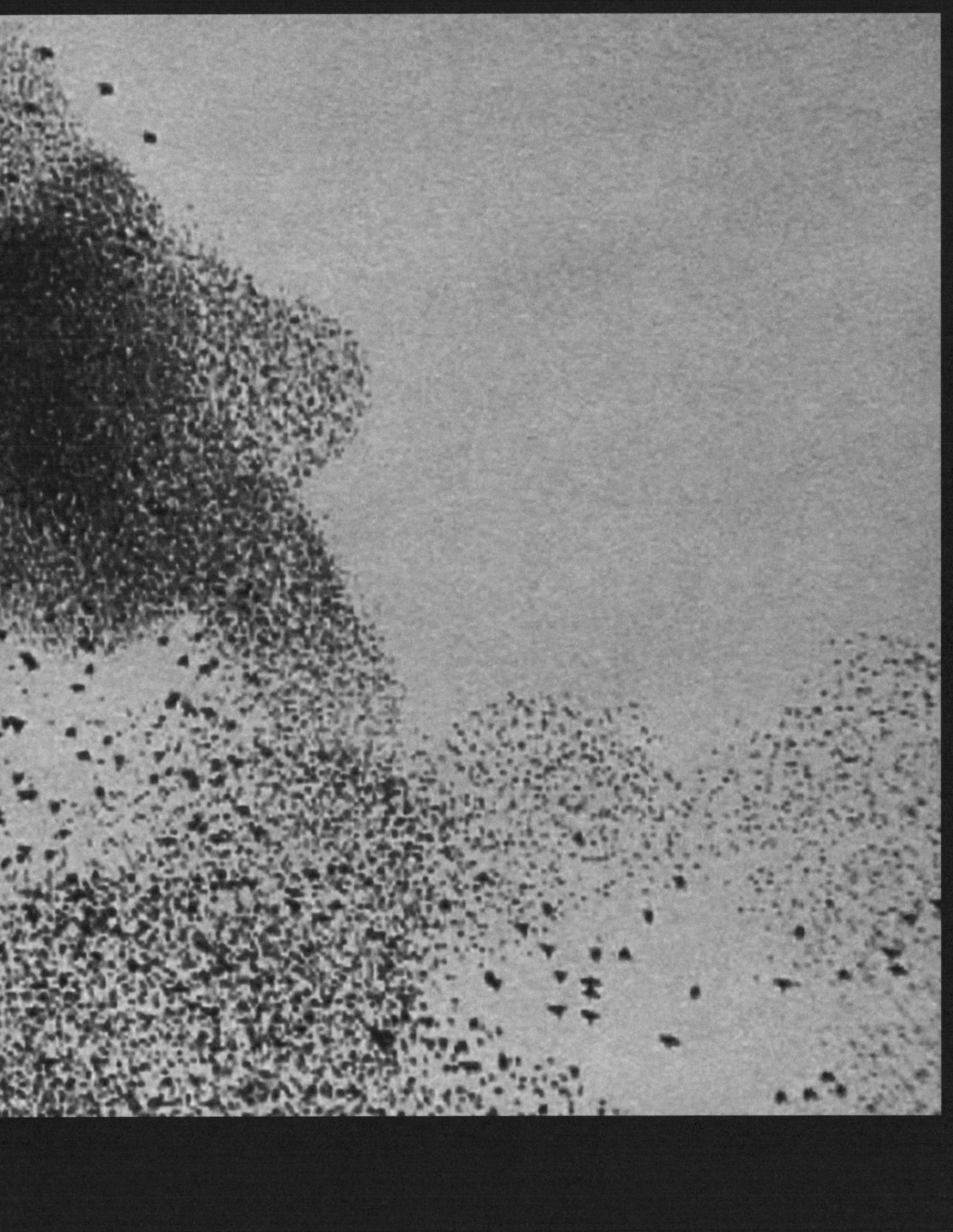

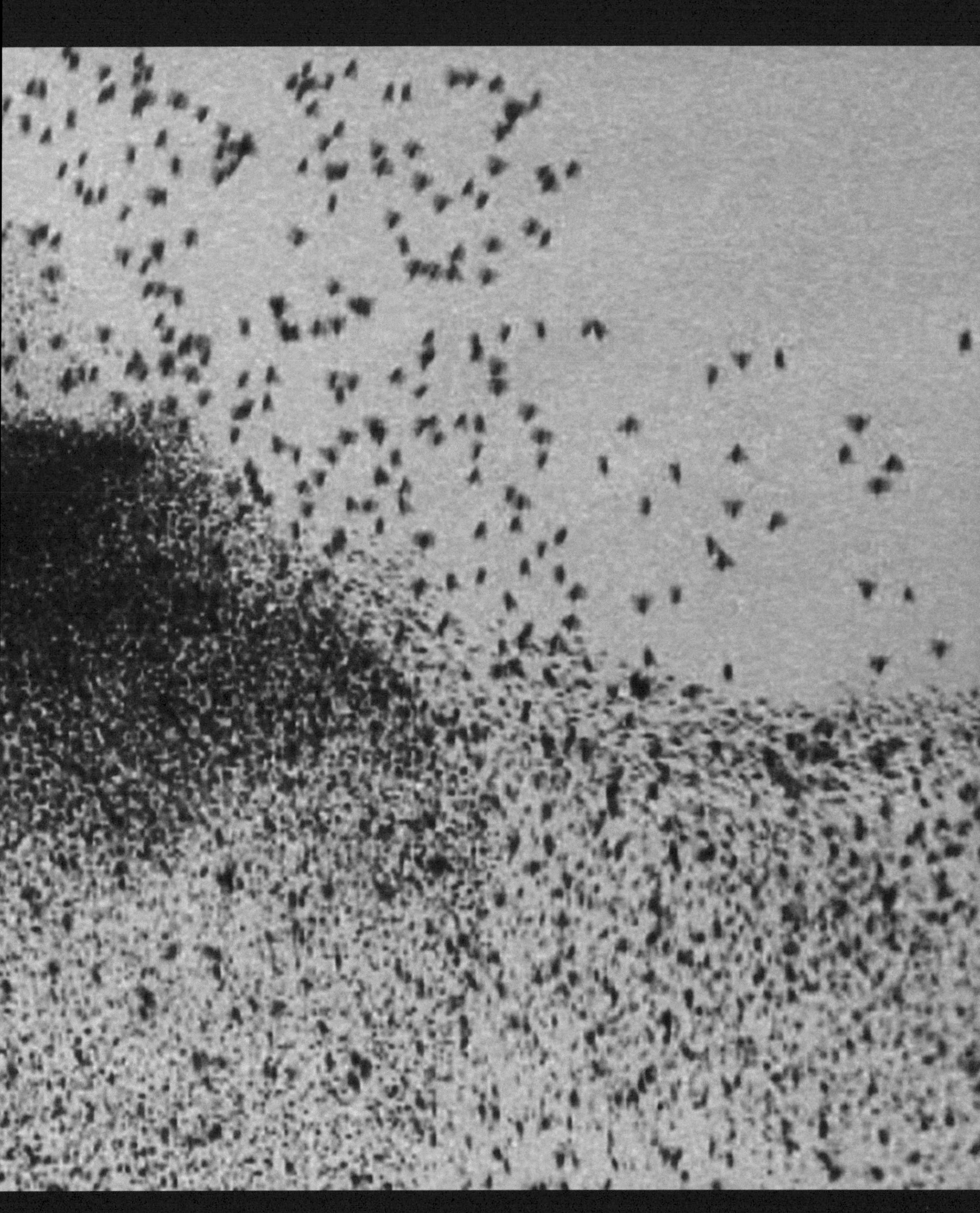

Der Katalog erscheint anlässlich der
Ausstellung
Choreographie der Massen.
Im Sport. Im Stadion. Im Rausch.

6. Juni bis 12. August 2012
Akademie der Künste
Pariser Platz 4, 10117 Berlin

Eine Ausstellung der Akademie der Künste,
Berlin, in Kooperation
mit gmp · Architekten von Gerkan, Marg
und Partner

www.adk.de
www.gmp-architekten.de
www.choreographie-der-massen.de

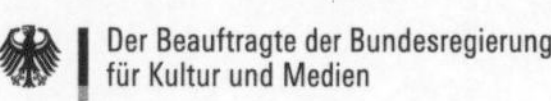

AUSSTELLUNG

Kuratoren Volkwin Marg, Gert Kähler,
Michael Kuhn
Projektleitung Akademie der Künste
Johannes Odenthal, Carolin Schönemann
Assistenz Akademie der Künste Jacqueline Saliba
Projektleitung gmp Hanne Banduch, Heidi Knaut,
Michael Kuhn
Ausstellungsgestaltung Hanne Banduch,
Heidi Knaut
Graphische Gestaltung ON Grafik, Hamburg
Digitale Bildbearbeitung Beatrix Hansen (gmp)
Redaktion/Lektorat Bettina Ahrens (gmp),
Martin Hager (edition8)
Übersetzung Hartwin Busch, Colin Shepherd
Korrektur Claudius Prößer

AUSSTELLUNGSFILME

Filmausschnitte zu
„Sport in der Antike", „Sport und Politik"
Konzept und Koordination Guido Brixner (gmp)
Produktion visionate interactive OHG, Hannover

„Im Rausch – eine filmische Montage"
Dramaturgie und Montage Hannah Leonie Prinzler
Klangkomposition Titus Maderlechner
Produktion Multivision Hamburg,
Knut Sodemann
Medientechnik vision_b, Berlin

PUBLIKATION

Ausstellungseinrichtung
Act!worX, Berlin
Jörg Scheil (Akademie der Künste)
Andreas Northe Möbeltischlerei, Hamburg
Matzat Museumstechnik, Berlin
Gärtner Internationale Möbel GmbH, Hamburg
P.O.P. Werbeteam GmbH, Hamburg
Wilking Metallbau GmbH, Berlin
Produktion Ausstellungsgraphiken und -drucke
René Birkner
DZA Druckerei zu Altenburg GmbH,
Altenburg
Reproplan graphics GmbH,
Hamburg/Berlin
Architekturmodellbau Monath + Menzel
Architekturmodellbau, Berlin
Werner Modellbau, Braunschweig
Logistik Dieke Eiben (gmp)
Leihverkehr Catherine Amé
(Akademie der Künste)
Presse- und Öffentlichkeitsarbeit Akademie der Künste
Anette Schmitt, Marianne König,
Stephanie Eck
Presse- und Öffentlichkeitsarbeit gmp
Christian Füldner

Begleitend zur Ausstellung ist eine Microsite geschaltet

www.choreographie-der-massen.de
Inhaltlich verantwortlich Michael Kuhn (gmp)
Content management Nicole Schindler (gmp)
Umsetzung SHAKEN not STIRRED, Hamburg
Design ON Grafik, Hamburg

© 2012, Akademie der Künste, Berlin,
gmp · Architekten von Gerkan, Marg
und Partner
Jovis Verlag GmbH, Berlin, die Autoren
und Fotografen
Alle Rechte vorbehalten.

Herausgeber Volkwin Marg für die Akademie
der Künste, Berlin
Autor Gert Kähler
Koordination Bettina Ahrens (gmp),
Michael Kuhn (gmp)
Redaktion/Lektorat Bettina Ahrens (gmp),
Martin Hager (edition8)
Korrektur Claudius Prößer
Graphische Gestaltung und Satz
ON Grafik, Hamburg
Umschlaggestaltung
ON Grafik, Hamburg
Repro Organisation DZA Druckerei zu
Altenburg GmbH, Altenburg
Druck und Bindung DZA Druckerei zu
Altenburg GmbH, Altenburg

Bibliografische Information der Deutschen
Nationalbibliothek:
Die Deutsche Nationalbibliothek verzeichnet diese
Publikation in der Deutschen Nationalbibliografie;
detaillierte bibliografische Daten sind im Internet
über http://dnb.d-nb.de abrufbar.

Jovis Verlag GmbH
Kurfürstenstraße 15/16
10785 Berlin
www.jovis.de

ISBN 978-3-86859-164-4

p. 79 **centre** ullstein bild – Imagno

p. 79 **bottom** ullstein bild – Hanns Hubmann

p. 80 **top left** Bundesarchiv

p. 80 **centre top** ullstein bild – Herbert Hoffmann

p. 80 **top right** Bundesarchiv, Graphic: Blez

p. 80 **bottom** ullstein bild – Wolff & Tritschler

p. 81 **top left** ullstein bild

p. 81 **top right** Bundesarchiv

p. 82 **top left** ullstein bild – TopFoto

p. 82 **centre top** ullstein bild – Wolff & Tritschler

p. 82 **top right** ullstein bild

p. 83 ullstein bild – Wolff & Tritschler

p. 85 **top** bpk/Hanns Hubmann

p. 85 **bottom** Johann-Karl Schmidt and Ursula Zeller (eds),
Behnisch & Partner: Bauten 1952–1992, Stuttgart 1992

p. 86 **top** Bundesarchiv

p. 86 **bottom** ullstein bild – Schäche

p. 87 **top left** Gert Kähler

p. 87 **top right** ullstein bild – Schlage

p. 87 **bottom** ullstein bild – Robert Hetz

p. 88 **top left** Gert Kähler

p. 89 **top right** ullstein bild – Minkoff

p. 89 **top** Gert Kähler

p. 89 **bottom** ullstein bild – Werner Schulze

p. 90 ullstein bild – dpa

p. 91 ullstein bild – Lehnartz

p. 95 **top** Wikipedia/ Harold B. Robson

p. 95 **bottom** Wikipedia/ Alan Cleaver/Lizenz: CC-BY-2.0

p. 96 **top** ullstein bild – histopics

p. 96 **bottom** Bundesarchiv, Graphic: Prien Kroll

p. 97 **top** http://www.juedische-allgemeine.de/article/view/
id/4108 (beide)

p. 97 **bottom** Foto: Friedrich Franz Bauer/ Bundesarchiv

p. 98 **top** © Bettmann/CORBIS

p. 98 **left bottom** http://spielverlagerung.de/2011/12/26/
eine-weihnachtsgeschichte-fritz-walter-die-todeself-
und-der-zweite-weltkrieg

p. 98 **right bottom** http://de.wikipedia.org/wiki/Todeself

p 100 **top** Wikipedia/© Photo RMN

p. 100 **bottom** Deutsches Historisches Museum, Berlin

p. 101 Bundesarchiv

p. 102 **left** http://www.emmemm.de

p. 103 **right** Wikipedia/Max Montecinos

p. 106 **right** bpk/Hans Hubmann

p. 107 **left** ullstein bild – Yavuz Arslan

p. 107 **right** ullstein bild – Sven Simon

p. 111 ullstein bild

p. 113 http://www.spartacup.schoolnet.co.uk/
Fbritishladiep.htm

p. 115 **top** ullstein bild – Public Address

p. 115 **bottom** ullstein bild – ddp

p. 116 **top** ullstein bild – CARO/Rupert Oberhäuser

p. 116 **bottom** ullstein bild – ddp

p. 120 **top left** ullstein bild – Yavuz Arslan

p. 120 **top right** ullstein bild – Sven Simon

p. 120 **centre** *Rom: Die Olympischen Spiele 1960 mit Sieger Tabelle*
by Joh. Jacobs & Co., Berlin: Erich-Zwirner, 1960. Printed
by Elsnerdruck/ Courtesy Eric Chaim Kline Bookseller

p. 120 **bottom** Deutsches Historisches Museum

p. 121 ullstein bild – Heritage Images/Land of Lost Content

p. 122 **top left** http://www.zhc-grubenlampe.
org/?Sponsoring:Werbung_am_Mann

p. 122 **top right** http://portal.krefeld-pinguine.de/index.
php?option=com_content&view=article&id=105&Itemid=
60&lang=de

p. 122 **bottom** ullstein bild – Werner OTTO

p. 123 **top left** foto: h.festag

p. 123 **top right** ullstein bild – Teutopress

p. 126 ullstein bild – Public Address

p. 127 ullstein bild – Reuters

p. 128 ullstein bild – ddp

p. 129 ullstein bild – Boness/IPON

p. 131 ullstein bild – Reuters

p. 132 ullstein bild – AP

p. 134 ullstein bild – Reuters/© Arnd Wiegmann

p. 135 ullstein bild – Reuters/© Christian Hartmann

p. 137 **top** Thomas280784 (aus de.wikipedia.org)

p. 137 **bottom** http://bathroomreader.com/tag/strange/

p. 138 **top** ullstein bild – CARO/Andreas Riedmiller

p. 138 **bottom** ullstein bild – imagebroker.net/J.W.Alker

p. 139 **top left** ullstein bild – CARO/Frank Sorge

p. 139 **top right** ullstein bild – Kreth

p. 139 **bottom** ullstein bild – AP/Tina Fineberg

p. 141 **top** ullstein bild – imagebroker.net/Thomas Frey

p. 141 **bottom** ullstein bild – Bullstein bild – Reuters/KAI
PFAFFENBACHoness/IPON

p. 143 **top left** ullstein bild – Public Address

p. 143 **top right** ullstein bild – Werek

S. 143 unten ullstein bild – Camera 4 Fotoagentur

S. 144 links ullstein bild – Team 2 Sportphoto

S. 144 rechts ullstein bild – imagebroker.net/Michael Weber

S. 145 http://hannani42.yoo7.com/t38571-topic

S. 146 ullstein bild – Sven Simon

S. 147 ullstein bild – Horstmüller

S. 148 links ullstein bild – Claus Bergmann

S. 148 rechts ullstein bild – imagebroker.net/Jochen Tack

S. 150 oben ullstein bild – CARO/Marc Meyerbroeker

S. 150 Mitte ullstein bild – Sven Simon

S. 150 unten ullstein bild – Pressefoto Ulmer

S. 151 links http://juniordesignerer.deviantart.com/art/
the-Thrilla-in-Manila-264177464

S. 151 rechts ullstein bild – United Archives/91040

S. 152 links ullstein bild – AP

S. 152 rechts ullstein bild – Reuters

S. 153 links ullstein bild – sinopictures/CNS

S. 153 rechts ullstein bild – Uli Winkler

S. 155 oben ullstein bild – Günter Peters

S. 155 unten Thomas Dietrich

S. 156 ullstein bild – Public Address

S. 157 oben Gert Kähler

S. 157 unten Johanna Kähler

S. 159 ullstein bild – Giribas

S. 160–161 © Olympiastadion Berlin GmbH

S. 181 oben rechts/links gmp Archiv

S. 181 unten gmp Architekten

S. 182 gmp Architekten

S. 183–187 Marcus Bredt

S. 189 oben rechts/links gmp Archiv

S. 189 unten gmp Architekten

S. 190 gmp Architekten

S. 191–195 Marcus Bredt

S. 197 Baukunstarchiv, Akademie der Künste, Berlin

S. 198 Auer + Weber + Assoziierte

S. 199 Meisterwerke der Kunst. Architektur II Hgg. zur
Förderung des Kunstunterrichts vom Landesinstitut für
Erziehung und Unterricht Stuttgart mit Unterstützung
des Ministeriums für Kultus, Jugend und Sport Baden-
Württemberg, 1999

S. 200 RKW Architektur+Städtebau

S. 201 Foster + Partners, Norman Robert Foster

S. 202 gmp Architekten

S. 203 Courtesy CSAC Archiv, Parma, Italien

S. 204 Karl Krämer (Hg.), Bauten der Olympischen Spiele
1972 München, Stuttgart 1969

S. 205 Renzo Piano Building Workshop

S. 206 A:AI Archiv für Architektur und Ingenieurbaukunst
NRW

S. 207 schlaich bergermann und partner

S. 208 Schultz + Partner Architekten BDA

S. 209 Zaha Hadid Architects

S. 210 Schuster Architekten Düsseldorf

S. 211 Otto Ernst Schweizer, Die architektonische
Großform. Karlsruhe 1957

S. 212 Souto Moura – Arquitectos, Lda.

S. 213 Tange Associates

S. 216–217 Multivision Hamburg

S. 218–219 Multivision Hamburg

S. 220–221 a&o buero

S. 222–223 a&o buero

S. 224–225 a&o buero

Trotz intensiver Bemühungen ist es nicht gelungen,
Urheberschaft und Herkunft aller Abbildungen zu klären.
Berechtigte Ansprüche werden selbstverständlich
abgegolten.

QUELLENNACHWEISE

Kapitel 1 – Sport in der Antike
_Xenophanes, Elegie, zitiert nach Ulrich Sinn, *Das antike Olympia*. H.C. Beck, München 2004, S. 26
_Lewis Mumford, *Die Stadt. Geschichte und Ausblick*. Deutscher Taschenbuch Verlag, München 1979, S. 271

Kapitel 2 – Leibeserziehung und Sport im 19. Jahrhundert
_Wilhelm Busch: Quelle http://gutenberg.spiegel.de/buch/4111
_Peter Ustinov: Quelle http://www.zitate.de/kategorie/Sport

Kapitel 3 – „Citius, altius, fortius": die modernen Olympischen Spiele
_Pierre de Coubertin, „Mein Programm", in: Deutsche Olympische Gesellschaft (Hg.), *Oympisches Lesebuch*. Hermann Schroedel Verlag, Hannover u. a. 1971, S. 15
_Peter Martin, „,Rassenkampf' im Sport", in: Peter Martin/Christine Alonzo (Hg.), *Zwischen Charleston und Stechschritt. Schwarze im Nationalsozialismus*. Dölling und Galitz, München/Hamburg 2004, S. 332
_Franz Miller u. a.: *So kämpfte und siegte die Jugend der Welt. XI Olympiade Berlin 1938*. Knorr & Hirth, München 1936
_Günter Behnisch, „Das Dach über der Landschaft", in: *Architekten Behnisch + Partner: Arbeiten aus den Jahren 1952–1987*. Hatje Cantz Verlag 1989, S. 43
_Fritz Auer, „Zur Entstehung des Olympiaprojektes". Unveröffentlichtes Manuskript, 1999

Kapitel 4 – Sport und Politik
_„Stell Dir vor: Während du zuhause Deinen Truthahn gegessen hast, plauderte ich da draußen mit den Männern, die ich ein paar Stunden vorher noch zu töten versucht hatte": Quelle http://werwiewo.wordpress.com/2010/12/22/das-weihnachtswunder-von-1914/
_Odd Nansen: Quelle http://www.zeit.de/online/2006/40/fussball_kz/seite-2
_Josef Goebbels: Quelle http://de.wikipedia.org/wiki/Sportpalastrede
_Herbert Zimmermann, 1954: Quelle http://web.ard.de/special/helden1954/pages/2463.php?ch=1
_Declan Hill, *Sichere Siege. Fußball und organisiertes Verbrechen oder wie Spiele manipuliert werden*. Kiepenheuer & Witsch, Köln 2008, S. 246 ff

_Johannes Müller, *Die Leibesübungen. Ihre biologisch-anatomischen Grundlagen, Physiologie und Hygiene sowie Erste Hilfe bei Unfällen*. Teubner Verlag, Leipzig 1926
_Bertold Brecht, „Die Krise des Sports", zitiert nach: Deutsche Olympische Gesellschaft (Hg.), *Olympisches Lesebuch*. Hermann Schroedel Verlag, Hannover u. a. 1971, S. 25

Kapitel 5 – Sport und Kommerz
_Oliver Hassencamp: Quelle http://www.sportwissen-schaften.info/dbquotations/seite-Kommerz-and.html
_Werbung für den ZHC Grubenlampe: Quelle http://www.zhc-grubenlampe.org/?Sponsoring:Werbung_am_Mann
_„Sie möchten bei den Krefeld Pinguinen werben?" Quelle http://portal.krefeld-pinguine.de/index.php?option=com_content&view=article&id=105&Itemid=60&lang=de
_Die „Coca-Cola-Spiele": Quellen http://www.coca-cola-gmbh.de/nachhaltigkeit/gemeinwohl/sportfoerderung/index.html
http://www.dosb.de/de/olympia/olympische-news/detail/news/neuer_coke_song_zu_den_olympischen_spie-len_2012
_Gunter Gebauer, *Sport in der Gesellschaft des Spektakels*. Academia Verlag, Sankt Augustin 2002
_Die Bundesliga-Rechte: Quelle http://www.soccer-war-riors.de/2010/08/09/entwicklung-der-tv-gelder-fuer-die-deutsche-bundesliga
_Markus Lamprecht und Hanspeter Stamm, *Sport zwischen Kultur Kult und Kommerz*. Seismo Verlag, Zürich 2002
_Die Mitglieder des Fifa-Exekutivkomitees: Quelle http://de.wikipedia.org/wiki/FIFA-Exekutivkomitee

Kapitel 6 – ... dann hat auch er gewonnen
_Der „Thrilla in Manila": Quelle http://de.wikipedia.org/wiki/Thrilla_in_Manila
_Die größten Zuschauer-Events: Quelle http://sportbild.bild.de/SPORT/sportmix/2011/02/02/die-10-groessten-sport-events-der-welt/millionen-vor-dem-tv.html
_Die größten Sportstätte: Quelle http://de.wikipedia.org/wiki/Liste_der_größten_Stadien_der_Welt

_FC St. Pauli – Freude schöner Fußballzauber [Joy, oh
football – game so precious]: Source http://www.
festgestaltung.de/fangesaenge/st_pauli1
_The Berlin Olympic Stadium as an example of a venue:
Source http://www.olympiastadion-berlin.de/special-
business-eventp.html

Quotations
_Gustav Le Bon, *Psychologie der Massen*. Stuttgart: Kröner
Verlag, 1982
_Étienne-Louis Boullée, *Abhandlung über die Kunst*.
Zurich and Munich: Artemis, 1987
_Elias Canetti, *Crowds and Power*. New York: Farrar, Straus
and Giroux, 1984, p. 15-30
_Johann Wolfgang von Goethe, *Italienische Reise*, Munich:
Stiebner Verlag 1999
_Peter Sloterdijk, *Die Verachtung der Massen. Versuch über
Kulturkämpfe in der modernen Gesellschaft*. Frankfurt am
Main: Suhrkamp Verlag, 2000